The Hitler Kiss

By Radomir Luza

The Transfer of the Sudeten Germans: A Study of Czech-German Relations, 1933–1962 (1964)

History of the International Socialist Youth Movement (1970)

A History of the Czechoslovak Republic, 1918–1948 (edited with Victor S. Mamatey, 1973)

Austro-German Relations in the Anschluss Era (1975)

A History of the Resistance in Austria, 1938–1945 (1984)

Československá sociálni demokracie (2001)

By Christina Vella

Intimate Enemies: The Two Worlds of the Baroness de Pontalba (1997)

The Hitler Kiss

A MEMOIR OF THE CZECH RESISTANCE

RADOMIR LUZA

with CHRISTINA VELLA

Louisiana State University Press ✦ *Baton Rouge*

Designer: Barbara Neely Bourgoyne
Typeface: Minion
Typesetter: Coghill Composition, Inc.
Printer and binder: Thomson-Shore, Inc.

Library of Congress Cataloging-in-Publication Data

Luza, Radomir.
    The Hitler kiss : a memoir of the Czech resistance / Radomir
Luza with Christina Vella.
        p.   cm.
Includes bibliographical references.
    ISBN 0-8071-2781-7 (alk. paper)
    1. Luza, Radomir.   2. World War, 1939–1945—Underground
movements—Czechoslovakia.   3. World War, 1939–1945—Personal
narratives, Czech.   I. Vella, Christina, 1942–   II. Title.
    D802.C95 L89   2002
    940.54'82437—dc21

2001007590

With deepest gratitude to Libuše
for her love, courage, and devotion.

CONTENTS

ILLUSTRATIONS

Maps

ACKNOWLEDGMENTS

Grateful acknowledgment is made to the Rockefeller Foundation, which in 1987 provided Radomir Luza with a generous grant and a residency at its study and conference center in Bellagio, Italy, so that he could gather material for a book on the Czech home resistance.

The authors both owe a great debt to Dr. Karl Roider, the manuscript's first, valued reader, for his encouragement and suggestions, as well as to Esmond Harmsworth for his good advice. Maureen Anderson of Fayetteville, Arkansas, worked hard on the initial transcription of many hours of Dictaphone tapes. Jeffrey Johnson of New Orleans was the computer expert who guided the authors—both craven resisters—in preparing the final disk version of the manuscript. Maureen Hewitt, Sylvia Frank Rodrigue, and Barbara Outland of LSU Press made significant contributions to the publication process. Most deserving of thanks is George Roupe, who has been unfailingly careful and kind through the book's editing. Finally, the authors want to acknowledge the patience of their families.

The Hitler Kiss

I

He didn't even take his slippers. As I look back on it, Father wasn't packing like someone who expected to live out of his knapsack for the next three years. A shirt, a change of underwear, shaving things, his eyeglasses, a stock—that neckpiece old-fashioned men were still wearing in 1941—were all he carried with him underground. Probably he had no idea what he should take, never having been in hiding before. He put aside the slippers with a casual pat and laced up his heavy shoes for the twelve-mile walk ahead of him. He had only two books, hardly enough to last a week, and a diamond ring Mother thought he could use in an emergency if he needed more than the few thousand crowns he carried with him. His warm Hubertus coat, green and protective, was ready by the door.

"Vojtěch, they are close. I can feel it," Mother kept saying. Father went on putting away his papers. He could not leave in daylight because the Gestapo was probably watching our house, and he did not want to get to Kravka's at an hour when outsiders who would recognize him might be there. Father's old friend and fellow legionnaire Čeněk Kravka lived near the main road from Brno to Prague.[1] When the Nazis invaded Czechoslovakia in 1939

---

1. In general, č indicates a "ch" sound: Čenek = Chen yek. Š usually indicates "sh": Beneš = Benesh; Eliáš = Eliash. A c with no mark is pronounced like the "ts" in bets. Nearly all Czech names are accented on the first syllable. Father's name, Vojtěch, is pronounced "Voy tyekh." The biographical section includes the pronunciation of most of the Czech personal names mentioned in the book and is followed by a listing of Czech place-names and their pronunciations.

and set up the German-controlled Protectorate administration, Father approached Kravka about finding a family who could shelter him when the time came to go underground. That time had come now. In September 1941, Hitler, noting that anti-German activity in our country was increasing, decided that Reich Protector Konstantin von Neurath was protecting us too much and needed a sick leave; the Führer appointed SS-Obergruppenführer Reinhard Heydrich—who was already the head of all security and police forces of the Reich—as the new Acting Reich Protector in Bohemia and Moravia. Though we Czechs were boycotting the newspapers in September, we nevertheless heard the official German announcements, and we knew that after his arrival in Prague on the twenty-seventh, Heydrich had declared martial law in the entire country—a tightening of the occupation and an all-around brutal business.

My father watched these events with mounting apprehension. General Alois Eliáš, the prime minister of the Protectorate government and Father's close friend, sent a warning through an intermediary: "Our situation is critical. You're in immediate danger. Two or three days at most." Then on September 28 we learned that Eliáš himself had been arrested. He would be sentenced to death three days later. Eliáš was the highest of the Czech officials required to carry out the policies of the German occupation of Czechoslovakia, but he was also a leader of the secret resistance, just as my father was. We all knew after the arrest of General Eliáš that it was only a matter of hours before the Gestapo would come for General Luža, too. And so on September 29, Father packed his knapsack and waited for the dark.

My mother, usually so high-strung, was no different now. Her eyes darted nervously from the door to the window and back to my father. There was a dooryard around our house, so the Gestapo would arrive first at the garden door downstairs rather than the entrance to our apartment. If they showed up now at that outside door, Father was prepared to jump out of our rear window to the backyard and try to escape. The Germans usually made their arrests between five and six in the morning, and since the Gestapo, like all other men, were creatures of habit and routine, we did not really expect them until the next day. Nevertheless, Mother couldn't keep her eyes off the door. Father was puttering, mentioning things as they occurred to him. We worked out a signal for letting him know when the Gestapo came. We usually pulled our shades down at night and raised them in the morning; however, I suggested that if we left our shades down during the day, that would mean the Germans had not come after all, and he might send someone with a message. If the shades were up, that meant the Gestapo had arrived, and no one was to come near us. Father, who was frugal with praise, thought this was an excellent idea.

At last the time came for him to leave. He was white faced, but he gave us his usual inattentive peck and embraced us as always before a short trip; then he set off into the cold September. Mother and I did not talk after we closed the door, busy with the racket inside our heads. I opened my New Testament and began reading, in Latin, of all things, which I detested and normally would have considered some sort of penance. After a while we went to bed, warm and miserable, thinking of Father, who had just begun his night journey.

Vojtěch Luža, my father, was born in 1891 in Uherský Brod, a town on the Moravian-Slovakian march. His father was a servant, not regularly employed, but hiring himself out wherever he could as a porter, valet, messenger, or the like. Father's mother must have come from a well-off family; her parents had enough money to disinherit her for marrying a man of low origin, thus abandoning her to a life of certain poverty. She thwarted their revenge by dying young, when my father and his brother Bohuslav were only four and three years old. They were reared by a kindly stepmother. The family supplemented its income by renting out one of the rooms in their small house to students. Father tutored these young men while he himself attended the local gymnasium, a seven-year institution that was partly high school, partly junior college.

Father was excellent in mathematics and science and in 1909 was awarded a scholarship and a stipend to further his education. Thus, at eighteen he went to study electrical engineering at the Brno Technical University, about sixty miles from Uherský Brod. As neither his stipend nor his family could support him in Brno, he had to continue tutoring. Even in Uherský Brod, in a yard hardly bigger than a pen, Father had worked out on a bar. He continued to keep up his exercises and even participated in the competitions sponsored by the gymnastics organization Sokol—contests that the whole nation followed.[2] In 1912 he passed his first state examination

2. Sokol ("The Falcon") was founded in the late nineteenth century as a gymnastics and cultural organization emphasizing egalitarian ideals and self-discipline. With its local, district, and central network, Sokol emerged as an effective force in Czech and Slovak independence movements. Sokol members were patriotic activists during both world wars.

and was preparing to take his second and final examination for college graduation. But on August 1, 1914, the Great War erupted, and he was immediately drafted into the Austrian army.

Father was a Czech, but there was of course no Czechoslovakia then, just as there is today no nation called Catalonia or Moravia. In the Middle Ages the Czechs had their own independent country, the wealthy Kingdom of Bohemia, consisting of the so-called historic provinces, Bohemia, Moravia, and Silesia, and surrounded by a natural border of mountains. The population of the kingdom was mainly Slav (which came to be called Czech in that area), but with a considerable admixture of Germans even then; the splendid capital was Prague. These Slavs and Germans, descendants of the grim tribes that invaded Europe after the demise of the Roman Empire, lived side by side unpeacefully through several centuries in the Kingdom of Bohemia. Czechs married Germans, and there were periods when the Bohemian upper classes pragmatically adopted the German language alongside Czech, but more commonly the two peoples intermingled their ethnic truculence with their religious and political antipathies.

The Slavs of the Czech lands might have reached across middle Europe to form a single ethnic mass with the Slav ancestors of Russians and Ukrainians. But the Magyars wedged themselves between them. From the Asian frontier the Magyars swept into the Danube Valley in the ninth century, conquering Slavs who obstructed their southward path and depositing themselves, a block of Hungarians (from the Latin word for Magyars), between the Slavs of central Europe and the Slavs of the steppes farther east. The area now known as Slovakia thus fell under Hungarian domination, a region of landless Slavs bound to Magyar landlords.

The Bohemian kingdom was eventually taken into that ragged amalgam, the Holy Roman Empire.[3] Having joined with the Holy Roman Emperor, an Austrian Habsburg, to halt a steamroller invasion of Turks in 1526, the Kingdom of Bohemia was not able later to reassert its independence. The Protestant Bohemians tried to throw out their Austrian overlords, literally, starting with the famous incident in 1618 when a group of Bohemian nobles

---

3. The Holy Roman Empire at times extended from France to Poland and Hungary but was made up mostly of Germans. The Austrian branch of the Habsburg dynasty held the imperial title continuously from the fifteenth century until 1806. In Bohemia, therefore, being in the empire usually meant being under the authority of the German-speaking Habsburgs.

tossed three Habsburg representatives out of a window of the Hradčany Castle. This rebellion, whimsically remembered as "the defenestration of Prague" inaugurated a humorless conflict which ended in the devastation and depopulation of much of Europe: the Thirty Years' War. The Catholic Habsburgs overran the Czech lands and crushed the vestiges of Bohemian independence. German was declared an official language alongside Czech. The lands of Protestants of all nationalities were confiscated. These estates were mostly parceled out to Catholic followers of the Habsburg rulers, largely German speakers, so that for the next centuries, the upper landed class in Bohemia was predominately German, while Czechs were reduced to peasantry.

The Czechs emerged from this ignominious condition, though they did not regain their independence. They reverted to Catholicism, became prosperous, and by the late nineteenth century were prominent in the intellectual life of the empire. The heavy industries of the Austrian empire were located mainly in Bohemia, Moravia, and Silesia, the areas richest in natural resources. But the political power of the Czechs in the empire was meager compared to their contributions. The ruling class remained German.

The decades preceding World War I were a time of political agitation throughout the whole Danube basin. Independent German states on the western fringe of Austrian dominion escaped from their centuries-old elastic federation with Austria. In 1871 they united under the leadership of Prussia and became the German state that we know today. However, one sixth of all Germans still remained outside of this new Germany; that is, they remained stippled over central Europe in the sympathetic embrace of the Austrian empire. With the rise of this unified Germany on its borders, Austria needed Hungary's military support more than ever and was obliged to yield to the Magyar demands for self-government. In 1867 the Dual Monarchy of Austria-Hungary was established, in which the two agglomerations, Austria and Hungary, became practically independent, joined by a common ministry and loyalty to the same emperor. The arrangement was well characterized by the Austrian foreign minister, who remarked to the Hungarian negotiator, "Now, you manage your barbarians and we will manage ours." By "barbarians," he meant primarily the Slavs, the third most important ethnic group, after the Germans and Magyars.

The Czechs of course clamored for a triple monarchy in which Bohemia would have the same degree of autonomy as Hungary. The Austrian emperor Francis Joseph decided against this idea, since it was opposed both by

the Germans living in the Sudeten mountains of Bohemia and by the Magyars, who feared that the example of an autonomous Bohemia would make
their own barbarians restless. At the outbreak of the First World War, then,
the Dual Monarchy stood for an Austrian state on one side—whose population was 36 percent German, and the rest a miscellany of Czechs, Slovenes,
Poles, Ruthenians, and Italians—and on the other side a Hungary in which
the dominant Magyars made up less than half the population, with Slovaks,
Croats, Serbs, and Transylvanians (Rumanians) making up the rest. The
Austrian-Germans were certainly more liberal toward their Slavs than the
Magyars, whose subject peoples such as the Slovaks and Serbs remained
poor and powerless. But the Austrians were not liberal enough. Francis Joseph was in the sixty-sixth year of his reign in 1914. He was the adversary
not only of Russia, Great Britain, and France—the foreign powers allied
against him in the Triple Entente—but of some Protestants, most democrats, and all nationalists within his own realm, including, eventually, my
father.

Just as the Thirty Years' War had begun with a violent gesture of independence from the Austrian Habsburgs, the First World War began in Sarajevo
with a murder and Serbia's determination to maintain its independence
from Austria-Hungary. Czechs responded to the general mobilization of the
empire—since they were conscripted along with everyone else, they had little choice—but they were not happy about defending Austrians and Germans who held them in contempt. Father belonged to a radical party
favoring equal rights for all citizens, especially women, and complete independence from Austria. He saw that the end of the empire could mean the
establishment of an independent Czechoslovak state. Father was not alone
in harboring the hope of Austrian defeat. Whereas in Vienna and Budapest
the announcement of war was greeted with the usual bellicose enthusiasm
such declarations arouse, in Bohemia and Slovakia the mood was sullen.
Father was one of the sullen Bohemians sent to the eastern front, where as a
junior lieutenant he fought against the Russians for nine months. Then in
August 1915, at about the time he would have finished his examinations
and left Brno as an electrical engineer, he was taken prisoner by the Russian
army.

Nationalists within Austria-Hungary had meanwhile become committed
to the complete dismemberment of the empire. In 1915 an underground
movement for Czech independence decided to seek support abroad. This
group of exiles, centered in Paris and substantially aided by the Entente, be-

came the Czech National Council for Czech and Slovak Independence, led by a philosophy professor, Thomas G. Masaryk; a Slovak astronomer, Milan R. Štefánik; and a lecturer from Charles University, the stripling Edvard Beneš. The committee organized volunteer units of over 100,000 Czechs and Slovaks to fight against Austria on both the western and eastern fronts, in Serbia, Russia, France, and Italy. In Russia the Czechoslovak Legion, as it was called, developed into a huge volunteer army of well-equipped troops. Slav conscripts in the Austrian army deserted to it by the hundreds, and its ranks were swelled by Czech and Slovak war prisoners held in Russia, my father and Kravka among them, who now agreed to change sides. I do not know whether this decision to turn against the Austrians was a difficult one for Father. By the time I was old enough to be interested in war stories, both he and I had another war on our minds. In any case, his joining the Czechoslovak Legion was significant, not least because the legionnaires later composed an old-boy military network in Czechoslovakia which served Father well. In the immediate term, being a legionnaire meant that he would never be taken prisoner by the Austrians as he had been by the Russians; if captured in battle, he would be hanged as a traitor.

When the Russian Revolution brought the Bolsheviks to power in 1917, the entire Russian army abandoned the war. The Czechoslovak Legion, some sixty thousand strong, began withdrawing through Siberia toward Vladivostok, my father with them in the Second Regiment; their plan was to leave Russia by way of the Trans-Siberian railroad, get back to Europe by sea, and take up fighting against the German-Austrian alliance on the western front. But in May 1918, the Bolsheviks in the middle Volga tried to disarm the legionnaires to insure that these foreigners could not help any of the anti-Bolshevik forces in the region. The Czechoslovak Legion, refusing to surrender its arms, thus turned on the Bolsheviks, launched a westward offensive, and became part of the anti-Bolshevik patchwork of the Russian civil war.

The United States had meanwhile entered the war against Austria-Hungary and had become the great guarantor of national self-determination. When the Czechoslovak Legion seized control of the Trans-Siberian railway in May 1918, President Woodrow Wilson was encouraged in his belief that Bolshevism was a temporary madness that could easily be crushed. The subsequent attempt to intervene in the Russian civil war was itself soon recognized by America as a form of temporary madness. Nevertheless, the Czechoslovak Legion, along with Masaryk's public relations campaign, influenced Wilson in favor of the Czechs. Just before the Dual Monarchy collapsed in 1918, having been destroyed from within, the United States recognized the National Council under Masaryk as the de facto government of a new Czechoslovak Republic that was officially proclaimed on October 28, 1918. Austrian authority melted away in Prague like the snow of an overlong winter. Czechs emerged to run Czech offices and police Czech roads; members of the beloved Sokol clubs patrolled the streets during the transition to the new order. Czechoslovakia became the pet of the Paris Peace Conference, which granted Czech nationalists nearly everything they had hoped to achieve during the war. In particular, the Treaty of Versailles granted to Czechoslovakia its historic natural barrier against Germany, the Sudeten Mountains, and with them, alas, the Sudeten Germans, some three million German-speaking Bohemians and Moravians, mostly scattered on the border rim.

As for Father, he was still making his way eastward through Siberia and upward through the ranks of the new Czechoslovak army. In 1918 he was a captain and commanding officer of the Second Battalion of the Second Legionnaire Regiment; by 1919 he was deputy commanding officer of the regiment; in 1920 he at last reached Vladivostok and the rank of lieutenant colonel. In those years he acquired a reputation for strength and bravery in battle, especially during the fighting in Siberia when he commanded an armored train. A story was even written about him by a prominent Czech writer and legionnaire, František Langer, describing his lifting a railroad car for what I hope was some good reason. Finally in 1920 he left Vladivostok for a circuitous voyage home, to his town with new street names, to his country with new anthems. In 1914 he had left an old regime whose tastes were set in Vienna, with its model of rigid court etiquette, its prominent men swathed in titles, all its women in long gowns. In 1920 he came home to the excitements of a young republic: democracy, equality, meritocracy, and legs.

Father was now twenty-nine, handsome, with a great deal of war experience and very little of any other kind. He met my mother, Milada Večeřová, at a ball in Uherský Brod when she was twenty-two. According to Mother, theirs was love at first sight, and I can well believe it. Father was six feet of muscle, black moustache, black hair, and bright uniform. Mother was tall and lissome and the first woman he had laid prolonged eyes on in months. It was not difficult for them to meet again in that quiet town where they both were

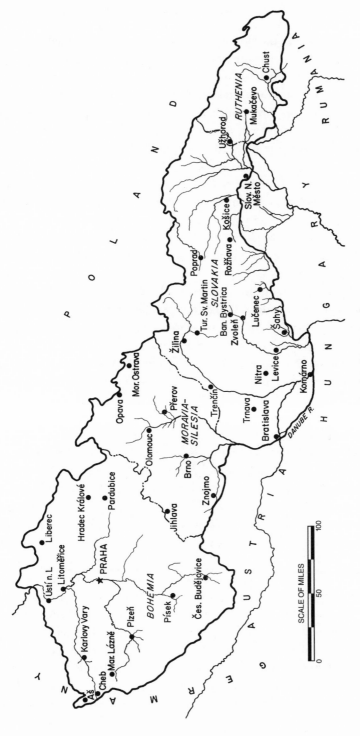

Czechoslovakia, 1918–38

born; they saw each other in Prague some weeks later at the all-Sokol congress, a great national gymnastics festival. Father was soon assigned to Prague, but he began visiting Mother in Uherský Brod, bringing her gifts of ham or some delicacy, and making all the appropriate courting gestures. Once during the train trip his new coat was stolen with Mother's present in the pocket—an event he was still complaining about long after I was born. They married in Prague in 1921, most patriotically, from the sound of it. After the ceremony in the Old Town City Hall, they had dinner at a restaurant piously named The Representation House. Then they spent their wedding evening—Mother reported this without so much as a flicker of amusement—watching a Smetana opera at the National Theater.

Mother was a well-bred girl from a professional family of half-German origin. Her mother, my grandmother, was cultured, a splendidly self-educated intellectual who loved the arts and German literature. She had become Czech by slow degrees during her marriage, and her friends in Uherský Brod were members of an international, not precisely Czech, society. Mother's father was an ardent Czech, a lawyer who could recite *The Iliad* in the original and would mutter Homeric consolations to himself to calm his nerves as he went about his business. He had known Masaryk in his student days in Vienna. One night the two of them had gone to an inn with some friends and were singing Czech songs when a German made some remark about the "Czech rabble" in the place. Whereupon Masaryk took the German by his belt—Grandfather gestured here as if Masaryk had waved the hapless German in the air in time to the music—and threw him out. My grandmother was never fond of my ebullient grandfather. In their old age, as she understood him better, she liked him even less. My mother took her side.

Mother had a few psychological defenses in place when she married Father, whereas Father, for all his superior intelligence, was simple, straightforward, and earnest. He was part of a generation that believed manliness consisted in working hard and fulfilling one's obligations in the priesthood of public service. Neither men nor women in my parents' day had much respect for the Tsar Nicholases of the world who cared more about their families than their public duties. My parents were well matched. I was never as compatible with either of them as they were with each other.

In Prague, Father became commander of the Fifth Infantry Regiment. He was happily assuming more and more responsibilities by the time I was born in 1922, working ten or twelve hours a day as an officer of the general staff, the general brains of the army. It was, after all, a great time to be young and driven, those optimistic first years of Czechoslovakia's independence. A democratic republic was a new thing under the sun in central Europe, an exhilarating and serious adventure, as important to Czechs and Slovaks as the independence of the thirteen colonies was to the founders of the United States. Our first, long-lasting president, Masaryk, was the son of a coachman; he had put himself through university and was respected as a scholar and humanist before becoming a statesman. Married to an American, Charlotte Garrigue, he was committed with all his will to a multinational democratic state on the French and U.S. model. Czechoslovakia emerged from the Great War a first-class economic power, having inherited 70 percent of the industrial production of the vast Austro-Hungarian Empire. When in 1924 Father became head of the operation section of the general staff, that is, the section responsible for war preparations and strategy, he might well have been organizing the defense of an exemplary democracy that would live forever.

There was of course the substantial problem of the Germans. When Czechoslovakia was founded, its population was about 13.6 million: seven million Czechs; two million Slovaks; minorities of Hungarians, Jews, and others numbering about a million; and over three million people of German descent and language living mainly in the outlying Sudeten mountain regions where the country projected deep into Germany. The eight territories in which the Germans were settled were separated from each other by broad belts of land peopled by Czechs. The German areas did not form one administrative or economic pocket. Nevertheless, these Sudeten Germans wanted to be united with Germany. The Czechs may have been, in the words of the Soviet foreign minister, Maxim Litvinov, "one of the oldest, most cultured, most hard-working of European peoples," but the Germans were unimpressed. Their past relationship with the Czechs had basically been that of master and menial. Most of them considered Slavs their inferiors and hated being under a government of their former servants. The Jeffersons and Madisons of the new republic were sincere in wanting a rapprochement with Germany, a strong alliance with France for security's sake, and a parliamentary democracy in which each citizen was equal under the law, with no one accorded special status such as the Germans demanded.[4] Prosperity, that

4. France and Czechoslovakia were linked by two treaties. The first, concluded January 25, 1924, stated that both parties would proceed jointly in all matters of foreign policy that might endanger their security and that they would undertake adequate measures for the protection of their common interests. In the second, concluded October 16, 1925, both states agreed mutually to render immediate help and support in the event of an unprovoked attack by Germany.

great mollifier of social unrest, seemed for a time to work its magic on the Sudeten Germans. By the middle of the 1920s, they had apparently accepted the Czechoslovak Republic and their place as citizens within it. All seemed right with the world.

The twenties was the right decade to be a child, set between the horror of the years before and the terror of the period after. We had a three-room apartment in a new house in the northern section of Prague and a servant, Marie. Thursday afternoons were for piano lessons, which I hated: Czerny and *Little Fingers I.* Sunday morning was the cinema, which I loved: Charlie Chaplin, Douglas Fairbanks, Deanna Durbin. Winter meant ski vacations in Šumava. I'd wipe the moisture from a window of the lodge to watch Father, who was good at all sports, zip down the slopes, a whip trail behind him in the whiteness. In summer we went to the Beskydy Mountains on the Moravian-Slovakian border and to the High Tatras in Slovakia. Swimming being my one athletic skill, I swam in the creeks and pools restricted to the military, surrounded by the kids of other officers. There were occasions, luminous in memory, when we rode on a train or in a motor car. Once in a while my parents took me to a Sunday matinee at the National Theater in Prague. My child's eyes saw it as huge and majestic, there overlooking the Moldau. I was surprised to discover later that it is one third the size of the Vienna State Opera, almost cozy in comparison.

We had in those years everything but money. We didn't enjoy the sheltered, rarefied atmosphere that surrounds the military in most countries, for ours was a young, not especially popular army which had inherited both the brash legionnaires and elements of the old Austrian army. Czechoslovak army officers were not well paid. They were respected, and their families had a few advantages, but if they had wealth, you could be sure they had inherited it or married it. We did not have much of Father, either. In 1925 he was promoted to colonel. Usually he walked to his office every morning at seven; on rainy days a carriage with two horses came for him. Once or twice a week before going to headquarters he would ride in Stromovka Park, the former royal hunting ground in Prague where the military kept horses. Then he went to his office, where he worked until evening for his low salary and his high ideals.[5] I was usually asleep by the time he got home, for in those days staying up late was considered sordid.

5. Father's salary as brigadier general in 1932 was about five thousand crowns a month; in 1937, as a division general, he made around seven thousand crowns. It is difficult to give an idea of how much this would represent today; it does not help to know that the exchange rate then

Father learned the French military doctrine and methods of training officers when he was invited by the military at the end of 1925 to come to Paris for three months. In matters of strategy, he was no doubt influenced by the ideas of the German general Heinz Guderian, whose book *Achtung Panzer* Father underlined and annotated until his copy was a dog-eared, illegible mess. The conventional wisdom of the Czech military was that northern Moravia and Silesia must be heavily fortified against possible German invasion. That was all very well, according to Father, but by the thirties he had become skeptical about the value of fortifications in western Bohemia. Father believed that some of our resources should be spent instead on tank divisions—tanks used not in the scattered way the French had employed them in the First World War but concentrated in large groups, "mobile fortifications." As for stationary fortifications, they should be strongest at the Moravian-Silesian "hallway" between Poland and Austria, the narrowest part of the Czech lands, so that the Czechoslovak army could not be cut off from its strategic retreat from Bohemia to the Beskydy Mountains on the Slovakian border. Father explained none of this to me. In the first place, I was too young; in the second place, he would not have discussed highly secret defense strategy with his family; and in the third place, he hardly took time to talk with me about the weather or my schoolwork, much less anything complicated. It is only recently that I have been able to piece together his ideas from his later comments, his notes, and my interviews with his colleagues.

Father was promoted to brigadier general in 1929, commander of the elite Second Mountain Brigade in Ružomberok, a Slovakian town that I remember as the place where he was given his first official car. I can see myself in the backseat in a heaven of wind as we flew through the countryside at thirty miles an hour. Slovakia was not urbanized or as economically advanced as Bohemia. Slovaks in general were painfully aware of their region's backwardness. But Father, who cared little for the smug sophistication of Prague, loved both Moravia and Slovakia, and felt completely at home in Ružomberok. I never heard him utter one word disparaging Slovaks or comparing them unfavorably to Czechs, and I grew up largely oblivious to the national tensions between the two groups. I remained in Prague with my mother, however, during Father's three-year tenure in Ružomberok because

---

was thirty crowns to one dollar. The rent on a three-room apartment for a middle-class couple might be three hundred crowns. A book with a good binding cost thirty to forty crowns.

of the linguistic difficulty I might have faced in a Slovakian school. The Czech and Slovak vocabularies are a little different. Czechs and Slovaks can understand 95 percent of each other's languages, the way an American can understand a Cockney although he cannot quite imitate him. Father was reassigned in 1932. He returned to Prague (without the car, alas) to command the Supreme Military War Academy for officers of the general staff; then he was appointed a division general, another step up in the military hierarchy.

The Great Depression came to Czechoslovakia in 1930. At first I knew it only from the adult talk of hard times and the economy. But soon the bell began ringing in our third-floor apartment—two, three, then five times a day. At the door would be some relatively well-dressed, hesitant young man. Had we perhaps some bread and soup, or a cup of coffee, or just bread alone? These were not people asking for small change but for food that they usually devoured then and there on the stairs. "You know who I think that younger one was?" my mother asked Father once after she had given the food and closed the door. "That was Voženílek, who used to have his notary office in the building with Dr. Knauer. Lord, he looks bad. And so confused." Within two years, Dr. Knauer himself was at the door, and many others like him—blameless, respectable people, begging for scraps, embarrassed to be recognized.

The Germans of Czechoslovakia suffered more during the Depression than the Czechs. The factories for consumer and export products—chinaware, elegant textiles, goods no one at home or abroad could afford any longer—were located in the German territories, whereas the Czechs were mainly occupied in heavy industries that were not so hard hit. The Germans turned on the Czechs with renewed resentment. The Depression not only rent lives; it broke the fragile entente between the two groups.

Father discussed the economic situation anxiously and often with Jaromír Nečas, his old classmate in the Brno Technical University and our neighbor in Praha Bubeneč. Eventually Nečas became Czechoslovakia's minister for social welfare, charged with relieving the hardship. The Germans respected him because, though a Czech, he was even-handed in distributing unemployment relief, food subsidies, and the like. His wife, I remember, was formidably intelligent and a feminist; their daughter was pretty but shy. When the Nazis invaded Czechoslovakia, they rewarded Nečas for his popularity among the Germans by making him head of the Protectorate Supreme Price Office. Of course they did not know he was also

a prominent member of the resistance. As his position became more dangerous and exposed, he was forced to escape the country alone in January 1940
to join the exile government forming in London. Eventually, the Nazis
gassed his wife and daughter in a concentration camp. The few Czechs who
learned about it could never bring themselves to tell Nečas. He died in Wales
in January 1945, mercifully ignorant of his family's fate.

Early on I became aware that there were Czechs and Germans in the
world, and that they were not the same. In 1933 Father invited a strict and
punctual German woman, an émigrée from the Reich, to tutor me in German, for languages were a normal part of a European education. She was
thirty years old, a social democrat probably, maybe even a Communist, and
anti-Nazi. I think Father wanted to help her. However, after a few months,
the Czechoslovak military intelligence warned Father that she might be a
German spy. Father did not believe it but he dismissed her, to my delight.
Next I was sent to my grandmother's friend near Carlsbad to perfect my
German. That was an interesting period in my adolescence, because in 1936
I got to know some boys and girls who approved of Hitler. I even dated a
pretty German girl. She was the picture of Hitler Youth in her white shirt
and black skirt, the uniform of budding Nazis. I must have been one irresist-
ible Czech, or so I tell myself, to get a German girl to go out with me.

That sort of fraternization was unusual then and it was soon to end
completely, for by this time Hitler was menacing central Europe. The
Czechoslovak government responded by trying assiduously to strengthen
Czechoslovakia's alliance system and by reorganizing and building up our
army. The number of divisions was increased from twelve to twenty. In 1935
seven army corps were organized; Father was appointed commander of the
one in Olomouc, in Northern Moravia, an assignment that required us to
move. At about the same time, the fall of 1935, the chief of staff of the Red
Army visited Czechoslovakia and invited Czechoslovak officers to come and
observe the Soviet military program. Father was thus appointed head of a
mission to attend the Red Army maneuvers near Moscow in the summer of
1936. He could still speak Russian, which he had learned during his years as
a legionnaire, and for ten well-publicized days he consulted with officers in
the Soviet Union who were close to Stalin, such as Marshal Voroshilov and
General Uborevich. He came back impressed with the efficiency of the Red
Army. The Soviets used tanks and armored vehicles in large units; their air
force made extensive use of paratroopers; their officers seemed competent.
In Prague it was considered correct to be restrained in praising the Red

Army. President Beneš, who succeeded Masaryk in December 1935, regarded Czechoslovakia as a firm part of western Europe, and was overly anxious, I think, to allay western fears that we would be drawn toward the Communist Soviet Union. As foreign minister, Beneš had inserted a protocol in the 1935 Mutual Treaty with the Soviets making Russian action contingent upon French assistance. In case of war, there was no automatic guarantee of help from our Russian ally, thanks to Beneš. Father's glowing opinion of the Red Army was therefore controversial and downright odd after 1936, when Stalin purged his top officers and practically everyone Father had met was executed, with the exception of Kliment Voroshilov.

By the time Hitler occupied the Rhineland in March 1936, Czechoslovaks knew that he intended to shatter the Versailles Treaty. His oft-stated principle that the German people formed a closed community which recognized no national borders was aimed squarely at Czechoslovakia's Germans; they were now bombarded with nationalist propaganda that ignored the existence of frontiers or citizenship. Czechoslovakia's defense was becoming a crucial issue, and Father was becoming a public figure. In 1937 the Czechoslovak military put on showy exercises near Olomouc to draw attention to what was now one of the most modern and well-equipped armies in the world. As director of the maneuvers, Father was mentioned frequently in the press. He was featured in the newsreels, explaining elaborate troop movements to President Beneš, talking with foreign military attachés. The publicity was part of Beneš' efforts to make the army popular, to get people ready for war. Vacations were out of the question for Father after 1936; the armed forces had to be prepared for a German attack.

At this time the army regional commands were divided among four generals, the respective heads of the military in the areas of Bohemia, Moravia-Silesia, western Slovakia, and eastern Slovakia. In late 1937, one of these generals was about to retire. Under his command were the two critical army corps in Olomouc and Brno. Who would be his successor? At home, that was the third most frequent topic of conversation, after Hitler and the nefarious activities of the Sudeten German party. Father's friend Major Voda thought Beneš would appoint Father. Sylvestr Voda was a grain commissioner and head of the union of reserve officers in Brno; he had met Father in Sokol during their student days. He was stocky and animated—"Major Motormouth," I called him privately, because he never stopped talking. A member of the rightist agrarian party, he was more conservative than Father, but the two got along fine, even in their constant political discussions. Visiting the Voda home was boring for me because there were only older girls there—his two daughters—but I liked Major Voda immensely. His liveliness was a contrast to my staid parents, and even when I was quite young, he talked to me without the patronizing air adults use when they are wasting time conversing with a child.

We received the first bulletins of the impending promotion from Father's brother, Bohuslav, Uncle Slávek: Beneš was favoring Father over all the other candidates. Uncle Slávek was a member of the central committee of Beneš' party and thus had an inside track on political information. He was director of a savings bank, mayor of Uherský Brod, and held other provincial offices. On important occasions, he liked to review the catechism of our family history. "Do you know how your father grew up? Without any advantages—none," he reminded me then, as if he had not pulled himself out of the same trench, "and now he will be a general with maybe the most important command in Czechoslovakia." Finally, Major Voda arrived with the confirmation. He ran into our house in Olomouc, his paunch heaving, his face the color of beet soup, with the syllables tumbling out: "Vojtěch got it! He got it! He's in!"

And so early in 1938, the last normal year of my youth, we moved to Brno in central Czechoslovakia. Our maid, our dear Marie, who had been with us in Prague and Olomouc, came with us to our five-room apartment in the new military headquarters on Kounic Street. We had an official car again, a blue eight-cylinder Tatra, and a civilian driver, Mr. Ličman. I was sixteen, well-behaved but hormonal, and full of nationalist, slightly right-wing political ideas. I made friends with Jiří Ingr, General Sergej Ingr's son, who lived on the second floor of our building, and with the family of General Antonín Hasal on the third floor, all children of legionnaires. I had a circle of friends, kids from the Realgymnasium: Míla Pechan, Odolen Drbal, Jiří Brada, and a dozen others. "Oh, are you finally getting some exercise?" Father would remark when he saw me going to meet them with my tennis racket or swim trunks. And he would add, inhaling sumptuously, "At your age, you should be breathing fresh air."

On Sundays a group of us would take bicycle trips and hikes in the woods. It wasn't respiration I was after on these weekends, but the platonic nearness of girls. I had been brought up in the implicit, certainly never stated, doctrine that girls were pure creatures who knew nothing of sex and would have abjured it if they had any notion of its existence. Neither the novels that I

sneaked out of my parents' library nor the servants I courageously questioned had disabused me of my chivalric ideas. So these easy, natural friend-
ships with girls my age were quite enlightening. I particularly remember
Věra Hložková, a big, pretty girl who was one of my favorite tennis partners.
With her open, frank face and easygoing air, she was too sisterly to arouse
sexual fantasies, though she did have a caressing alto voice. I was surprised
to find out that after the war she became intimate with her boss, the Communist Viliam Široký, then the deputy prime minister of Slovakia, and a
nasty piece of business. Despite her connection to him, she was one of the
first people arrested and tortured in 1949 at the start of the purges. For, once
the Communists began gaining control in Czechoslovakia, they played out
the old Soviet story of persecutions, arrests, confessions, and executions of
high-ranking party members, a vortex that Věra was somehow swept into.
Later, in Vienna in the 1970s, I was about to board a streetcar when I heard
that distinctive voice calling, "Rád'o! Rád'o!" It was Věra, who had survived
and been "rehabilitated" by the Communist regime. She had that strange
look and nervous volubility of people who have endured too much. She
talked disjointedly about being kept naked on the cement floor of the notorious Koloděje prison and about her torture, which somehow caused the loss
of her breasts. I saw her again some years afterward in Vienna, accompanied
by a man who I suspected was a secret policeman. She looked very ill, ravaged by disease and memories.

Although in general the Czechoslovaks were not deceived by Hitler, I remember hearing conversations in those years remarkable for their naïveté.
Brada, the brightest student in our Realgymnasium, admired the Germans,
especially their stand against the Jews. Even after the start of the war, my
Jewish friends had no inkling that there was a holocaust coming to Germany. Some of them were still speaking German at home in preference to
Czech. Those who sensed the seriousness of Hitler's intentions had only a
vague notion of the scale of the persecution. I remember that some Jewish
friends came to ask us to keep their jewelry in case the Nazis invaded and
arrested them. We could hardly make them understand that we might be the
first people the Germans would round up, and their valuables with us.

In March 1938, Hitler moved into Austria and completed the union of
Germany and Austria that he had long been threatening. The *Anschluss*
added six million Austro-Germans to the Reich; Germany now completely
surrounded the historic Czech provinces and controlled our north-south

trade lines. With our three million Germans, we would be the Führer's next target.

The Sudeten Germans had embraced National Socialism by 1935; Hitler was almost as popular in the German areas of Bohemia and Moravia as he was in Germany.[6] He was sending regular financial subsidies to the Sudeten proto-Nazis; in return, the Sudeten German party leader Konrad Henlein assured Hitler privately that he was ardently striving to bring all of Bohemia, Moravia, and Silesia into the Reich.[7] Publicly, Henlein professed loyalty to the republic. He repeatedly stated to foreign leaders that his sole aim was to achieve an understanding between Czechoslovakia and her "mistreated" German minority. He shuttled back and forth between London and Berlin while the British obtusely believed his assertions that he had no connection or contact with Hitler. To the British, Henlein shrewdly described Czechoslovakia as a state tainted with Bolshevism—the kiss of death in western diplomatic circles.[8] Using Henlein as his mouthpiece, Hitler thus turned the German question in Czechoslovakia into an international issue.

The Sudeten Germans, ecstatic about the occupation of Austria, began holding demonstrations in which hundreds of thousands of overstimulated *Übermenschen* demanded incorporation into the Reich. Hitler at the same time gave vitriolic speeches in which he screamed that he would no longer tolerate Czechoslovakia's oppression of its German population. The propaganda succeeded in inciting the Sudetens. In May 1938, the Czechoslovak army put down riots in the German areas, almost without bloodshed, and partially mobilized for war with Germany. At the same time, in municipal free elections held throughout the spring, almost 90 percent of the Sudeten Germans voted for the Henlein party and espoused Nazi aims. Britain and France, frantic to prevent a situation that would involve them in a war with

6. More than 60 percent of German voters in Czechoslovakia cast ballots for the Sudeten German party—the Henlein party—in 1935.

7. Secret report from Henlein to Hitler, Nov. 14, 1937, in *Documents on German Foreign Policy 1918–1945, from the Archives of the German Foreign Ministry, Series D (1937–1945)* (Washington, D.C., 1949–51) 2:56–57.

8. Henlein publicly stated in March 1941: "The Sudeten Germans succeeded in a short time in endangering the internal stability of Czechoslovakia so thoroughly and creating such confusion that she was soon ripe for liquidation. . . . We knew that we could only win if we succeeded in making three and a half million Sudeten Germans into National Socialists, but if we were to avoid Czech interference, we had to pretend to deny our allegiance to National Socialism." E. L. Woodward and Rohan Butler, eds., *Documents on British Foreign Policy, 1919–1939,* 3 vols. (London, 1949–50), 2:556.

Hitler, pressed Beneš to accede to every German demand. But in the wake of a violent speech by Hitler on September 12, 1938, Henlein followers poured into Bohemian towns, shooting policemen and smashing the windows of Czech and Jewish shops, intent on seizing the public buildings. The Czech police restored order, again almost without shooting, and the government imposed martial law. Henlein fled to Germany and, dropping the veil of loyalty to Czechoslovakia, issued a call to arms against "the Hussite-Bolshevik criminals of Prague."

This was the Munich crisis, in which Hitler threatened to attack Czechoslovakia unless we surrendered the Sudeten territories, a demand that Britain and France pressured President Beneš to accept, finally presenting it to him as an ultimatum on September 21, 1938. The Germans had five armies massed on the frontiers, preparing to attack Czechoslovakia. People of my generation have a precise recollection of September 23 at 10:20 in the evening: that was when the government decreed general mobilization and the sleeping streets throughout the country were suddenly alive with thousands of conscripts hurrying to their regiments. We moved some forty divisions—our entire army—into place. What would the western allies do? Honor their treaty commitments or let us fight Hitler alone?[9]

It was a crisis for Father, too. We had a stream of visitors to our apartment and incessant phone calls from officials who hoped the military would persuade Beneš to fight—without allies, if necessary. The senior military staff was passionately opposed to giving in. So was the rest of the nation. If ever there was a country ready for war, it was Czechoslovakia in September 1938. As soon as people heard about the western ultimatum, they gathered in the squares, and the gatherings developed into massive demonstrations urging war. They demanded that the government be turned over to army officers who would not capitulate. The next day at school we heard what sounded like a buffalo stampede. Thousands, then tens of thousands of people were pouring into the streets of Brno. One group stopped in front of the military command headquarters on Kounic Street and began to chant, "Give us weapons! Give us weapons!" Father appeared on the balcony, raised his arms, and the crowd quieted.

9. By September 28, 1938, the Czechoslovak armed forces numbered some 1,075,000 men, deployed over 9,000 fortified posts throughout the country. The four armies contained over forty divisions. For more details of the military preparedness, see Radomír Luža, *The Transfer of the Sudeten Germans* (New York, 1964), 22.

"My friends, you must go home," he said, his voice echoing down the crowded alleys. "We are trying to work here, trying to do exactly what you are telling us to do. But we can't accomplish anything with all this roaring in our ears."

Similar demonstrations were going on all over the country. Czechoslovakia had become a war camp. More than a million men were under arms. All the main roads were mined and blocked. We were covered by a total blackout. Mother and I went to Uherský Brod, Father to Račice Castle, the headquarters of his Second Army during mobilization. The northern Moravian barrier that Father commanded was to be held against the expected pincer attack from Austria and Silesia. The government left Prague on September 27, expecting the capital to be bombarded that very night.

But there would be no fight. Eduard Daladier and Neville Chamberlain went to Munich, where on September 29 they met with the Führer and his ally Benito Mussolini. Without the presence of any representative from either Czechoslovakia or the Soviet Union, the four leaders decided to surrender the Czechoslovak territory demanded by Hitler. Beneš was called back to Prague to receive an ultimatum not from Hitler alone, but from the four powers together. If Czechoslovakia refused to yield the Sudetenland, thus "provoking" a German invasion, France would not honor her treaty commitment to Czechoslovakia, and Great Britain, whose obligations were contingent on French intervention, would also be absolved of facing Hitler.

Meanwhile, the commanding generals of the four Czechoslovak armies, including Father, met in Moravia and deliberated whether to fight an invasion. The generals believed they could hold out against Hitler for three months, provided that Poland would pledge not to join Germany in an attack. After three months they hoped the western allies could be shamed into honoring their treaties. They decided further that if President Beneš refused to fight, they would replace the president with a military government and go ahead with defense measures.

Then the army representatives went to Prague on September 29, faced their supreme commander, and demanded that he reject capitulation. "They entreated, threatened, begged, some wept," according to Beneš' own account. I don't know if my emotional and flammable father was one of the weepers or the threateners, but as a son and a historian, I wish I could have witnessed that scene. Beneš, in an agony of uncertainty, finally prevailed over the generals. According to General Hasal, who later described the meeting to me, the president said that war against Hitler would come soon anyway, and he could not accede to what might be a slaughter of the country. "The generals left dissatisfied, embittered, and in a desperate mood," Beneš later wrote.[10] Evidently they had changed their minds about throwing him out.

Unlucky Beneš. The decision to capitulate haunted him for the rest of his life. It seems clear now that Poland would not have remained neutral in the event of war between Germany and Czechoslovakia, and it seems doubtful that after three months of watching Czechoslovaks wage a desperate struggle the French and British would have been any more willing than in September to be "digging trenches and trying on gas masks here because of a quarrel," as Chamberlain airily described it, "in a faraway country between people of whom we know nothing."[11] Nevertheless, neither time nor the thousands of words I have read about Munich have weakened my conviction that Father and his colleagues were right and Beneš was wrong. Aside from the question of morality, there can be little doubt that the sacrifice of Czechoslovakia which began at Munich handed the Germans a huge endowment of war matériel and a strategic geographic advantage on both the western and eastern fronts.

Germany thus moved unopposed into the fringe of the Bohemian lands containing mountain approaches and fortifications. Czechs, Jews, and anti-Nazi Germans fled to the rump republic, leaving their property to be confiscated by Germans. President Beneš, denounced by everyone, resigned in October and went into exile in Great Britain. A judge with no political experience, Emil Hácha, was then elected president, with a new cabinet. Hácha was only sixty-six, but he was fragile and declining from what had never been a strong personality. In the weeks following Munich the Poles and Hungarians behaved like neighbors who, observing that the next-door house is on fire, take the opportunity to raid its storage room. The Poles seized the Těšín district. Hungary, with German and Italian approval, seized five thousand square miles of Slovakia.[12]

10. Beneš in London, on January 8, 1941, reported in *Central European Observer* (January 17, 1941). See also Edvard Beneš, *Mnichovske dny* (Days of Munich) (London, 1955).

11. Chamberlain made the famous remark on September 27, 1938, in a broadcast during the Munich crisis.

12. Czechoslovakia lost 93.5 percent of its lignite mines, 55 percent of its coal, 46 percent of its supply of electrical energy, and fully a third of its population, including over a million Czechs and Slovaks. The republic was reconstituted as Czecho-Slovakia; Slovakia and Sub-Carpathian Ruthenia received wide autonomy, with their own cabinets and diets.

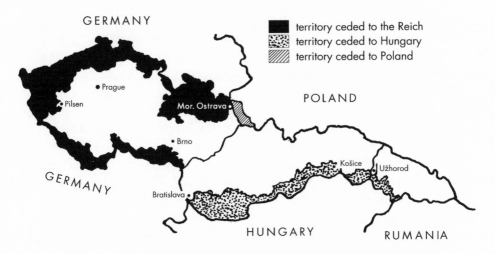

Czechoslovakia's territorial losses, 1938–39

At home, we all went into shock over Munich, Father especially, for he had never expected French and British appeasement to go so far. It is a strange thing to see the population of an entire country personally depressed, to look into every face and see bitterness. Father, who tried never to let his feelings show, exercised more self-control than usual, but in his gray-green eyes I could see anger, ugly and relentless. He was pale with exhaustion. Nothing after Munich would ever be the same.

Despite Hitler's promises that he wanted "no more Czechs," and despite the solemn pledges of the western powers to defend the remainder of the country, the Munich Pact was broken in just six months. Hitler marched into Bohemia and Moravia in mid-March 1939 and declared the country a Reich protectorate, an invasion that the rump republic, deprived of its fortifications, was powerless to resist.[13] At about six o'clock on the evening of March 14, 1939, just after Father got home from work, we began getting agitated phone calls. The Germans were coming; their troops had moved into Moravská Ostrava, the industrial center of northeastern Moravia, and

13. With the occupation of the Czech lands and western Slovakia in March, 1939, the German army seized 1,582 of our airplanes, 591 antiaircraft guns, 2,175 pieces of artillery, 469 tanks, 43,876 machine guns, 1,090,000 rifles, and a vast store of other war matériel. In addition, huge reserves of weapons in Slovakia and Ruthenia were now available to the Germans. See Hitler's speech, April 28, 1939, in Hans Volz, *Dokumente der deutschen Politik,* ed. Paul Meier-Benneckenstein (Berlin, 1939–40), 7:150.

there was fighting in the neighboring city. Though at first he could get no confirmation from Prague of an invasion, Father issued instructions to begin burning documents. A snowstorm fell on the entire country as the military authorities worked through the night destroying confidential files, personnel information, and every sort of anti-German paper. Mr. Ličman, Maria, and even our former maid Božena Foral came to help us remove the materials from our apartment. The photos of Father with Marshal Voroshilov and the Russian officers were the first things we threw into the flames. Outside, the odor of cinders hung in the air; every family in our compound had been doing the same thing. All the windows as far as one could see were flecked with snow and ashes and bits of singed beige paper, the military's official stationery.

Around eleven the next day the Germans arrived at the offices, but they did not disturb the private quarters for another two months. Eventually, our apartment was taken over by a Colonel Freytag, the new military commander of Brno. He seemed a decent sort, but his wife made sure we understood from her manner that she would disinfect the place to get rid of the Czech germs as soon as we left. The Czechoslovak army was disbanded, its soldiers and officers barred from all military facilities. As we moved to a four-room apartment on Wurm Street, we decided to do without maids so that we could indulge in anti-German invective or make plans for our future security without endangering anyone who might overhear us.

Czechoslovakia disappeared from the map of Europe. Slovakia was declared an independent republic—independent, that is, from the Czechs—and became a German satellite. Hácha remained as the state president within the Reich Protectorate of Bohemia and Moravia, the hesitant and unwilling instrument of Hitler's Reich Protector, Konstantin von Neurath. Karl Hermann Frank, the deputy leader of the Sudeten German party and anathema to all Czechs, was named state secretary—his title was Higher SS and Police Leader—and was given control over security matters. He wielded disproportionate power. The Czechs in the Protectorate government were not ministers in the usual sense. Although they were charged with administrative duties, they exercised almost no authority in political affairs and were constrained to carry out German orders. Those orders involved expropriating Czech property, harassing the Czech intelligentsia, and Germanizing the rest of the population. Hácha appointed General Eliáš prime minister of the nonministers. Respected and well known in diplomatic circles, Eliáš was personally acquainted with Neurath, whom he had met abroad. They communicated with each other in French, which perhaps kept Neurath in mind of the world beyond the aberrant Reich.

Two weeks after the occupation, Father and Eliáš decided to risk meeting face-to-face to plan the future. They came together in a peaceful weekend cottage near the Sázava River. For these two soldiers, the ultimate goal was clear: armed insurrection by the Czechoslovak military against the German occupiers. But the time had to be right. There could be no question now of a crippled army taking on Germany alone, even with massive popular support. For the present, Father and Eliáš agreed, the work of the resistance was not to plan futile uprisings, but to gather intelligence and smuggle it abroad, to help in a war that at first would be fought by others. They believed that the Germans could not permanently occupy Czechoslovakia and that war would come to free us. But unlike many of their colleagues, they believed it would be a long war and hence a long occupation and that Hitler's defeat would require the involvement of both the Soviet Union and the United States. The resistance they endorsed could only be an adjunct to Allied military operations.

I hope Father and Eliáš embraced as usual when they ended their meeting, for there was not to be another. Eliáš began his perilous double life in the Protectorate, complying with the Nazis sufficiently to maintain his position as prime minister, while secretly using that position to send information abroad, help the families of political prisoners, and defend Czech interests as well as he could in his daily dealings with the Germans.

In July Father had a chance to learn what the Soviets thought of the Czechoslovak situation. A high Soviet official—probably a member of the Soviet military intelligence—was passing through Prague and asked for a secret meeting. Father still had his official car, thanks to the slow metabolism of bureaucracy; he picked up the Soviet at Wilson Railroad Station, and the conference took place in the backseat.[14] As the driver slithered around the city for two hours, the official set out Russia's position. War was inevitable. Stalin intended to fight Hitler in his own time, after the British were firmly engaged in the war. Stalin's exclusion from the Munich conference had completely alienated him from France and Britain. He trusted them less than ever, knowing that they would be happy to allow the Soviet Union to

14. Father was accompanied by Major Voda (who also spoke Russian), Josef Appel, who would bring Father's report of the meeting to Eliáš, and General Rudolf Hanák.

fight Hitler alone, but he foresaw that the cooperation of all the anti-Nazi powers would be necessary to defeat Germany. Soviet intervention in any case would come to relieve Czechoslovakia, and at that time the Soviets would expect the help of the home resistance.

When the Nazi-Soviet Pact was announced on August 23, 1939, the Czechs went into collective shock: our only remaining friend was striking a deal with our killer. But Father, remembering his conversation with the Soviet official, adopted a wait-and-see attitude that kept him relatively sanguine until Hitler discarded the neutrality pact and attacked the Soviet Union in June 1941.

After the invasion of our country, Father stood aloof from the mass resistance organizations that were forming, especially ON (Obrana Národa), Defense of the Nation. The military men who started ON were convinced that Germany would be beaten as soon as France and Great Britain decided to take action. They did not, therefore, take pains to set up their groups so that they could survive long years in secret. They met almost publicly in such places as coffeehouses, kept files and made up lists of their members, and had far-fetched plans for igniting a mass revolt against the occupiers.

General Ingr, one of the leaders of ON, was himself sane, but he was out of the country after June 1939, having been secretly dispatched to Paris to be ON's representative abroad. Ingr, Beneš' minister of national defense in the exile government in London, was unusual among military men in that he possessed political sense, if not political ambition. He smoked some sixty cigarettes a day which he rolled himself, daintily tapping his tobacco bag over little paper troughs and leaving what afterwards looked like an arrangement of larvae on any conference table where he sat. We were glad that Ingr escaped before the Gestapo uncovered ON and, just as Father had repeatedly warned, arrested practically all its members. ON had been the largest resistance group in Europe, yet in a matter of months in 1939 it was virtually wiped out. It was wrenching for Father to learn about the executions of his colleagues, men he had known for decades. ON's destruction convinced him that the resistance had to operate through loose circles, not from one central command.

Since the Czechoslovak army had been dismantled, Father retired in the summer of 1939 and resumed university studies to complete an engineering degree. He was organizing his own clandestine nucleus of ten or twelve individuals, both military and civilian people, which included, as I later found out, Otakar Žalman, Jaromír Appel, František Peller, Ludvík Tůma, František Jedlička, and, of course, Sylvestr Voda. Father held to his belief that anti-German attacks by the resistance could only annoy the Nazis at this point, snarl up a few of their plans, and momentarily distract them from their military efforts, but the damage we Czechs could do with nuisance terrorism would not be worth the retaliation we would invite against both ourselves and innocent people. We had to wait for a war that would start outside our country.

I had begun studying Polish, for we believed that Hitler would next invade Poland, where the West would at last intervene. It was one of those peculiar coincidences that the night the war broke out, I had just finished reading my first book in Polish, General Wladyslaw Širosky's *France and Poland*. I was restless for hours, gave up trying to sleep around 4:30, and was listening to Polish Radio Katovice. Suddenly I heard, "Uwaga! Uwaga! Uwaga!" (Attention! Attention! Attention!) and an excited announcement that German planes were bombing Polish airports. Later in the morning I heard Hitler's speech declaring war on Poland. In a few weeks came the news of the Polish collapse. We were sorry for the Poles—there are times when Czechs do pity Poles—but we were overjoyed that France and Britain finally declared war. The West was not after all resigned to Hitler's swallowing central Europe.

But with the outbreak of war, the Nazis were more than ever determined to keep the Czechs under tight control, to wipe out our leaders and anyone likely to challenge German authority. On September 1, 1939, simultaneously with the declaration of war by the Allies, the Germans arrested no less than two thousand Czechoslovak public figures. Among those taken prisoner that day was Uncle Slávek, who had become a member of our national parliament. He died in Buchenwald in May 1945, just a few days after the camp was liberated.

The Czechs were getting over the shock of occupation by now and were energized by the outbreak of war. They began gathering in mass demonstrations under the guise of national or religious commemorations. Some of these demonstrations were spontaneous, and others were planned by resistance organizations. Often they involved up to 100,000 people. They made the Germans more than uneasy. Czechs boycotted the Protectorate press; newspaper sales plummeted. Transmitters from abroad were being smuggled into the country to assist the home resistance. Until these were destroyed by the Nazis in 1941–42, the underground sent thousands of cables to London, providing the Allies with information about troop and supply movements, war production, and all sorts of vital intelligence that could only be uncovered by people inside the Protectorate. A resistance mentality therefore pervaded the country.

There was no single center of the resistance in those days, and no clear division between the Czech nominal government—those Czech officials whose every move was watched by the Nazis—and the resistance. Underground groups sprang up here and there through the cracks in the Nazi system. Like ON, some were large organizations loosely connected to each other through people who were active in several groups. Some examples of these organizations were PÚ, Political Center; PVVZ, or literally, the Committee of the Petition "We Remain Faithful," named after a manifesto published before the Munich Conference; and KSČ, the Communist Party of Czechoslovakia, which followed its own star, according to the dictates of the Comintern. All of the resistance organizations, eventually even the Communists, recognized President Beneš as the country's leader and the voice of free Czechoslovakia, a voice we heard regularly and riskily over the BBC. For the most part, military people nursed their plans for a popular insurrection that would overthrow the Nazis, while their followers engaged in passive sabotage—boycotts and huge public demonstrations consisting simply of massive, apparently submissive gatherings.

On the anniversary of Czechoslovak independence, October 28, 1939, the underground in Prague organized the largest anti-German demonstration ever held in occupied Europe, a flagrant display of rebellion in the middle of war. Germans and Czechs scuffled; a Czech student was shot and eventually died. Then the student's funeral on November 15 became the occasion for more demonstrations in Prague. Declaring that "a group of Czech intellectuals has been attempting . . . to disturb peace and order in the Protectorate," Hitler retaliated with measures that were purposely arbitrary. He closed all Czech universities and ordered nine student leaders, chosen at random, to be shot without a trial. All students living in dormitories were arrested, and more than twelve hundred were sent to concentrations camps. Father learned of these developments when, arriving at the Brno Technical University to take his final examinations in engineering, he found the buildings seized by the German police. Like thousands of other students, he never graduated.

Strangely, the mundane rhythms of life continued in the vicious climate of the occupation, though now I cannot quite explain how. I went to school from eight until one, Monday through Saturday. There were reports to write and streetcars to catch by 7:15, even while terrible news blared from the radio: the German occupation of Norway and Denmark and then Belgium and the Netherlands. To alleviate the manpower shortage, we students were required to work for six weeks, so as soon as classes recessed for the summer, I went with Odolen Drbal to his father's limestone quarry near Hranice. The work was hard but I enjoyed earning my manly wage and making new friends. Then came the astonishing collapse of France in June 1940—France, which we had counted on to make all the difference. Only Great Britain remained at war with Germany. We huddled at the radio each night as if gathering for prayer to hear fifteen cherished and illegal minutes of news from the BBC. I can hear the theme music now, through the static of fifty-odd years.

Yet what I remember just as clearly about 1940 is Mr. Kadlec's dancing classes, where we young Czech patriots were authorized to press the belts and backs of nubile females and to slide them around on a hardwood dance floor that was far away from war. Kadlec even gave a few evening dances after the Battle of Britain, or so the chronology seems braided in my mind. If Britain fell, all was lost, and if I had been younger or older, the stark outlook for our side would have thrown me into the most morbid despair. But I was eighteen in 1940, and as summer rusted into fall and then was covered by winter, I was a happy almost-man, having fallen in love with Věra, a sweet young thing I met at the dances. I had been seeing her for a year when it was required that I ride my bicycle to her summer house and meet her parents, a formality I dreaded but had to endure for the sake of my Věra. The family was nice enough. Her father was a legionnaire; her mother was Russian. I began to understand that love was important in life, perhaps even as important as nationalism. Věra was a whole country in herself. My only dissatisfaction with her, which I discovered as we became closer, was that she was intent on preserving my virtue, which I would have sacrificed to her without hesitation at any time during our relationship. She worried about me in other ways, too, often warning me to be careful, not to do anything that would draw the attention of the Germans.

When Father talked to me about the resistance in that second year of the war, it was mainly to warn me not to take part in any illegal group or activity. He expressly ordered me, in his best military fashion, to stay absolutely clear of any underground business. I guess he thought if I was not afraid of the Gestapo, I might at least be afraid of him. I was, but I nevertheless asked Major Voda confidentially what I might do to help the resistance effort. I had the nucleus of an organization, ten or fifteen fellow students, including Pechan and Drbal and two boys from Hranice, all prepared to undertake some task. I had been careful not to hold meetings or to let my friends know the names of the others in our group; I was the only link connecting us. Major Voda suggested that we might help support the family of Štěpán Drásal, a resister who had been arrested in a sweep of the Sokol underground. With thousands of breadwinners in Gestapo prisons and thousands more fleeing to join the liberation movement abroad, there were families all over the country suddenly without any income whatever. None of us fledgling resisters had much cash; we had to give up practically all of our pocket money. But there were enough of us that we managed each month to help Mrs. Drásal and her children with some necessities. She never asked the name of the young man who brought her the money or the source of his largesse. Major Voda promised to observe my foremost rule of conspiracy: he was not to tell Father.

How were larger sums raised for the resistance? Father's main go-between with Eliáš was Mr. Appel, a lawyer and Sokol member. Eliáš saw to it that Appel was appointed to the central committee of National Solidarity, the new official political movement that was supposed to replace our old party system. National Solidarity was the only legal outlet for political expression. Ninety-eight percent of the male voters joined it as a way of showing more solidarity than the Nazis had bargained for; therefore Appel was in touch with all sorts of people. Father sent him the names of families urgently in need of money; Appel handed the lists to Eliáš or a Solidarity official, who then funneled relief, either private donations or public funds that he could quietly divert. Appel, who also gave legal advice to political prisoners, was in many ways an ideal conspirator: well dressed, repressed, tenacious, and trusting no one. He avoided arrest until 1944 and even then survived three interrogations by the Gestapo.

Another such official was Jaroslav Mezník. In 1940 he was appointed provincial president of Moravia, with access to certain moneys. In their last meeting, in a forest near Brno, Mezník told Father he was proud to report that families of resisters and exiles were being supported from these public funds. He was arrested a few weeks later, in October 1941, and brought to the Kounic Student Home, which the Gestapo was using as a jail. Afraid of the torture that he knew was in store, he committed suicide by leaning out of his cell between the bars and shouting so that a sentry shot him.

Father believed that above all we had to concentrate on gathering intelligence. We needed communications facilities—transmitters to keep us in contact with the resistance abroad, ways of sending warnings and messages between individuals and groups at home. So he arranged a meeting in a park with Alois Šilinger, yet another legionnaire, who was a communications expert. Šilinger had a good position waiting for him in Brno when Father persuaded him to take instead a lesser job in Uherské Hradiště, where he could help the resistance. Šilinger thus became head of telephone service maintenance, moving freely all over that district on the Slovakian border.

Meanwhile, one resistance group after another was being devastated by arrests. No large organization could remain secret for more than a year before its members were rounded up one by one. Time and again, fragments of the shattered organizations would regroup and attempt to rebuild, only to be smashed in a new spasm of repression.

Father had escaped arrest for two years since the occupation began, but his time was running out. After the Germans attacked Yugoslavia in April and the Soviet Union in June 1941, his situation became more dangerous each day. Once the Czechs knew that the Soviets were in the war, their defiance resurged. Individual sabotage, strikes, passive resistance of all kinds increased—random acts that made Hitler furious and invoked the violent retaliation of Neurath's deputy Frank. A new wave of arrests thus washed over the Protectorate during the summer of 1941; there would be over ten thousand by the end of the year. And every resister in prison, subject to interrogation, meant much greater danger for those still free. The Gestapo began jailing Sokol leaders all over the country—nearly a thousand. Within eight months, only a few were still alive.

Mr. Appel brought General Eliáš' last communication to Father in early September—a warning. Appel's smooth features were contorted with anxiety as he delivered the message: the situation was critical. On the twenty-seventh came the news of Heydrich's appointment and the declaration of martial law. Then more executions, starting with two generals, leaders of ON, who were friends of Father. The next day Eliáš was arrested and charged with high treason. Father could either wait for death to drive up for him in a black sedan, or he could flee.

That was how it happened that on the midnight of September 29, 1941, I lay awake with my Bible, wondering if Father was safe at Kravka's and thinking about the deep vein of malice in human beings. How unexpected it was that

torture, having long died out everywhere in the West, was again commonplace in the twentieth century in one of the most civilized countries in the
world. Two blocks from our house executions were going on every day at
the Kounic Student Home, watched by German spectators who were perhaps educated and liked Brahms, but who nevertheless gathered willingly to
see Czechs with bloody faces lose their lives. Then I tried to stop thinking
altogether while I waited in the dark for the Gestapo.

II

At six in the morning, the shrieking of the front bell told us they had come for Father. While we tried to get into our clothes, they were beating the door, cudgeling it as if it were shielding some secret, and ringing the bell of our landlady, Mrs. Břečka, who lived in the basement below us. By the time Mother and I got downstairs, the Germans were already in. "The gentlemen are here," Mrs. Břečka said with a quaver, as if she, too, had spent the night expecting them. There were three of them in shiny boots and long leather coats looking at everything in the entrance hall but us.

"Where is General Luža?" the first one snapped as he bent to investigate a sideboard.

"He left yesterday," my mother answered. With my racing heart, I was surprised to hear the evenness of her voice.

"To go where?"

"He's visiting friends."

"What friends?"

"He didn't tell me. But probably he'll be back in a day or two; that's his usual stay," she said. And then, as cool as you please, she added, "Why? What's happened?"

The Nazis, of course, knew the script and knew they had missed their man. Irritated, one of them gave the house a cursory search while the others remained with us, each in a separate room.

"Should I raise the shades?" I asked.

"Ja, Ja," the officer replied with a wave of his hand, content that things should appear normal in the neighborhood.

I gazed out for just an instant before I sat down with my Vulgate Bible. My mind, however, was on the newspapers just now coming out on the street corners of Brno. The German-controlled press had begun featuring boxes on every front page with announcements of people who had been sentenced to death. There were ten or twenty each day, workers, peasants, journalists, captains, and colonels, including many of Father's friends: Czech resisters. But Father would not be one of them.

As for ourselves, we, too, were guilty of all sorts of offenses that were shortly to qualify as capital crimes—even my apolitical mother. Had she not managed to get sugar and oil for us, even an occasional chicken, beyond the rations we were allowed? Hadn't we spoken to some Jew we knew, despite its being a grievous offense? Hadn't she listened to foreign broadcasts? We were all obliged to remove the device in each radio—we called it the "Little Churchill"—that enabled us to receive shortwave broadcasts. Each radio bore a sticker warning its users that listening to foreign broadcasts was a capital crime. We removed the Churchill in our set, at least until it was time each evening for the BBC news; then we put it back again for the broadcast. Many people, perhaps most, committed these "crimes." Though these were acts that could get you into plenty of trouble, you generally got by with them unless you ran afoul of the authorities for some other offense. Besides that, I was guilty of bona fide resistance activity by collecting money for Mrs. Drásal.

"What is that?" the Nazi officer asked me sharply. He was looking at an antique pistol hanging on our wall. Having an unregistered gun was absolutely punishable by death.

"It's an old weapon that my father received as a gift. It dates from the Napoleonic era," I answered, then added helpfully, "1812. It doesn't work. It's over a hundred years old."

Jesus, Maria, please don't let it work, I thought. Were we going to be shot because of that stupid gun in our hall? But the German took my word for it and put the pistol back. By now the search had been completed, and the officers were satisfied that my father was not hiding in the house. It would only be moments before they left.

"You will come with us," the first one snapped again. My mother's eyes grew wide, as mine must have. The last thing we had expected was that we would be arrested. They put us in the back of one of the two-door Opels that were parked outside. Mother, in her housedress and no makeup, looked wary and baffled as she stared out of the car window at people going to work in the cold rush hour. I was let off with one of the Germans at the Gestapo section of the police city jail, while the car continued to the women's prison.

The policeman at the front desk was a Czech who looked at me disinterestedly, relieved me of my shoelaces, belt, the contents of my pockets, and my Bible, and gave me a list of what he had confiscated. Upstairs, a stricter-looking German guard led me to my little cell. The door opened and the door closed, and suddenly I was alone with four soundless walls. The room contained a French toilet sunken into a corner of the floor, a small bed, a washstand, and me. There was no stench. The only window was a tiny opening near the ceiling. My heart was pounding and I felt strangely giddy. I had an inchoate sense that what was happening to me was going to be one of my life's great experiences, undoubtedly painful, and possibly the last.

I dreamed that an SS officer was shouting at me, something unintelligible, and I was afraid he would hit me for not obeying him. I opened my eyes and found that the steel door to my cell was open, and an SS officer was indeed bellowing at me in German. It took me a few seconds to understand him. Apparently I had failed to rise to attention and give my cell number and my prisoner's number when he entered. He proceeded to scream the prison rules. I should make up my bed military style every morning. This was of the foremost importance—I could tell from the way the arteries in his neck were compromised each time he repeated that instruction. I was not to sit down, ever. Food, what there was of it, was to be consumed inside my cell, standing. Breakfast, I soon learned, meant that a guard handed you a piece of bread and an empty bowl into which he ladled some warm liquid that resembled formaldehyde. Lunch, the main meal of the day in central Europe, was more "soup" and bread, with perhaps turnips and a lump of potato. Once a week there might be a few threads of pork or some other meat. Supper was bread and turnips.

I began walking around the little cell, walking and talking to myself. I suppose this was what every solitary inmate was doing all over the prison; after all, you couldn't just stand in the cell, shifting your weight from one foot to the other from dawn until dark. I began longing for other voices, and wished the bawling SS officer would come back. Without clocks, time became liquid. One had to tread ceaselessly or be enveloped in an ocean where no shore was in sight. After perhaps a week, I began speaking in

French and German, so as to concentrate, but also to disassociate myself from the prison, to put a mental barrier between myself and my surroundings. A few times I caught myself mumbling; then I would take pains to enunciate clearly, to establish some sort of daily schedule, to hang on to normal behavior. I did push-ups and deep knee bends, gave lectures to imaginary students—every mental and physical exercise I could conceive. Minutes crawled by like days. I was not too worried about my mother; I assumed she had been taken to a women's prison and was not worse off than I was. But I was sick with thinking about Father. Since some time had passed and they were not questioning me as to his whereabouts, did that mean they had already captured him? Were they interrogating him that very moment? Even if the Germans never touched me, I thought I might not survive more than a few months in prison, for I was losing weight, perhaps as much as a pound a day. I had plenty to occupy my mind, too much, in fact; I couldn't focus on anything long enough to start making sense to myself. Was this how people went crazy?

What saved me were the prison nights, for from the very beginning, I had fabulous dreams. I would go to sleep in pain from the constant hunger, dream of steak and coffee with my family, and wake up momentarily full. I spent whole nights caressing my Věra, chatting with Mother, doing my homework on our flowered sofa. After seven or eight hours of warmth and plenitude, I was able again to face the barren, lonely, hungry dawn. Sometimes, as I paced and chattered frantically, I could work myself into a woozy zone where dreams and daydreams merged. I was in that half-world, fidgeting in a corner of my cell, when Teta Tíni, my splendid great-aunt Tíni, came once to take me away.

She appeared at the prison smiling her mischievous smile, her eyes as bright as her abundant jewelry. No one moved to stop her, though they surveyed her wondrously from her feathered hat to her felt shoes as she swept past them, as dazzling as a tropical bird alighting in that drab male place. The steel door to my cell opened for her, and she led me out of it down the gray hall and stone steps of the prison, down to her landaulet with its clean, cushioned seats. We set off in the fresh sunshine through the streets of Brno, our carriage rattling across the intersections while cars waited and drivers leaned out of their windows to observe us. A little way into our journey, however, I saw that the cars and cross lights were gradually vanishing, and the pavements, too, and that we were picking our way on dirt roads. There were horses where the cars had been, and here and there a pile of feculence, as we traveled a quiet highway, past towns and decades, back to villages I had known in my childhood, and finally to the countryside near the Slovakian border, to a time before I was born.

We went far along a provincial railroad track to the hillside houses of Uherský Brod. We were climbing up toward the elegant house of Teta Tíni's sister, my own beloved grandmother. Our horse knew its way through the dirt streets and vegetable patches to the central square, where my grandparents lived in one corner. Suddenly before us was my grandfather, Karel Večeřa, talking with a neat young man who had stopped his own cart and taken off his cap. The man was the local veterinarian. I knew what Grandfather was saying to him, for I had heard the story many times. "My wife's sister Tíni is coming for a visit. We don't get to see her often. She and her husband live near Prague. We are going to have a nice dinner. Why don't you come?" And indeed, Grandmother had put out the good china, started the fire in the parlor, and welcomed Teta Tíni with kisses.

"When you come, my dear, it's as if all the lamps in the house were suddenly lit," she said.

We had a long, happy meal and a great deal of wine. The veterinarian, whose skin under his Sunday suit looked as if he had scoured it, drank too. As no one took the least notice of me, I stuffed myself and relaxed with Grandmother's books surrounding me at the table. At the end there was champagne, which we brought with us to the next room as Teta Tíni, a bit unsteadily, seated herself at the piano. Like all the women on my mother's side, she was an accomplished musician. Grandfather dozed a little by the fire; Grandmother hummed softly as Teta Tíni played, her rings catching the gaslight. The veterinarian at first took a low stool near the piano, and gingerly stroked Tíni's arm. Soon he was on his knees a few inches from her elbow. As her treble hand moved toward him in a rising arpeggio, he would catch the fingers with his lips and cover them with kisses before they glided back down the keyboard. Once, in a quick phrase, he missed the little fingers entirely and kissed a high B-flat. Now and then my grandfather awoke and regarded the scene with a detached, aqueous gaze. Grandmother hummed on comfortably.

Ah, the weeping and shame the next morning! We all had headaches and queasy stomachs, but my grandmother's dignified conscience tormented her worse than any hangover. "To think that such a thing could have happened in my house," she wailed. "A married woman, my own sister, in the plain sight of God and everyone." Teta Tíni's eyes were puffy from crying. My grandfather lowered his head in remorse, for the party had been his idea.

"Let's clear out when she subsides a bit," I whispered to Teta Tíni, and soon we had descended the broad slope to the railroad station, and Uherský Brod was behind us. As we reached the open road, Teta Tíni began to regain her good humor, and within a few miles, she was herself again. Our carriage flew over cereal fields and mountain paths, and in only a moment, we had covered hundreds of miles and were in Brunn, on the outskirts of Vienna.

"Your great-uncle Franzi's pharmacy," Tíni remarked, indicating a big brick building. "Do you know how he got his fortune?" I did know, of course. Everyone in the family knew. "He mixed up a cure for lice," Teta Tíni said, scratching her head expressively, "and sold it to the imperial army during the Great War. Naturally, the infantry needed all he could supply, and so he got rich."

Our talk was of other great-aunts and uncles as we made our way back across the border. The carriage stopped before the apartment where I was born in Prague. I was suddenly cold. It had become Christmas without my noticing, and there was a stately fir tree in our hall decorated with white paper baskets full of nuts and sweets. A little blond boy—it was I, with long, embarrassing curls—was crying as if his heart would break, and Boženka, the maid, was trying to distract him by getting him to blow out the candles burning on the tree. Even my hard-nosed father, who had little patience with tears, looked helpless and miserable at the deluge of grief. Of course! That was the first Christmas after my Vašek had gone back to the Ukraine. Vašek, my "nanny," was Father's military servant, a moose of a man with a beard soft as sparrow's feathers and a vest that stank gently of lamp oil. I cried for days after he left, and ached for him for months, especially on that first Christmas. I told Tíni I did not want to stay to open the present he had left for me. So we went down to our carriage and, in an afternoon of deepening shadows, went across town to another decade.

We came to the house of General Eliáš, "Lešek," and his wife Jaroslava, whom my parents fondly called "Slávka." I knew what we would meet inside, and I couldn't wait to see Teta Tíni's face. The Eliáš mansion just outside Prague was rumored to have cost a million crowns; Slávka was wealthy. Lešek Eliáš was a prince of a fellow, warm, urbane, calm, five feet eight inches of cosmopolitan civility. We stepped through the foyer to a grand dining room, which looked exactly as it had when I first saw it with my father, when I was about twelve. There I was again with Father, looking with wonder at the carved chairs; the long, elegant table; the sparkling crystal chandeliers; the mantle lined with porcelain decorations; and the monkey.

It was a big, nervous monkey, excited by the presence of strangers, emitting wild cries and flinging himself around the room and through the door. I followed him to the next room, where he had bounced with a random crash into a tray of glasses and was scratching some papers on a desk as if they were so many banana leaves in a pile. Being a quite domesticated primate myself, but still hardly permitted in our front parlor, I admired that monkey's unfettered access; but even I could see that he was completely destroying the place. "I would not have believed it if I hadn't seen it with my own eyes," had been my father's comment. "A monkey loose in a house like that." Teta Tíni could hardly believe it, either.

"They have no children," she observed, as we drove away. But they certainly formed a devoted family, Slávka and Lešek and the ape.

The thought of General Eliáš sobered me. Where was he now? Under torture, probably, never to see his wife, his pet, his house again. I knew that our excursion was wearing out; I began to feel the bleak present pulling me back to Brno. Without saying a proper good-bye to Teta Tíni I returned to the prison, where there were no shadows because there was no sun. I resumed pacing back and forth in my cell, thinking of torture and of slight, brave General Eliáš, while Teta Tíni quietly drove off to enjoy the rest of her life.

My desperate loneliness and self-pity were relieved at last when late one night a man of about forty was pushed into my cell. At first he reacted to all my questions by eyeing me with a distant, preoccupied look, like someone tuning an instrument; but when he learned my name he confided his identity, Antonín Jahoda, and his offense. In late summer 1941, the Soviets had dropped two small parties of Czechoslovak soldiers into the Protectorate to make contact with the resistance. He had helped some of those who landed in central Moravia. He had been tracked down through an informer, a Czech secret agent of the Gestapo. This was serious business, and I felt that my roommate was not long for this world. Though I tried not to get attached to him, we were close friends by the time he was taken out for interrogation. I believe he was dispatched without a trial to a concentration camp for liquidation. Meanwhile, other prisoners were arriving: a middle-aged Communist worker—when they went to war against the Soviet Union, the Nazis began arresting Czech Communists by the thousands; a parish priest; a youth about my age; and many others. As the cell filled up, our captors brought in pallets at night and removed them in the morning. Eventually there were about nine of us, occupying every square foot of floor space except for our single toilet in the corner.

There was social ranking in the cell; though we were all friends, each of us knew who in the room was professional, who was proletarian. The lower-class people distinguished themselves especially by their obsession with food. All of us were hungry. But whereas the priest and others would talk of food, family, politics, food, God, the occupation, and food, the workers and poorer fellows talked of food, food, food, and food. We were glad to receive every newcomer, however, because each one could bring news of what was happening on the outside.

Our most welcome roommate was an inmate from another cell who had been in the prison several months. He taught us how to make contact with fellow prisoners during our weekly shower and how to communicate with other cells by banging on the latrines. Most important, he told us that it was a good idea to fall sick and have to visit the prison physician, a Czech named Přemysl Kočí. I set to work at once coughing and complaining of what I hoped sounded like contagious strep throat. I remarked darkly that I had had TB, and it could be recurring. Before long, I found myself in Dr. Kočí's bare examination room.

"What's the matter with you?" he asked wearily in Czech.

"My throat. I can't swallow. And it hurts."

He looked for a moment, and then carefully examined a swab he had prepared. "Your aunt is concerned about you," he said without expression, while my mouth was open. "She says to let her know, through me, if you need anything." He glanced at the door, ran the swab over my shocked tonsil sockets, and sat me up. "That should take care of you," he said, and turned away.

From that moment, I suddenly felt that I was not alone. Within a week, small packages of food began arriving—only the most meager rations made it through to me in the cell, and these had to be shared with my cellmates, but each little parcel was a party. Through the doctor, Věra found out where I was. She began picking up my dirty laundry each week and delivering fresh linen. I was not allowed to see her, nor to exchange notes. But each time I opened the bag of underwear, looked at the whiteness that Věra had folded with her own hands, and took in the wholesome emanations of bleach and sunshine, the real world of love and soap and domesticity seemed near to me.

On October 17, my birthday, the moment came that I had been dreading and waiting for: my interrogation. A sentry called my name and brought me to an office where two Gestapo took me over.

"Just so you know what to expect," one said casually, "you are going to be court-martialed. We are taking you to headquarters for trial." There were three possible verdicts by a summary court: you could be released; you could be sent to a concentration camp; or you could be executed. There was no appeal.

I don't know how I got down to the car, for my legs and arms had gone weak. Since the day Heydrich had instituted martial law, the word court-martial meant execution. Even in prison we knew that. How many men had been taken directly out of a kangaroo court-martial, thrust against a wall somewhere, and shot? Hundreds? Thousands? I looked out of the car at the streets of Brno, at housewives pushing carts, children whining, people shopping, and realized that I was a dot in the world, and that after I was erased, the world would continue as before. Someone might hear the shots that would shatter my body and would perhaps look up from his work, but soon he would remember he had a job to finish and would go on about his business. We arrived at the law school, the new Gestapo headquarters. My guard stationed me in front of an imposing hall where I soon realized summary courts-martial were in session. Prisoners were being taken in and, ashen-faced, removed. I looked at the light coming in from windows near the ceiling. This was the first day of my nineteenth year, and I would never see another.

In the grisly ranking of my war experiences, there are some incidents that are carved into me and others that scored me for a time but which I somehow got over. But nothing was as excruciating as the anguish of that day in front of the hall of sentencing. The fifty minutes I stood outside that chamber was the haunting worst hour of my life. Even now, the memory of it agitates every nerve ending of my body. The swinging doors of the hall burst open upon me when I least expect to see them, blasting quiet thoughts. A death sentence drenches my dreams: an arrogant German voice enunciates it clearly—I have been hearing it for this half century—and ends my case with the bang of a gavel.

However, I never heard the real sentence, for the trial never happened. After a time, a uniformed guard motioned to me, but instead of leading me forward through the doors, he turned right and brought me up a staircase to the office of a German in civilian clothes. I had worked myself into such a state of desperation over my impending execution that by the time I arrived before the young Gestapo officer, I was going into something like shock and felt absolutely nothing. I was therefore not flushed with relief, as he probably expected, and definitely not gushing forth information to my "savior."

My interrogator acted incredibly nice as he began questioning me about my father's departure. A radio was on. In between marching music, there was an announcement that in the Ukraine the armies of the Reich had achieved another of their splendid victories. Despite the distraction of the radio, I gave a careful portrayal of a languid young scholar completely bored by politics. I told him my father had gone to tend our rented garden, where he sometimes stayed overnight, and that he would doubtless come back. This was the story my mother and I had concocted so that our explanations would match. He questioned me for about an hour in Czech. Then he took out some ominous documents.

"I have some important questions here. You will answer them truthfully for, if you lie, you will be interrogated by other officials who will certainly not be as gentle as I am." Then he asked me about an illegal group which used a youth of my age as a contact man. Was I that contact man? He peered into my face, alert for any twitch. I pondered how difficult it must be for him, a conscientious Nazi, driven by duty like my father, to have to smile all day and be friendly to us Czech slime. Fortunately, I knew nothing of this underground group, and my interrogator knew nothing of the group I really was involved in. So we continued to get along. Finally: "Do you understand German?"

"Not too much."

He spoke to a cohort in their native tongue. "I don't think this Luža kid is part of it. Send him back."

Outside, the noises of the streetcars and buses were a kind of greeting: "Well, well, you're still alive. So far, so good." My cell almost seemed like home. My friends had kept lunch cold for me, and covered me with furtive questions and affection. Dr. Kočí, too, had good news for me on my next visit.

"You say the cramps are here?" he asked. Then: "Your mother is in the female prison Cejl and she's doing all right."

Still, I expected to be sent to a concentration camp, since the Gestapo could not keep me in that overcrowded cell forever. I was losing weight, like everyone there, and in early November I had developed blood poisoning from a splinter in my foot. On the morning of November 12, a guard called my name and screamed, "Take all your things with you!" My fears seemed about to be realized. I was brought downstairs to two Gestapo officers, given a brown bag with my belongings, even my Latin New Testament, and presented with a release paper stating that I would never divulge one single word about my detainment. By that time I guessed that I might be let go; I would have signed a promise to wear a dress for the rest of my life. They took me by car to the center of town and opened the door. I was free.

I boarded a streetcar. When the conductor came to me I said, "I have no money. I was just released from the Gestapo prison." She stared at me, saw that my clothes hung on my frame, and moved away, disconcerted. There was a newspaper on a seat nearby, the first reading I had seen in weeks, but I was afraid to look at it for fear I would find some friend on the list of people the Nazis had executed. I walked to our house from the streetcar stop, strangely dismayed at the sensation of moving straight ahead for blocks and blocks, unconfined. My mother arrived home an hour or so after me. We hugged each other wordlessly. I had stored up so many things to say to her, but now I could not begin. She was horrified at the amount of weight I had lost; she, too, was emaciated. We retrieved our stash of provisions from the top of the closet, little packages of sugar, rice, and flour, hardly enough to last a month, but sufficient to convict us of hoarding if the Gestapo had noticed them in their searches. My body was unaccustomed to food. I threw up at first and had to eat a little bread at a time. We sat at the table chewing appreciatively. Some starlings outside the window were arguing noisily in a foreign language. We looked at the birds and each other and said nothing.

III

We were pretty sure we had not seen the last of the Gestapo, who had only released us so that we would lead them to Father. After jail and during that entire year before I myself went underground, I felt as if I were in a place whose peculiarities I had yet to learn. Our little routines—winding the hall clock, setting the table—took on an air of unreality, as if the things around us were props and we were actors who would soon get back to our own lives. The morning after my release I dragged my infected foot to the hospital and was operated on by the father of one of my friends. When I went back the next week for a checkup, the doctor was gone. The whole family had vanished into the camps because the mother was partly Jewish.[1]

Knowing we were being watched, we waited for a message from Father. Sure enough, on an afternoon too wet and cold for casual visits, Marie Žalman rang our bell. Major Otakar Žalman was Father's friend and confidant, but we had met his wife only once or twice.

"Will you have something hot to drink, Mrs. Žalman?" I asked. But without waiting for the answer, my mother signaled me with her eyes to leave.

"Are you in contact with my husband?"

"No, but Oto sees Kravka," Mrs. Žalman told her. "We can pass messages

1. Josef Podlaha was deported to Mauthausen; his wife and their two sons were sent to Teresienstadt. They survived the war and I saw them again in 1945. Podlaha had been a professor in the medical school of Masaryk University, one of the country's most prominent surgeons.

to him. Mrs. Peller can bring letters back and forth between you because her husband actually visits General Luža." František Peller was a prosecutor in the Brno district court; his wife came from a political family Father had known years before in Ružomberok. The letters Mrs. Peller eventually brought from Father were purposely innocuous, and we destroyed them at once. I can still remember flushing at the sight of Father's small, sure script. We were not told where he was living, but it was apparently in the country, since he sent us a little food. On farms, eggs and garden produce were still relatively easy to come by, though meat was precious everywhere.

What the Žalmans and Pellers offered may sound inconsequential now—the mild kindness of people habituated to doing the right thing. But as they knew, helping us meant they were ready to lay down their lives alongside ours. To live anywhere in the Protectorate without registering your address at a district office or gendarmerie was to be an enemy of the Reich. If you were found without an identity card, you could end up being shot, along with all those who helped you and their families—spouses, children, parents—anyone who lived with them or knew they were harboring you. People old and young were being shot like dogs at the Kounic Student Home for nothing more than failing to turn in an unregistered person. Once someone helped you, he could never again feel safe. If you were caught later, long after you had lost contact with your protector, you might be tortured until you revealed every link in your underground survival, going back months and months, so that one arrest generally meant death for dozens of people. If Father were ever captured, or even if Mother or I were interrogated, the Žalmans and the Pellers could expect to share our fate.

Father's friend František Jedlička had been advising me about whom to talk to, whom to stay away from. He thought he could get Father across the Reich frontier to Switzerland. What he described sounded feasible to me, but I don't know how practical this plan of escape really was, and so I need not torment myself now over my father's refusal. Father replied through his messengers that the underground needed people in Czechoslovakia more than the liberation movement needed people abroad, and anyway, it was his duty to stay home in this terrible time. So that was that.

Despite everything, Mother and I were getting along well—in fact, these were the best years of our complicated relationship. Mother had been apolitical when she was arrested, self-centered and a bit narcissistic. But one of her cellmates had been Mirka Sigmund. The Sigmund pump factory was smuggling technical information and money to Great Britain, according to the Gestapo, whose information about such people was generally first-rate. After six weeks of being shut up with the likes of Mrs. Sigmund, Mother emerged a brave militant, twitching with ideas about how a self-respecting Czech should resist the Germans.

It is not surprising that a few people like my mother were enraged and radicalized to the point of resistance by the occupation. Humans, after all, tend to fight when cornered. What is remarkable to me is the degree to which the occupation brutalized the occupiers. For every Czechoslovak who was shot or hanged or beaten, there was someone, a fellow European, willing to fire a gun or open a trapdoor or otherwise rise to the sadistic occasion. The mistreatment of thousands of helpless people cannot be accomplished with only a handful of barbarians; it takes many thousands, more than just the hard core of brutal officers the Germans might have culled from their ranks. Where did the Nazis find them? Some of the torturers and execution-ers must have started out as normal people and were barbarized somehow, by training, to be sure, but also by a complex mental transformation. The surprising thing to me was not that the occupation created so many martyrs willing, if necessary, to die for others, but that it produced so many monsters willing to kill.

I had been permitted by the Gestapo to return to my Realgymnasium. I passed my final examinations with distinction in May 1942. It was impera-tive that I find a job immediately after graduation; otherwise, the labor office would find me one, something suitable for a Slav prodigy, such as pouring molten metal in a foundry or mining coal in Germany. "Get out of town," Mr. Jedlička advised me. "In Brno, the police know exactly where to find you. If they are ordered to produce 10,000 Czech hostages, they'll come for you first; but if you're not here, they'll be too busy rounding up the other 9,999 to track you down." So I got a job in the enormous Baťa shoe com-pany in Zlín, fifty miles away, working in the chemical lab and then in the plant itself, so that I qualified for extra food rations as a worker. I watched people in Zlín pouring out of the trains every morning and wondered why they were so eager to get to work to make boots for German feet. And those Czech officials checking my ration card—didn't they realize that they were cooperating with the Nazis and making it easier for the animals to win the war? Maybe some of them thought that no matter what they did, they could not affect the outcome of the struggle, so it was useless to expose themselves to danger. But the majority were not thinking at all. They wanted the Ger-mans to lose and certainly did not wish any harm to people in the underground. But Czech officials were used to taking orders; if the Protectorate authorities told them to investigate this or report that, they simply did it without considering whether or not they were making it easier for the Germans to occupy our country. As for the workers, they hated the Germans as much as anyone. But no one could refuse to work, and whoever worked, worked for the Reich. When they put in overtime, or in some other way "cooperated" with the occupiers, they said to themselves, "I should make fifty extra crowns this week." Not for a moment did they think, "These three hours of overtime will help the German army fighting on the eastern front." On Saturday night they came home, glad to have the extra money, just as I was glad to get my extra rations, and maybe they listened illegally to the news as I did and prayed that, boots or no boots, the Germans would die in Russia.

The Germans were in fact in trouble. Having begun the invasion of Russia in June 1941, German troops had fought their way across eastern Europe and were approaching Moscow just as I was arrested in September. But when I was released in November, I discovered that the Red Army had launched a counteroffensive. By December the Germans were exhausted and overextended across a vast front where they were attacked by the Russian winter. Throughout the Protectorate came the demand to donate winter clothing for German soldiers who, we were told, were still fighting in summer uniforms. Mother and I gave a pair of worthless old skis, being careful not to show how delighted we were that Nazis were freezing. Then came the news of Pearl Harbor and the entrance of the United States into the war. The day of infamy was a wonderful day for us.

We soon learned that whenever the Germans encountered reverses in the war, they reacted by tightening the occupation. Anything could make us vulnerable to arrest: not covering our windows sufficiently during a blackout, concealing a few scraps of leather or cloth, holding back a little something that was requisitioned. Because of Heydrich's controls, life was fraught with anxiety, not only for people like us who were genuine resisters, but for average Czechs who were simply trying to get along. There was no body of active collaborators in Czechoslovakia as there was in France or Norway, no significant pro-German group among the Czechs. But neither was there a widespread determination to oppose the regime. Only a small minority of our millions were active resisters. The Germans succeeded in keeping the rest under an incubus of terror.

On the other hand, everyone was a passive resister. In order to eat, city

people often had to involve themselves in some black market transaction—
exchanging a dress for a little meat, swapping a child's toy for a few eggs.
Since everybody was doing it, it seemed that you could get by with it; but
you could never be sure. There were continual executions of so-called black
marketeers. Country people had to register their livestock and were required
to deliver a certain quantity of meat, eggs, and dairy products at certain periods. Every farmer and villager kept some animals illegally, despite the fact
that the authorities would show up now and then with the official goose or
pig list and compare it to the tails they counted in the yard. If you went to
the countryside, to someone willing to trade his illegal products, there was
always the possibility that you would be caught with the food on the way
home. What would they do to you for having a black market chicken? No
one was sure. A quarter kilo of sausage or a little jar of pig fat under your
coat might doom you if the bus were searched, or it might not. If you had
children in school, you had to worry about what they could say that would
put you under suspicion. Every life was scored with constant small lies, compromises, and anxiety.

It was lucky indeed that I graduated in May and left Brno, for that was
the month of Czechoslovakia's most sensational act of resistance, and it was
followed by sweeping reprisals. On May 27, 1942, afternoon radio programs
were interrupted: "Attention! Attention! An important announcement! Acting Reich Protector SS-Obergruppenführer Reinhard Heydrich has been in-
jured by a bomb thrown into his car!" For the second time in eight months
we were under martial law throughout the country. "Anyone harboring the
culprits," we were warned, "or having knowledge of their identity or whereabouts and failing to report it will be shot with his family." A manhunt for
the attackers turned into a frenzy of revenge when Heydrich died a few days
later. In no less than five thousand villages and towns, German police went
from house to house searching for suspects. Though the bombing had been
the work of only a handful, thousands of Czechs were arrested during the
next six weeks, and over a thousand executed, including the imprisoned
General Eliáš. The slaughter was mainly directed against intellectuals and
former army officers. At the height of the terror, the Germans burned down
the village of Lidice not far from Prague, shot all of the men, and put the
women in concentration camps. About one hundred of the children were
gassed; a few selected on the basis of their Aryan looks were put out for
adoption by German families. "This measure has evoked great satisfaction
and in many instances open joy among the entire German population," the

German Security Service enthused in reporting the burning of Lidice. "There is a feeling of satisfaction because energetic measures have now at last been taken. The opinion prevails that this kind of action should have been taken sooner." Two weeks later the small community of Ležáky was burned and all of its inhabitants shot. By that time seven paratroopers, including the two Czechs who were ordered by the London government to kill Heydrich, had died in a Prague church where they were cornered.[2]

With our stomachs churning, we learned about Lidice from red posters tacked up on the streets of Brno. Even that was not going to be the end of the reprisals. There were rumors that Hitler had ordered the execution of every tenth Czech, in which case my mother and I would surely be murdered, no matter where we were in the Protectorate. I was afraid to leave my room in Zlín and afraid to stay there. I walked the streets, feeling the tension like some live thing jerking my insides; there was nowhere to hide.

However, my arrest was foiled by Božena Foral. Boženka, our maid in Prague when I was very young, now lived in Brno and cleaned our house each week. I loved her like my mother. Before Father went into hiding, when our situation was not so dangerous, he had asked Boženka and her husband František to hide our meager arms—one or two hunting rifles, a general's saber, a revolver, and some rounds of ammunition in an aluminum tin. We were certain that sooner or later our house would be searched and it would be fatal to have these weapons in our possession. Boženka's husband was a worker, a member of the class the Nazis exalted in their propaganda. Workers were seldom molested, so we thought it unlikely that anyone would search their home.

But by 1942, the Germans were bearing down on everybody, workers included, and Boženka and František wanted by all means to get rid of the weapons. Nearby Wilson Forest had a steep hill with a hollow tree at the bottom that would be a good hiding place. One evening František was dispatched with the weapons and the tin of ammunition. He concealed the saber in his slacks, but he was not tall and the point of the thing kept thumping the ground with each step unless he walked on his toes. Nevertheless, he tiptoed through the woods and down the hill and was almost to his destina-

2. After the arrival of Heydrich in Prague on September 27, 1941, and the arrest of Prime Minister Eliáš, President Beneš ceased communicating with the home government, though not with the resistance. The Czech cabinet in the Protectorate, having become the unwilling puppet of the Germans, was no help to the resistance effort. President Hácha had become so ill by the winter of 1942–43 that he could not even sign his name.

tion when he saw an obstruction in the darkness ahead. A light glared in his face and suddenly there were two policemen in his path, asking him to produce his identity card. It was difficult for him to move while keeping the saber still, and he took some time getting the card out. They didn't ask him to open the can with the revolver and bullets. That would have meant his certain death. Instead, the two policemen moved on, and František completed his mission.

Boženka was a stout-hearted little thing. A few weeks later when she and my mother were tidying up the attic, they found a rifle. It was June 1942, just after Heydrich's assassination, and every day five minutes away from us people were being hanged and shot because unregistered weapons were found in their houses. I am profoundly embarrassed to report that my mother wrapped the rifle in paper, put it in a grocery bag, and, with the untroubled conscience of a general ordering his men into battle, asked the maid to get rid of it. Boženka took her burden. She was afraid to go home the shortest way, through the forest, since that was where František had encountered the police. She took the longer route, which ran alongside the Kounic Student Home, with its execution stand set up in the yard. She figured that, package or no package, no one would dream that a woman would be carrying a gun near that place. But she did not count on hearing people being executed. As she approached the building, a shot rang out, followed by a cry or some desperate, human sound. Then, after a few steps, another shot. Then another pause and the drama was repeated. Tears welled in her eyes. She began sobbing, and the more she tried to control herself, the more agitated her weeping became. Two Sudeten German women standing near the building saw her and laughed. "Look at that. The Czech bitch is crying." But nothing worse happened. She regained her composure within a few blocks. A woman she knew approached her and offered to sell her some eggs. The normal ration was four eggs a month; it was unusual to find them on the black market, so Boženka had to look regretful and explain that she had no money with her. At last she made it home with the rifle.

Nor was that the end of my debt to Boženka. On Thursday, September 17, 1942, she was cleaning our house when two Gestapo men appeared in the hall. "Where are the Lužas?" one of them barked. A Czech policeman was with them, standing behind them. He put a finger to his lips to signal Boženka.

"I don't know. Mrs. Luža is due back on Saturday," Boženka answered.

Mother had absented herself from Brno after Heydrich's assassination by visiting one of her women friends, a dentist named Dr. Káňa.

"What about the boy? Where is he working?"

"In a tannery, I think. I don't know."

The officers conferred for a moment in German, then addressed Boženka. "Listen, you come back here on Saturday, and as soon as you see Mrs. Luža or Radomír, you call us. Here is the number. You warn them that we're waiting for them, and you'll be hanged."

Poor Boženka was quite rattled, but she contacted Věra at once, who in turn called me at my hotel. When I heard Věra's voice, I knew there was an emergency, and my teeth went numb. "I need to talk to you before you go home," she said.

"I'll meet you in our usual place at eleven."

Mother, too, was instructed not to return. The Gestapo apparently was watching our house and when we failed to show up, went directly to Boženka's apartment.

"You must have warned Mrs. Luža; otherwise, she'd be back."

"I received a letter from her," Boženka said. "She's staying another week."

"Show us the letter."

"It was only a postcard. I threw it away."

"What about Radomír? Doesn't he come home on weekends?"

"Maybe he decided to spend Sunday where his mother is," Boženka suggested.

They questioned her about her husband and then demanded that she produce the slip of paper on which they had written their number; but as she needed to find some keys to get into the room where she had left the paper, they lost interest in seeing it.

"Just watch yourself," they said from the door, "because if we find out something about you, you will go to the gallows alongside the Lužas."

Mother had no choice but to stay with Dr. Káňa as long as she could. Božena Káňa was about forty-five, mannish and rough. Her husband, Bonifac, had been a colleague of Father's, a brigadier general, whom the Gestapo arrested in Brno in 1941 and tortured so brutally that when they finally dumped him in the hospital, his bladder was crushed. The prison physicians, who knew Dr. Káňa, called her so that she could see him before he died, but by that time, General Káňa was already in a coma. After her husband's death, Dr.

Káňa was willing to do anything against the Germans and, since only death could reunite her with her husband, she was absolutely fearless.

When I met Věra on Saturday night a couple of blocks from her apartment, her pretty face was swollen from crying. I could see that the Nazis had not come on a whim; they were actively looking for us. It would only be a matter of days before they would track me down in Zlín, since they were now interning the family of any prominent Czech who had escaped abroad or was living underground. Leaving Věra was hard that night. Now that I, too, was going underground, it was possible I might never see her again. As I tried to calm her, she kissed my hands again and again in her intense Russian way. In the last embrace we permitted ourselves, she pressed her soft body against me as if to print me with the memory of it.

Around midnight I rang the bell of my friend Míla Pechan who had been one of the members of my clandestine group. His father was a gymnasium professor and would let me stay until I could talk to Mr. Jedlička and get a message to Father. Mrs. Peller came on Sunday night with instructions for me from "someone in the underground." I was to go to the bus terminal in Brno at ten o'clock the next night, carrying a two-day old newspaper with the headlines plainly in sight. Someone would make himself known to me and get on a bus. I was to follow him inconspicuously and go wherever he went. The next evening I was waiting at the station when a young man who seemed to me rather malevolent walked out of the gloom of the garage and wordlessly handed me a bus ticket. "Thank you," I said. He smirked in reply, and moved away from me, falling into the line forming for one of the suburban buses.

The man I came to know as Malý, the Little One, got out at Bosonohy, a suburb of Brno and much too close to the city, I thought, to be safe. I followed him at a distance until we were out of sight of the road. "Will I see Kravka now?" I asked him as we crossed a field. He smiled his cryptic smile, but neither answered nor looked at me. We came to a clearing with a group of houses, all close to each other, and stopped before one of them where the entrance was already half-open. The Little One looked around quickly and pushed me inside. Before my eyes had adjusted to the change of light, someone else, a woman I think, pushed me through another door. From the corner a large man lunged toward me. Even as I flinched, I felt relief spreading down me, for before I could actually see him, I knew it was my father.

*　*　*

It had been a year since Father had left us. He had a mustache, but he looked fresh and serene. I felt safe. Everything would be all right: the Germans would lose the war; we would all be reunited; I would finish growing up and would become a scholar with a beautiful wife and intelligent children. Father's eyes were shining with emotion that for once he did not try to suppress. He held my shoulders and filled his eyes with me.

We talked through most of the night. We began with Father's movements from the time he left home to go into hiding. The day after his departure, he sent someone to find Mr. Voda, but our friend had himself been imprisoned that very morning. Still unaware that Mother and I had been arrested, Father went with Kravka to Javůrek, near the main road from Brno to Prague, where he was sheltered by the village schoolmaster. The schoolmaster had a name quite common in Czech: Karel Novák. He protested at first that he already had one person hiding in his quarters. But when Kravka confided Father's name, Novák said, "Of course we can't refuse *him*. We'll do whatever we can for him."

They placed Father not in the overcrowded Novák house but with Novák's mother, a lively woman nearly eighty who was not especially afraid of an early death at the hands of the Gestapo. She liked Father. The only problem was that the old grandmother had no radio, and the broadcasts from London were the only thing that kept Father sane. He had to stay in one room, just as in other places he would stay in an attic or a cellar of someone's house, keeping very still, for the houses were small and the floorboards squeaked. His window was tightly covered. The room was unheated so as not to arouse the suspicions of visitors or relatives. In the daytime he did not go out of the room even to go to the bathroom unless it was absolutely necessary. At night his lights stayed off. The radio news was sometimes his only stimulation, his one connection to the world. The BBC offered news in Czech three times a day; there were other broadcasts in the languages of occupied countries. Father would have liked to hear them all. During the time he stayed in the grandmother's house, he slipped around the village every evening to get to the Nováks' radio. Often, Mrs. Novák came to get him and walked with him. They never saw anyone on those foolhardy trips, but it was an absurd risk for someone normally as prudent as my father.

Eventually, the Nováks were able to take Father into their own house. He felt fairly secure with them, despite the usual constraints—solitude, inactivity, anxiety, and helpless dependence on his contact men, Peller and Kravka. During his many months in Javůrek, he gave Mr. Peller a number of messages for us that we never got, as he found out when he and I were able to talk.

Father was upset at how bad I looked. Our ration allowances were meager, and in Zlín I had no chance to buy on the black market. Father's retirement pension had been stopped, but he had money from donations made to the resistance, and his keepers had at least a little opportunity to get black market supplies. They had to be careful not to buy too much, lest someone suspect they were feeding an unregistered appetite. Father had tried to send us a little food; Peller stopped it, not because he wanted it himself, but because he thought sending it was dangerous. Messages that a woman could carry in her head were one thing; packages of food, which in a hungry city would be noticed, were something else.

When I try to explain to someone how a resistance group forms, I think about the early months of my underground experience. Our "organization" at this time was unorganized. It evolved, beginning with the people we had to take into our confidence to secure a hideout. There was Kravka, the fellow legionnaire whom Father first approached, and the Pellers and Žalmans, who provided the contacts between Kravka and Mother. Peller committed the extraordinary indiscretion of telling his wife exactly where Father was hiding. That was dangerous for her as well as for Father and the Nováks. Perhaps Peller disclosed the location to Žalman, too—we were never sure. Then there were the Nováks, husband and wife, who actually hid Father, and the Nováks' daughter and son-in-law, who also lived in the house with their newborn baby. Karel Novák's mother did not know where Father went after he left her house. Next was Malý, the Little One, who had escorted me to Father and seemed so sinister at first, though not after I realized he was merely studying to become a tough guy. Malý was a mechanic in the Protectorate transportation system, working in the Brno garage where buses had to stop every day. He thus met many people outside his own domicile and could transmit messages. In case one of us required immediate treatment, we took a doctor into our circle of confidants.

Another important ally was the head of the Czech gendarme station near Javůrek.[3] Kravka recruited this valuable man, Karel Weingart. He did not

---

3. Gendarmes were the Czech state security agents (policemen) stationed in the countryside. They were under Nazi supervision. Police were the security agents in the Czech cities. The Gestapo was the German secret police in charge of anti-German actions or political offenses against the Nazi regime. The SS was a selected group of Nazi followers bound by the oath of blind obedience to the Führer. The military branch of the SS headed some antipartisan actions near the end of the war.

tell Weingart my father's name or who was sheltering him, only that if rumors reached the gendarmerie about someone hiding in the area, or if the Germans were about to search, or if they made an arrest, or anything else that could affect an underground person, then he was to send a message to Kravka immediately. Another man Father selected was the mailman Josef Hlaváček, whom we referred to as the Fast One whenever we had to speak or write about him. Coming down the road with his lopsided trot, he looked like John Barrymore lurching across the screen after the voice of his father in that early *Hamlet* where everybody, even the ghost, walked with a limp. It's easy to see why we wanted to recruit the mailman. He went all over the area and spoke to nearly everybody. Mail was delivered twice a day. Without doing anything at all unusual, he could take messages to practically anyone on his route and find out all sorts of information that people gave up innocently as they chatted with him. Again, it was Kravka who knew and trusted the Fast One and took him aside. "Look, Josef," Kravka told him, "a group of us are in the resistance. We want you to be part of our organization. If you agree to help us, you will be a contact man to a very prominent person, a public figure from Prague. His cover name is Václav Pech. But are you absolutely sure you can keep everything in the strictest secrecy? Because you know it is a matter of life and death for all of us."

"I felt I had suddenly grown two meters taller," Hlaváček wrote years later, when he described his first meeting with Father:

A few days later Mrs. Novák brought me into her kitchen to meet Mr. Pech. He was a big man with warm eyes. "Brother Hlaváček," he said, "We need you. You will gradually become part of our organization. What we want from you is to help guard us. Keep your ears open for what people are saying. If anybody mentions that something looks peculiar here, or shows you that his curiosity has been aroused, please let us know. I would appreciate very much if you could deliver any boxes or papers which Brother Kravka gives you for me. That will eliminate the need for Kravka to come here constantly, which might look strange." After three or four months I was finally told that Brother Pech was the Moravian military commander, General Luža.[4]

Hlaváček and the others made up the core of Father's support group in the spring of 1942, individuals who eventually put him in contact with other

4. "Thee," "Thou," and "Brother" were customary forms of address in Sokol, the gymnastic organization. These terms were later used among the Czech legionnaires, and still later in the underground. Though Kravka was just a soldier and my father a general, they both used the egalitarian "Brother" in speaking to each other.

individuals. He often remarked that he did not have an organization and did not want one until the defeat of Germany was within sight and we could become an adjunct to the Allied military operation.

Then came May 27, 1942, the attack on Heydrich, and the new declaration of martial law. The Germans were going from one village to the next, searching every house. The Nováks were nervous to the point of exhaustion. Father needed a safer hiding place, but Kravka could find no one who could take him. As a last resort, it was decided to scoop out a space under the kitchen large enough to conceal Father beneath the floorboards. It was no easy task to dig a hole as big as a grave without attracting the attention of neighbors only a few feet away on either side. Moreover, the dirt from this excavation had to be disposed of; it wouldn't do to let it pile up next to the house. Kravka, Father, and the Nováks dug at night, quietly. Father, wearing bedroom slippers to muffle the sound of his steps, carried the dirt to the backyard and spread it around. They lined the hole with wood and covered it again with the kitchen flooring, the linoleum and some carpet. They were then as ready as they could be for the Germans.

Three weeks after Heydrich's assassination, the Germans searched Javůrek. They appeared suddenly before dawn, a noose of police surrounding the entire village, cutting off any escape to the woods. Father's careful selection of protectors paid off. Weingart saw the arrival of all the Ordnungspolizei cars near his gendarme station; he woke up Kravka, who sent Malý running to tell the Nováks. Father rushed into the hole and lay down. Fortunately most of the hollow space was under a kitchen cupboard, but a little part of it extended beyond the cupboard, so that the Germans walking in the kitchen with their massive jackboots would notice that their steps made a different sound as they crossed that part of the floor. The Nováks' daughter somehow had the presence of mind to fill a little tub with water and place it over that hollow spot. When the German police finally got to the Nováks' house—six of them, who combed the bedrooms and then went to the kitchen—they found Jiřina Novák bathing her baby near the cupboard. They stood only a few inches from Father, who, because of the dust and sawdust loosened by the German boots, needed badly to cough and sneeze. The Germans left, without Father, and the entire family collapsed like broken wires. Even the baby who had been screaming dropped into a depleted whine. None of them could survive another such ordeal.[5]

5. Between May 28 and July 3, 1942, 3,188 people were arrested in the Protectorate, 1,357 were executed, and 4,715,511 were required at the least to present their identity cards. Five thou-

The Nováks were relieved of their burden by a bus driver, Jan Sec, and his wife Fanynka. Sec worked with Malý and also knew Kravka; he agreed to take Father in. Mrs. Novák—Father called her Little Spruce—was actually sorry to see Father go, and kept reassuring him that he could return in a few weeks or months. She was a cultured, intelligent woman, a Chekhovian character trapped in a narrow village until Father's arrival brought fresh ideas, a strong mind, change, and danger to her dreary life.

The Secs lived in Bosonohy, west of Brno and fourteen miles from the Nováks' home in Javůrek. Although Father stayed within a twenty-mile area during all of his time underground, even a short move such as this one was difficult and risky. There were sentries all over the place, for we were still under martial law because of Heydrich's assassination; Father dared not walk from Javůrek. Instead, Sec picked him up after his last run from Brno to Bíteš at ten o'clock, before he had to get his bus back to the Bíteš garage at eleven. They flew to Bosonohy, driving about seventy miles an hour, because Sec had at all costs to avoid meeting the oncoming bus driver, who would be leaving Brno at eleven o'clock on his last run. If anyone tried to stop them, Sec was instructed to drive through them and keep going.

Sec's two-bedroom house was only three or four hundred yards from the main road going from Brno to Prague. There were no immediate neighbors, but there was a child, the Secs' eight-year-old son. Generally, we never hid in a house with children because they could not understand the gravity of our situation and might tell somebody about their family's secret boarder. Father thus had to make himself invisible in that cottage so the youngster would not be aware that he was living there. The boy did see Father, twice, but was told that he was a repairman. With the money Father gave them, the Secs were able to buy enough on the black market to feed all of them well without arousing suspicion. The chubby wife liked to cook and was not unhappy to have someone around who was appreciative of every mouthful and could pay for groceries. Jan Sec was a genial man of the people. He was about forty, crafty, practical, and remarkably calm, considering the nerve-wracking task he undertook in sheltering Father. In a different decade he would have been regarded as quite ordinary, but in those hysterical times, steadiness—the ability to keep one's head in any situation—was a national ideal. Father had been with the Secs a few weeks when I arrived. They did

---

sand villages and towns were searched by the German security officials. Report by the Reich Security Main Office, August 5, 1942, at the YIVO Institute for Jewish Research, New York.

everything they could for him, even sending the boy away for two days so that I could stay with them temporarily. That was why the house was open for me when Malý brought me to Sec; it was Mrs. Sec who pushed me into Father's room and closed the door.

My few hours with Father were running out, for we had to find a permanent shelter. Father had no place to send me except to the Nováks, the school-master and his wife who had protected him for almost a year. "Ludmila— Little Spruce—is the manager in the family; she makes all the decisions," Father told me several times. I was not ready to leave Father when Kravka and Malý came to get me for the bus trip to Javůrek. I still had so much I wanted to say and hear. "Malý will be your only contact with your father from now on," Kravka said. "The Nováks are both very nice. However," he could not resist adding, "Mrs. Novák is the one who wears the pants."

We waited in the forest until dark before we approached the house. Karel Novák was about sixty and tall, with a white wad of fluffy hair that made him look more unusual than he was. He welcomed me as if I were really a guest and not a curse on his family. His wife was indeed his boss, and both of them seemed to like it that way. I had never before seen a henpecked husband up close—they weren't common among the army officers who were our friends. Though the schoolmaster was fairly well educated, his wife was brighter and noticeably more dynamic. She contradicted him freely, amiably corrected his grammar or his statements, and issued directions: "Karel, get the blankets for Radomír, and separate that trash so you can burn the paper tomorrow. Why have you waited so long to get rid of it? What do you mean, the bread at the baker's contained millet? It was filled with sawdust, like your head." None of her quacking affected his character-istically pleasant mood; they were not tense when together. But my first im-pression—that he was able-minded and energetic—was changed completely after I observed him with his wife. By the time my underground life was over, I had learned that no matter how transparent a man seems, you don't really know him until you see his wife. Whether their relationship is good or bad, married people are like two sides of a lake: you have to know both shores before you can claim to know the water.

In seventy-two hours I had gone from being a free man with a home and a job to being a criminal confined day and night to a few feet of space, en-gaged every moment in life and death calculations. It was Ludmila Novák who helped me calm down. Mrs. Little Spruce was smart, interested in world

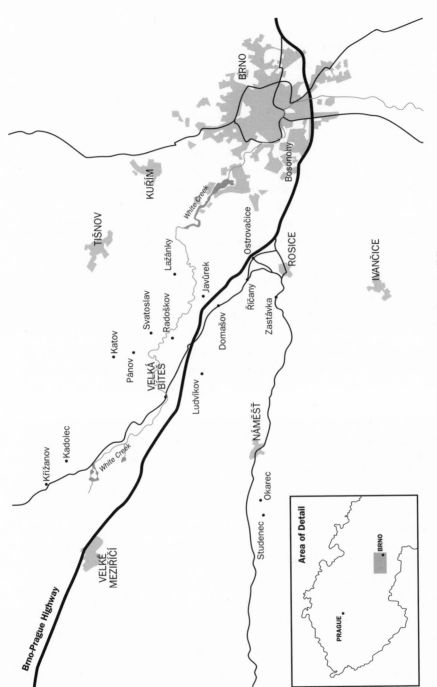

Villages between Brno and Velké Meziříčí

affairs, and eager to talk when she had time. She subscribed to *Lidové noviny*, the Brno daily. It was full of German propaganda by that time but also contained literary articles one could look forward to. The family had a nice collection of nineteenth- and twentieth-century authors, perhaps three or four hundred books. Eventually I read them all, including my first pornography, Frank Harris' *My Secret Life*. I loved Czech and foreign fiction, and was conscientious about studying German, though my only good textbooks were the few Father was able to send me through Kravka. I was burning to learn everything there in my cubbyhole. I had grand plans to get a law degree one day, study philosophy, go into politics, and burst upon the postwar world with my enlightened insights.

I saw little of the Nováks' daughter and even less of her husband, the Young Master, a draftsman who left for Brno every morning at six and returned from work at seven in the evening. He was chilly toward me, but toward everyone else, too. I tried to be inconspicuous. I got up early in order to eat at the same time as the family, and then I was locked in my room. I could read all day or I could watch the linoleum wear out and fight depression. So I read.

I could hear almost everything that went on in the cottage, and I became aware for the first time of the relentless drudgery of housekeeping in a family with no servants. Dust had to be constantly rearranged. Shopping required going to the next village on a bicycle every two days—there was no refrigeration—and making separate stops at the baker, the greengrocer, the butcher. At each store one had to wait. That was boring enough for the village women who had nothing but vermicelli in their heads; it must have been awful for Mrs. Little Spruce, who had Tolstoy and Kafka waiting at home for her few spare minutes. Cooking a chicken meant catching the thing and killing it, then plucking it—a long, nasty chore—and cleaning it before cooking could even begin. The animals in the yard had to be fed twice a day, the animals in the house three times, and what's more, they expected every meal cooked. The stove was the center of endless labor. While the women cooked, they heated water for cleaning. And how they cleaned! The floors, which were scrubbed daily or every other day, were far cleaner than the people walking on them, who only bathed once a week. When the fire was finally allowed to go out, the heavy iron box of ashes had to be emptied.

Our meals were modest by today's standards, but compared to most people in Europe during the war, we ate well. Rabbits did not have to be registered, so we had rabbit every Sunday, one of the gentle creatures I could sometimes see in the backyard, tame and soundless like me in its pen. I was a city boy, accustomed to thinking of every domestic animal as a pet. I remember when the butcher came early one morning to slaughter a pig illegally. One moment there was an animal peacefully going about his business in the yard, observing my window now and then with his intelligent eyes; the next moment there was the desperate squealing that took days to forget. Almost before the echoes of it had faded, someone presented the boiled head of the pig on a platter, still warm, surrounded by horseradish and beautiful pieces of homemade bread. I gobbled down the delicious pork—for once, I could eat my fill—and hated myself. The whole family then worked as fast as possible to cut up the pieces and get them smoked before the crime against the Reich could be discovered. Either the pig had been unregistered, like me, or it had been registered and the family would claim they slaughtered it because it was sick, in which case eating the meat was forbidden. For a few days we had pork every day. Then we returned to our usual lean diet with an occasional serving of the salted, bitter remnants of my backyard friend.

My simple life was made a little more complicated by Karel Novák's mother, who lived close by and came in and out of the Nováks' house several times a day without knocking. Although she had sheltered my father, Babička was adamant that it was too dangerous to hide any resister under the same roof with her grandchildren. If she found out about me, she might frighten the already frightened and persuade them to turn me out. "Babička is coming!" hissed through my door was like a command: "Be absolutely still." Noise of every kind was my enemy. "You are a big man," Mrs. Little Spruce gently reminded me. "You have a big voice, and a heavy step." I was six feet three inches tall and afraid of my shadow, which was even bigger and could give me away even when all of my substance was out of sight.

Once in a while I would go out into the yard for a few minutes at night, to my great peril. I looked at the open sky and tried to memorize the spatterings of stars so I could reproduce them on my dark ceiling inside. I inhaled the trees and countryside. If it was snowing, I had to be careful about leaving tracks, but I loved going out in the rain because I did not have to worry that dogs in the vicinity would hear me and start barking. The danger was that one of the neighbors might look out of his door at the weather and see me standing in the rain in the Nováks' yard.

The only relief from my loneliness came from Mrs. Little Spruce, who was lonely, too, surrounded by the sapless intelligence of her husband and neighbors. "It's a kind of ghetto," she once said dispassionately of her seclusion in the village. "Living here is like being in exile." She never once complained about her husband, but she didn't have to. The intellectual gulf between them afforded few bridges. They could discuss who had been fired from his job and the wisdom of boiling the baby's diapers, but by and large Mrs. Little Spruce was isolated on her side of the marriage with her books and thoughts and responsibilities. Novák was so passive that she could not even depend on him to help her make decisions. Whatever she said happened. He said nothing at all until she had spoken, and then whatever he asserted was a rephrasing of her opinion.

Mrs. Little Spruce detested Malý. Whenever he came around, her eyes turned neutral and her mouth dropped into a special impassive shape that all Czechs had added to their facial vocabulary after the German occupation. A story had come to her that the Little One once boasted in the bus garage of personally assisting a high military official in the underground. Talking too much was no minor transgression; it was a deadly mistake. I asked Malý about it and he denied everything. I wasn't sure what to think.

Father, who had none of the usual arrogance of the high military, was at home with common folk like Malý and Kravka. He could make himself one of them without losing his own personality; as a result they were at ease around him and generally adored him. Nevertheless, Father was out of patience with Kravka and even more with Peller for deliberately keeping him isolated from any other resisters. Father knew better than any of them what was possible and what was dangerous, and he had no intention of recruiting fighters yet. Just the same, Peller persuaded Kravka to ignore requests to get in touch with certain people, and the two of them held back information that was intended for Father. When Kravka lied to him about having made contacts, Father felt betrayed. Even though he was General Luža, he would not have lied to Kravka.

Poor Kravka. He was only a rank-and-file soldier, but he was performing impossible feats for us. One night very late I was startled by a knock at the Nováks' door. It turned out not to be the police, as I feared, but my mother. Her arrival in that crowded house could only mean that Kravka could find no place to put her and had brought her to the Nováks in desperation. Mother was miserable with anxiety. She kept mentioning this or that little thing which was left at home, a home she had not seen for several months and might never return to. In fact, we later found out that the Gestapo had already confiscated our apartment on Wurm Street. All of our belongings were sold to Gestapo members for a pittance—carpets, dishes, photographs, sewing boxes, souvenirs, everything. We never saw any of it again except for our Louis XVI bedroom set, which turned up in Austria years after the war, gouged and dilapidated.

For several days Mother remained in my little room at the Nováks. We could not speak much, for the walls were thin and there was a fair amount of coming and going through the house. Mother complained that when Kravka came to get her at Dr. Káňa's, he talked entirely too much. He divulged to Dr. Káňa's unwilling ears not only the area where we would be hiding but the names of the villages and proudly informed her that he was in constant contact with my father. First the Little One, now Kravka! These people were saving our lives with one hand and signing our death sentences with the other. I wrote at once to Father about Kravka's indiscretions, sealed the letter, and with my twenty-year-old's naïveté, gave it to Kravka to deliver. He opened it, read my stinging words about him, and never forgave me. Despite that grudge, Kravka came almost every day to report that he had talked to someone about keeping Mother but had been refused. Most people simply did not have the practical means of hiding anyone, and those who did were too scared.

In the middle of all this, Kravka and I got into a stupid political argument; he complained to Father, and I was instructed, in effect, to cool it. Kravka was not a person with whom one could debate politics. He was deeply provincial and had a high opinion of himself. But though we did not understand each other at the time, I still recognize that he was among the most dedicated of the people who helped us in the underground. He saved our lives many times over.

In December, Kravka came for Mother. I found out much later that the Secs took her in, keeping her in the same room with Father. After two difficult months—the little boy still did not know anyone was living with them—Father was finally able to place her with the family of a gamekeeper near Velké Meziříčí. Josef Pavlas lived on the estate of Count Alois Lichtenstein-Podstatzky, a German.[6] Though his employer was anti-Nazi, Pavlas would not risk confiding in him about Mother. She was introduced to everyone as his wife's aunt and was assumed to be a poor relation who had come to help with the three children. The Nazis were not strict about checking on

6. The count and his wife, Josephine Lichtenstein, born Harrach, gave between two and three million crowns to the Czech resistance.

the registration of women, but because Mother was living almost openly, it was necessary to procure a false identity card. Someone in the district office distributing identity cards smuggled out a blank one that was then filled in with Mother's false name. Like all illegalities, this was risky for everyone involved, as the German police counted the cards as they were printed and counted them again as they were handed out personally to the applicants. Uncovering Mother's false identity would have led to uncovering the worker in the district office who got her the card.

Kravka did something else that was quite wonderful. He conceived and helped to build a hideout in an alcove in the Nováks' basement. The niche was big enough for two people to sit down and was covered by a big piece of cement which, when closed, looked like part of the painted wall. Hlaváček the mailman, the Nováks, and Kravka all helped, as did my father, for Kravka began this project while Father was still living with the Nováks and finished it while I was there. As with the previous hole, dirt was stealthily carted away, and the whole enterprise was carried out without the grandmother noticing. The hiding place was so expertly built that it would have been impossible to detect in a general search, although if the Gestapo had targeted the Novák house because of an informant, they probably could have found it. With this model hiding place, which took about six weeks to complete, I felt much more secure and the family was considerably less fearful of a raid, and it was all thanks to Kravka.

With whom I had another dispute in January. Now, I had only Malý left to make contact with my father. When I needed something, I let him know through Hlaváček. I had brought five thousand crowns with me to the Nováks. I now gave it to the Little One so that he could take better care of himself. But after so many months of doing our bidding, he was no longer very punctual, with or without rewards.

Despite Peller and Kravka's trying to keep him isolated, Father had managed to make an important contact with a former officer, another legionnaire.[7] Jan Moravanský was a former artillery major who had set up a small resistance organization. Father's appointment with him was charged with sus-

7. It happened like this: Sec, the bus driver sheltering Father in Bosonohy, had learned about a teacher near Křižanov who was in the resistance, though still living legally. Sec talked to the teacher, František Maloušek, who mentioned that the leader of his group was a former captain. Sec in turn confided that he knew General Luža was hiding somewhere in the area. Sec and Maloušek then conspired to get the two military men together for a meeting.

pense. They met in a ditch around midnight using a military map to locate the spot, some godforsaken village field near Brno. Moravanský traveled twenty miles to get there. Father and Sec arrived an hour early to make sure no one was watching the place. Then Father waited for the signal, a flashlight that flickered three times, for without a signal, the Gestapo could have walked up to him as well as Moravanský. Next came a man with the password and, finally, Moravanský, who recognized Father at once. They talked softly in the darkness for two hours using only cover names, discussing the possibilities of raising an underground force. Moravanský's group was centered in Velké Meziříčí.[8] He had a list of fourteen hundred former soldiers living legally, six hundred of whom he thought would respond if called to an uprising. There was the possibility of getting heavy weapons from Slovakia, forming a brigade, and harassing the rear of the German army when the front approached the Protectorate from the east. The nominally independent Slovak state was a German satellite, its fascist government closely monitored by the Germans; however, Slovakia was not occupied, and the resistance had more freedom to operate there than in the occupied Czech lands. As in the Protectorate, one center of the resistance was the army. It had not been disbanded in Slovakia, and it still contained many of Father's friends, former members of the Czechoslovak military. Father and Moravanský in effect began merging their supporters that night as they shared information about possible confederates.

Moravanský put us in touch with two general staff officers who would become closely attached to us—Father met them at almost exactly the same spot two months later. The first, General Staff Captain Josef Robotka, had been a member of ON but had so far avoided arrest. The second was another general staff captain named Karel Štainer; at that time his cover name—he had plenty of them—was Karel Veselý. An early member of ON, Štainer had joined the Petition Committee of We Remain Faithful after ON's destruction. In March 1940 the Gestapo surrounded the house where he was living, but he ran, firing his revolver, and managed to escape. He had thus been underground a long time when we met him. He introduced us to a third man, Dr. Josef Grňa, who had been a professor of economics and finance until he was forced to go into hiding. His wife was in an internment camp

8. Called Slezák, then later the Tau, Moravanský's group was subsumed in the Council of Three in 1943–44. Moravanský described the meeting with Father, which took place in September 1942, in a report he wrote at the end of the war.

near Brno. These three, Robotka, Štainer, and Grňa, became Father's most important cohorts in our most pressing underground project: staying alive.

At the end of March 1943, I noticed that Mrs. Little Spruce suddenly seemed quite tense, and as usual, the rest of the household reflected her mood. Karel Novák generally propelled himself by inhaling from one direction and exhaling in the other, his shirt a white lateen as he tacked across the high sea of the front room. But now he was walking briskly through the house, around the yard, in and out of the rooms, as restless as if he had some place to go. Mrs. Little Spruce would not tell me what was upsetting her; apparently it was something her son-in-law had learned in Brno. But soon the Little One brought me a letter from Václav—Father—with the explanation, camouflaged in the verbiage we used in our written communications: Major Žalman had been arrested by the Gestapo.

"Žalman doesn't know where we are," I told the Little One. "Why is everybody getting excited?"

"You can't be sure what he knows," Mrs. Little Spruce interjected. "Peller knows exactly where you are, and he told his wife; maybe the fool told Žalman, too."

"If he is tortured, Žalman will implicate Peller at least," said Mrs. Little Spruce.

The Little One added, "You can be sure that if the Gestapo arrests Peller and so much as shows him a club, he'll vomit names as fast as he can get them out."

Torture, far more than death, was what everyone feared. We knew about the nightlong, agonizing interrogations; we all knew of someone, a close friend, an acquaintance, a friend of close friends, who had been trampled, beaten with rubber hoses, mutilated, hung for hours, revived when he had become mercifully insensible, or subjected to a hundred other brutalities. The Gestapo understood psychology and pain. An interrogator would ask a question, hear the expected denial, apply some grisly torture, and then give a fairly accurate answer to his own question, so that the victim naturally concluded there was no point in trying to bear the unbearable, since it appeared that the Germans already knew everything.

Though I still thought we were being hasty to move, Father sent a note saying that he was coming for me the next day to go to a new place. At least we would be together for a while. I had so much to say to Father that could not be confided to any messenger, things too complicated to express in the vague, symbolic small talk we had to use in letters. I even jotted a list of what I wanted to discuss with him. I had not counted on Mrs. Little Spruce, who apparently had her own list. Father stayed with her in the kitchen hour after hour, enjoying the black market chicken, cake, and rapt attention she saved up for him. She was middle-aged and portly, so that even now I have to doubt that my middle-aged and prudish father had the slightest male interest in her, notwithstanding his cloistered situation. I thought each hour that he would surely excuse himself. But they went on into the night, discussing Peller, Žalman, Kravka, Hitler, and the universe while I fell asleep resentfully in my room.

I didn't like walking in daylight, despite Father's reasoning that it aroused less suspicion than being in the woods at night. We were not even sure we were going the right way to the Hermit's brick factory, our destination. The Hermit was a former officer, a lowly one, since eccentrics like him don't go far in the military. Robotka, from Moravanský's group, was bringing us, and I was uneasy about him too. He was young—about thirty-five—and exquisitely groomed. As a member of the elite group of general staff officers, he was sharply conscious of his position, not to mention his hair.

Father's knapsack was full of books and he was already tired from talking all night with Mrs. Little Spruce. I didn't offer to carry the cement knapsack—a few hours of mild revenge which I have had fifty years to regret. In any case, Father was oblivious to my sullenness. The respect of people in general—people like Jan Sec and Mrs. Novák, or even complete strangers—fulfilled him as much as any close relationship, for he had even less aptitude for intimacy than most men of his reserved generation. He loved me, I knew that much. Yet he was most comfortable with me when I was out in the audience admiring him and not backstage. None of these insights made me happier as I trudged along behind him to Robotka's house, where we had to stop before going on to Hermit's.

Father, however, was relaxed and expansive. Mrs. Robotka—Helena—was dressed as if she were giving a cocktail party out there in the sticks. She introduced the other officer recruited by Moravanský, Karel Štainer, whom I would come to know all too well. We dined, for a change, like city people, on good china, and Helena amused us with the sort of urbane talk that had become so unfamiliar I was almost tongue-tied when she turned the conversation to me. Father was anything but tongue-tied. After his long confinement, he couldn't shut up, even when everyone but Mrs. Robotka was falling over with fatigue.

"Father, this whole business of the Hermit scares me," I told him when we were in bed on Robotka's sofa.

"I'm not comfortable about it," he confided, "but it's the best we can do for now, until things ease up."

"And what's wrong with you?" I asked, "Couldn't you see those two fellows were bored out of their minds, and yet you went on and on." I was half-expecting him to say that he hardly needed lectures from me on etiquette. But instead, I felt his smile in the darkness.

"Your garrulous old man starting to embarrass you? Why, I didn't even tell them my idea about the tank formations."

"Tell it to me. I'm tough."

"Land reform in Slovakia. That's what I really wanted to get into. Maybe tomorrow."

"Do it. I'll sprinkle water on their faces from time to time." I forgot what I wanted to say about the Hermit. There was a nice space between us in spite of my premonition.

IV

Two or three miles before we reached Pánov we could see the Hermit's black chimney on the horizon. I was tired when we approached it and had to keep warning myself to be ready for anything until we were safely inside. In a curve of winding road stood an abandoned brick factory with a house, the Hermit's house, attached to it. If the Gestapo found out where we were, they could easily surround the place. On the other hand, we were so isolated there that it was unlikely they would come upon us accidentally. We had the first floor of the house to ourselves, as the family lived upstairs. The Hermit's excitable wife came down to meet us.

"She cursed me and told me I wouldn't go to heaven," she said, without any greeting or preamble. "All because I wouldn't lease my shed to her." She wasn't talking about a neighbor, because there were no neighbors. "I feel sorry for her," the Hermit's wife went on. "Old. She's not normal. Anyway, I'm not sure I want to go to heaven, considering some of the people there. You know," she said, lowering her voice, "Father Petr's in heaven, who they say starved his mother, and I'm sure he's not the only one. Father Benedetti, the Italian, with those severe penances to the children. Whose sins was he trying to wash away, I wonder." From the corner of my eye I saw Father's temple mildly ticking. Robotka, too, was watching Father. Hermit's wife smiled an edgy, dimpled smile, not completely unaware of the effect she was having on her listeners, but not fully focused on us, either. She began describing the bitter cold of some place whose name she neglected to mention. "It's always winter there," she said to me as a personal aside. While the others moved off, I talked with her or, rather, listened—she could hold a conversation without your saying a word.

The Hermit himself was an arresting figure with his biblical beard and forthright manner. His name was Bohuslav Indra. A tall, sturdy man about my father's age, fifty-two, he was utterly charmless—one of the things I immediately liked about him—and strikingly intelligent, although as a staff captain in the auxiliary sanitation services, he had occupied the lowest and worst of all career military positions. When the regular Czechoslovak army was disbanded, some consolations were handed out to the men forced into retirement. Hermit had been given the brick factory. But then new construction declined during the war, and neither bricks nor the factory were needed any longer. Hermit was bitter toward the Czechoslovak army, in which he had met so little success, but as a nationalist, he wanted to help the resistance. I was at first fascinated by him. Later, I grew to love him and eventually even called him "Father."

Hermit's daughter, Milena, was about twenty and thin. Her breasts were notable, and since I had not seen young contours for many months, I stared at them involuntarily the first time I saw her. In the space of one or two minutes she informed me that her father was married for the second time, that her stepmother hated her, and that her father cared little for either his wife or her, since he was still grieving over a son who had died more than a decade earlier. "Why does your mother dislike you?" I asked courteously.

"She's not my mother. She hates me because—I don't know," she shrugged. "You'd have to ask her." I raised my furtive concentration from Milena's bosom, expecting to meet her owl face, but instead looked straight into the iron eyes of the stepmother. She was standing in the hall behind Milena and had heard every word. She gave me her decorative smile, turned away quietly, and loathed me from that day forward.

I had a queer sense while we stayed with Hermit that I had been detached from March 1943 and was living somewhere outside time. The house was about eighty years old, with a wood stove that had warmed forgotten ancestors. The furniture was of some antique style and old too. Hermit was an intense man full of blunt kindliness. Even after I got to know him well, he always seemed to me a little outlandish. He was an extreme conservative and ardent admirer of politicians active around the time of the Great War. The issues that preoccupied Hermit were the burning questions of 1918, and the public figures he talked about were mostly men who had passed from the scene, in some cases before I was born. Like many right-wing Czechs, he was disgusted with Masaryk and Beneš for cleaving to the "liberal, appeasing, hypocritical" western democracies. "Masaryk is no true Czech!" he once exclaimed. "If I had to, I'd vote for a Communist like Gottwald in preference to those groveling, Anglophile, so-called humanitarians who delivered us to the Nazis." Hermit and Father had several heated exchanges, but their political differences only seemed to make them fonder of each other.

We could shake off the archaic atmosphere only through reading, and since Hermit had hundreds of books on every subject, I studied almost the whole day: paleontology, astronomy, Jane Austen, pipefitting—they eased my anxiety about what poor Žalman might be divulging to the Gestapo. Father, too, had a reading schedule. Though he had no good textbook, he was studying English, for even in confinement he had the determination of the self-made man to make every hour yield something. Trotsky's history of the Russian Revolution and all the wonderful volumes of Ferdinand Peroutka's *The Building of a State* were among his books.

Hermit worked as if stillness were sin, building fences, repairing the house, planting a garden, putting in fruit trees. His wife cooked delicious meals for us—never had we eaten so well in the underground—and was affable when we saw her face to face. But the Hermit told us she constantly harangued him to get rid of us, more insistently every day. Once she pleasantly asked if we had enjoyed our apricot pudding (there had been no pudding, but we complimented her on it anyway), and then one hour later we heard her shrieking to Hermit that if he cared about her nerves, he would put us out. I was surprised to see that Hermit, like Sec and Novák, was afraid of his frangible wife. We learned from overhearing their arguments that Hermit had never prepared her for our stay, telling her we were only going to stop briefly. At each of her outbursts, he would say, "Just a few days longer," not admitting that the arrangement was supposed to last for a couple of months. The truth was that we were trying frantically to find another place, but we simply could not. Robotka was living legally in Velká Bíteš and working as an insurance agent. He went as far as thirty miles away asking at least one person a day to shelter us, but was always turned down.

Apprehension gnawed at me throughout my stay at Hermit's. Nevertheless, it was there that I thought out the details of recruiting an organization. I would start by getting a false identity card so that I could walk around the area—that was no simple item. Once organized, my group was not going to undertake any active resistance such as derailing trains or setting fire to supplies, nor was I thinking about an uprising yet. My goal was to set up cadres in each village I could reach on foot, cells of three or four key people. Each person I contacted would be told to have a friend or two in mind whom he would approach only when the time came to enlarge our operation. The most important thing was to create the units of resistance but not to link them. The people I eventually recruited did not know each other except by cover names. Each person was exposed only to me but not to others in his group, and each one knew nothing of the existence of any other group. If the Gestapo captured one man, that victim could lead them to me and, at worst, one or two others, but then the trail would stop. There would be no line for the Germans to follow connecting one cadre to another, as I was the only one who knew about any others. I was now armed with a 6.35-mm pistol to use at very close range if I were seized and there was a possibility of escape. If the gun could not help me—it wasn't much of a weapon—I had been provided with a single capsule of cyanide. I carried it like an amulet to protect me from unthinkable horrors. We all have to die sooner or later, I kept reminding myself, and if I were in the hands of the Gestapo, sooner was certainly better—for me, for Father, and for all of us. I just had to remember, in my haste to get to the safe afterlife, not to drop the pill before I could swallow it. If you were going to be tortured to death, it was best, of course, to receive the Hitler Kiss while being captured—a fatal bullet that you did not have to give yourself. Known resisters were rarely kissed that quick way. The Nazis much preferred to empty their victims of information before disposing of them.

The underground was now barren. Almost nothing remained of the great resistance organizations—ON, the Petition Committee, PÚ (the Political Center), and their coordinating committee, ÚVOD—except a few scattered and frightened souls without leaders. Josef Grňa, the former professor of finance from Bratislava, was surviving. Like Father, he had gone underground when Heydrich announced the first martial law. Grňa and Štainer were hidden at different times by Cyril Musil, a famous Czech ski racer. They were now practically the last permanent members of the Petition Committee who were not in prison.

Father did not get to other underground fighters such as Grňa by tripping over them on his furtive nighttime walks; meetings with anybody were incredibly difficult. For Father's first conference with Grňa in January 1943 (two months before we arrived at Hermit's), both of them traveled to Kadolec, a village midway between their two hideouts, and spent the night. Štainer brought Grňa from his location in the Bohemian-Moravian hills— twenty miles on skis. That was fine for Štainer, who was a competition ski racer, but not so invigorating for poor Professor Grňa, who arrived white as an aspen and wheezing. He had to go to bed for several hours before he could confer about anything. Father was an excellent skier, but only when he had skis. He had walked the last fifteen miles through deep snow and was also dead tired when the meeting began the next day.

Father explained to Grňa that he had stayed away from all the large resistance groups because no mass association, in his opinion, could escape detection for two more years. That was how long he expected the war to last. Any uprising of the resistance would have to take place at the end of the war, in conjunction with an Allied invasion. Meanwhile, the resisters had to stay alive. Like all of us in the underground, Father assumed that at the end of the war the revolutionaries—that is, the resistance leaders who had carried out the projected uprising—would take over from the defeated Germans and run the country until President Beneš returned and elections were held. It was expected that the major resistance leaders would be offered ministerial positions in any postwar government. Whatever interim program the revolutionaries put in place would be, we thought, taken into Czechoslovakia's postwar political system and might even provide the basis for the permanent government's policies. So Father gave a great deal of thought to what we would do in that transition period after the German defeat. He and Grňa decided that the revolutionary organization would have a military leader (Father) and a political leader (Grňa by default), since we knew no one left in the resistance who was remotely qualified for government.

Štainer and Robotka, our new collaborators, began visiting us regularly at Hermit's. Not that we were delighted with either of them. Robotka had the polish of a young aristocratic officer of the old Austro-Hungarian Empire. He was not tall, but everything about him was narrow and straight, from the impeccable path in the middle of his head to the keen crease of his pants. Like most officers, he considered civilians an inferior, unranked class. Even out of uniform, he was quite a picture in his immaculate gloves, there in Europe's Appalachia. He always wore what we call in Czech a "butterfly," a bow tie, a most unusual appurtenance in the provinces. Once you noticed him, though, you tended to forget he was nearby, so faintly did his personality press upon his surroundings. He spoke softly, in succinct, well-crafted locutions, and sparingly, so that you could project onto him almost any character you wanted him to have. I had not met many people with his self-awareness, and I imagined at first that he had hidden reserves of experience and was accustomed to great responsibility. Neither was true. Robotka was a follower, an attendant lord, properly turned out for each occasion. His visits to Hermit's were big events and much appreciated because he brought us books, newspapers, and attitudes from the real world. He tried to discharge whatever tasks Father gave him, and when he could not be frank he was at least correct. But in relying on him, one relied on the judgment of an impressionable junior officer.

Karel Štainer was resourceful, talkative, and slick. He was completely a man of the people, a sports enthusiast who dressed like a rustic and seemed part of the landscape as he went from village to village on his bicycle. Though he was not registered and was therefore living illegally, he had a false identity card to hand the authorities when they stopped him on the road. Štainer defined everything in terms of left and right, privation and privilege. He was jovial on the surface, but captious underneath, full of borrowed ideology that he worked into every discussion. He never used a moderate phrase if an exaggeration would do. The first time he met me he delivered himself of the opinion that General Zdeněk Novák was a capitalist, as evidenced by his wealthy family and the fact that he was one of the few members of ON who had not been arrested. In Štainer's short glossary, "capitalist" was the moral equivalent of slave trader. The only worse judgment he could make was to call a man a "bourgeois element." Novák had been Father's close friend for years and was an active resister. According to our information, he had advance knowledge of the assassination of Heydrich. So I protested that if he was a capitalist, he was a capitalist with guts. That momentarily shut Štainer up, but the comment was sufficient to prove to him that I was, as rumored, an agrarian, another of his catchwords. Štainer was neither educated nor cultivated. He read cowboy and detective serials, when he read at all, and liked to use political and scientific terms that he did not precisely understand, mispronouncing them slightly so that you did not always understand them either. His favorite subject was Marxism, which he explained in terms coined in his own mint. But what he lacked in intellect he made up in temperament: he was nervy and stubborn as an oak stump about his convictions, especially the wrongheaded ones. He gave a great deal to the resistance, nevertheless. With his long experience in the underground, he often was indispensable. During the time I knew him, his wife was in an internment camp for the families of resisters.

It irked Father to have to explain himself constantly, especially to people who were unsophisticated in matters of warfare, conspiracy, public policy, and military ethics. Štainer and Robotka had the notion that we should work exclusively with left-wing sympathizers, preferably Communist supporters. As silly ideas go, this one was somewhat understandable. In those months our whole nation looked toward the advancing Red Army to liberate us from the anti-Communist Nazis. Our political thinking as a country was moving to the left. But Father was eager for support anywhere he could find it. He especially wanted to get in touch with General Novák, who was working legally as a brewing executive while secretly trying to rebuild ON. Robotka was deputed to make the connection. When he returned to Father, Robotka reported disdainfully that "Uncle," as we called Novák, had contacts to former agrarians in Slovakia and was in communication with the right-wing underground in Prague. "So what?" asked Father. Jedlička, Dr. Káňa, and many others helping us had similar connections. "In the army," he reminded Robotka, "General Novák and I were not the instruments of any one party. We fought for the country. That's the way it must be in the resistance. If people are willing to fight with us, we don't inquire into their private political beliefs."

Father was unsettled about other things, too. He was aware that he was well known and esteemed. He didn't want his name attached to any ragtag underground initiative. Štainer and Robotka were young, obscure captains. Štainer had in fact been so impressed with Father's prominence, he couldn't at first believe that he was meeting General Luža and not a pretender. Claiming to be Father's representatives, these two could approach important people, people who would otherwise dismiss them, and draw them into all sorts of projects without even informing Father. On the other hand, the very fact that Father might be recognized prevented him from going himself to make the contacts he needed, so he was dependent on Štainer and Robotka for any substantive underground work.

As for Grňa, he was no politician and hardly a leader of men. He was a typical academic: intellectual, to be sure, which was a relief from Štainer's superficiality, but idealistic, impractical, and plodding. He would never have achieved a position of consequence in the underground except that he was almost the only choice left after the Gestapo devastations of the underground.

*   *   *

By the spring of 1943, our situation at the Hermit's was critical. The wife was still as gentle as milk when she spoke to us, and she cooked wonderful meals (we were paying for the food, of course). But every day on the floor just above us she created a scene with Hermit. Once we heard a fierce commotion and wondered if we should intervene to keep him from killing her. It was actually Hermit who was in danger. He came to us with his nose bleeding into his beard and his hand slashed where she had attacked him with a claw hatchet. We didn't know where to go. There was nothing, nobody who would shelter us.

Then Hermit's wife discovered the dead man. It was about nine o'clock in the evening. We heard her shouting—that was nothing unusual—but then she came running downstairs hysterically. "He has no coat," she said, beginning the conversation as was her habit, in medias res. "There's no blood." At the back wall of the brick factory she had found a man, simply dressed, with no discernible wound, and so recently alive that there were still tiny white bubbles around his mouth. I had never seen a corpse except for brief visits to well-dressed relatives in funeral caskets. We concluded that the dead man had been a fugitive, like us, who died from a heart attack, stroke, or simple exhaustion. If the police were chasing him, they would soon catch up with him, investigate the grounds, and find us. We had to get rid of him. After much agitated discussion, we decided to carry him as far away as we could and leave him in an inconspicuous spot where he would not be immediately noticed.

Hermit and I thus started out around ten o'clock with the terrifying body between us. He was a big, overweight man, heavy as an automobile, it seemed, with hair that fell from side to side as if he were tossing his dead head and eyes that now and then opened to stare at me incuriously. We had to cross the creek into the forest without leaving wet tracks, though we were staggering. There was a full moon lighting our humid way, what we call in Czech a fish-eye moon. We wished it would rain, so as to obliterate our marks and lessen the danger that we would meet someone, for it would be pretty hard for the three of us—Hermit, me, and the Quiet One—to go by unnoticed. Hermit and I finally found a place we thought we could leave him and let our load fall. One of his knees bent as we dropped him, and the joint cracked a weak farewell. We got back home about one in the morning, feeling dead ourselves with fatigue. I thought again and again about the dead man, a poor wretch fleeing like me. He became a symbol of exhausted humanity, alive and struggling desperately one minute and erased from existence the next. If forced to leave Hermit, I could perish in just this way. We later learned that some children looking for mushrooms found the body five weeks later. The story was put out that he was a worker who died of tuberculosis, but I doubted that. Except for being dead, he had looked pretty healthy.

Hermit's wife changed as a result of the incident. Perhaps she became aware of the fragility of all of our lives; perhaps, like me, she suddenly realized that today or tomorrow one of us could be in the dead man's place, with foam around our mouths. In any case, she softened toward Father. She began saying that if necessary, he could stay, but she absolutely would not have me in the house. I was getting used to the separate view people had of Father and me. Father was a national figure, though that made him a dangerous person to shelter. I was a twenty-year-old nothing figure and an ally, she thought, of her stepdaughter. There was some talk of my going to one of the summer cottages in the countryside. I protested that everyone in the area knew which cottages were supposed to be vacant. At the first sign of life in one of them, there would be reports to the owners and the gendarmes. Father finally put an end to that discussion by declaring that if I had to go to a weekend cottage, he would go with me.

Father and I nevertheless wound up in a bitter argument, or so I hear it now in my mind, for in the deep, closed corridors of memory, all our disputes ring loud. I overheard him tell Štainer that I was young and inexperienced. Compared to Štainer, who was twice my age and adroit in the business of illegal life, I was indeed a green plant, having been the only child in a home where no one smoked, drank, played cards, or fought. When my father was not working, he read. For recreation, my mother had headaches. Neither of them uttered one single vulgar word in my hearing. I was not prepared for the fucks and shits that would splash on me when I left their roof, nor for life's more serious inclemencies. But I was tough minded, at least. I didn't fall for every casuistry that was presented to me. Father had no business encouraging Štainer's condescension.

As if our nerves were not already jangling, it was about this time that a car full of German officers pulled up to the brick factory. Hermit sounded the alarm. Father got to a hiding place we had dug out in the floor. I had time only to slip into the bathroom with my revolver. I held my breath, waiting for the door to burst open. But after a while, I heard the car drive away, the Germans having only wanted some water for their radiator. The incident was not entirely harmless, however. Now some Germans had noticed the factory; they would keep it in mind the next time they were ordered to do a sweeping search of the villages.

We finally learned of our hideous reprieve: Major Žalman, expecting torture and fearful of what he might reveal, had hanged himself in prison the day after his arrest by the Gestapo. Thanks to our courageous friend, Father could now return to the Secs without worrying that the police were following his trail from Žalman to Peller to Jan Sec. The Secs were willing to have Father back, but because of their little boy, they could hide only one person, and that with difficulty. There was still the problem of what to do with me.

The remainder of 1943 is a blur of faces in my memory, the names in my diary a chronicle of increasing despair as I went from one person to another. I remember that on June 1 it was already hot as I put my few things in a briefcase and buried Father's letters in a jar in Hermit's yard. Robotka was taking me to a hideout Štainer had found. After being passed through a relay of escorts, I found myself walking alongside František Zajíček, who was, like Štainer, a former member of the army's ski team. He was well known in Czechoslovakia before the war and, having had to resign his lieutenant's commission, now worked at the district office in Velké Meziříčí. With hardly a word, he led me around the perimeter of the town at a gallop before stopping at a house. He went inside the yard and returned frowning. "Well, I thought I had a place for you, but somebody is still there who was supposed to leave. Now I don't know what to do with you." Then he brought me within sight of a little house. "Go there," he pointed. "Say that you are a teacher who was a good friend of that lady's husband. She's a widow who lives with her mother and daughter. Don't tell the little girl your situation." I wanted to ask whether the lady knew that I was unregistered, but Zajíček had already left.

Růžena Šenková was a pleasant and courageous young woman about thirty years old. She had one room that I could use for a few days, but as she needed money, she would have to rent it out soon. Her husband had been a forester and hardly an intellectual, yet Růžena had a nice little library. I remember I read Pearl Buck's *The Good Earth* from her shelf. The women were delightful, all three generations of them. Or perhaps it was merely that after the terseness of my good Hermit, the shrieking of his wife, and the moroseness of his daughter, I was starved for amiable chatter. Zajíček came that night and every night to bring me food, since the ladies could not afford to feed me and I had no ration card. We all enjoyed him. He was witty and full of fun and card games no one had ever heard of. On Růžena's radio I listened to the BBC's report of the German retreat from Kursk—the turning point of the war, though we didn't know it then. Just as we were detaching the Churchill, Růžena heard the jackboots of German soldiers approaching the house. "Under the bed!" she hissed. They were only asking about the room for rent and were soon gone, leaving us trembling and aware, as always, of our peril.

Zajíček came the next day to move me. It was hard for me to leave Růžena. I had no romantic interest in her—though perhaps Zajíček did—but I had begun to recognize how much one needs acceptance and pleasant conversation. Within a mile, he turned me over to another man, since it was safest for him and for me to have intermediaries—we called them cutouts. I was left at a crossroad where a rangy fellow approached me and identified himself as Maloušek, the same teacher who the previous winter had taken Father on that long trip through the snow to meet Professor Grňa. Maloušek told me we were going to the estate of a wealthy landowner with a house that overlooked the road, so that I would be able to see any Germans approaching and have time to escape. As I still did not have the one thing that could keep me alive, a false identity card, I was looking forward to this refuge. I did not ask who had made the arrangements—it was always better not to ask—and so I did not know whom to blame for what happened when we arrived.

The landowner's face fell when he saw me. He would save us the trouble of making our request, he said, since his wife wouldn't hear of my staying. He offered us some money, which Maloušek indignantly refused, and a meal, which the teacher did not permit me to accept. Maloušek discharged a stream of complaints as we walked off the estate under the eyes of the owners watching our retreat down the hill: "These are the very people we are risking our necks for. There are men being shot every day, people suffering in concentration camps, people being tortured in some prison this very minute, all for these louts, so they can live in comfort and not put a hair of their heads in jeopardy." I did not commiserate with him, for it was the end of the day, and I still had nowhere to go.

I had no alternative when I left Maloušek but to return to Růžena's. If the Gestapo made any sort of search there or discovered me accidentally, it would mean certain death for her mother, her daughter, herself, and me, but even so, I had to knock on her door and say, "Hi, I'm back." It was getting dark. As I got into the middle of Velké Meziříčí, where people were coming home from work, I suddenly noticed that my new shoes were making a lot of racket on the sidewalk. I was trying to be invisible, yet people a half block up the street were turning around to glance at me. Squeaking raucously and aware that I was getting more lost by the minute, I turned a corner and ran headlong into Zajíček. He did not seem surprised to see me back on the road and was happy to lead me to Růžena's so that he would have an excuse to visit her. "Why don't you tell her I went to the new place," I suggested, "but voluntarily relinquished it to a resister who needed it more than I did? If she finds out other people are turning me away, she'll be more fearful than ever about accepting me." Zajíček agreed with me completely, marched up to her door, and told her instead the whole dispiriting truth.

I was touched that she received me warmly. Late that night she came to me where I was reading, her face grave. I waited for her to tell me I would have to go the next morning, but instead she took something out of her pocket, stroked it hesitantly, and laid it on the page in front of me. It was the identity card of her late husband. Zajíček could take the card to the district office and exchange it for that priceless thing, a perfectly new, blank identity card. I would have everything I needed to survive except a place to live.

My next hiding place was temporary—an attic in the house of a man we called the Proletarian. He lived near the dangerous center of Velké Meziříčí, where he made Venetian blinds, not the type we have today, but a wartime blind that shut out every splinter of light. He had plenty of work; every single window in the country had to be black at night. When the Proletarian found out no one would keep me, he said, "Well, the young fellow will just have to stay with us until you can find a safer place for him." Though frugal, he and his wife had many good books, mostly German authors. I was happy in their attic. Their son was a friendly young engineer, an active resister, who came every day. They were a devoted family until May 1945, when the son was murdered by the SS.

Zajíček soon brought my new identity card with a picture Hermit had taken of me wearing glasses, which I did not yet need. Štainer helped me fill out the card, for the lies had to be put down with great care. Since this was an adult card, and not the special youth card required of people younger than twenty-six, I had to pretend to be twenty-six. That was easy; I felt forty. I was going to enjoy having a new name, having people react to me, and not to General Luža's son.

I could now walk a little in the countryside with the Proletarian. If the gendarmes stopped me, I was Ladislav Zezula, living in Meziříčí. They could check and find out that the address was fictitious, but they were unlikely to do that unless they had some reason to suspect me. "My, how you've aged since last week," the Proletarian joked. "I think I detect a few wrinkles around your eyes. Štainer told us we were getting a clumsy kid who couldn't even pack his own knapsack, but you matured quickly." Then, seeing my change of expression, he said gently, "Be cautious around him. I don't think he would deliberately harm you or put you in danger, but he's impulsive and he resents you."

Štainer's remark nicked me because there was a prick of truth in it, as in nearly all criticism. Was I an oaf who got in everybody's way? I couldn't help noticing that people who looked on Father as a type of civic god, or at least a clergyman in the religion of patriotism, regarded me as something of a nuisance. At first I thought Father's admirers were opportunists eager to please an important man. But after a long time in the underground I saw that most of the people around Father only wanted the same things from him that I wanted: attention, approval, a sense of being part of someone they thought of as higher or more valuable than themselves. Perhaps all hero worship has some sort of father complex as its nucleus, a craving somewhere below thought. It certainly seemed that in our closed society of the underground there were several people trying to be good sons in some incoherent hope of garnering Father's sparing praise.

My next futile excursion, a few days later, was forty miles away to see if Mrs. Tůma would take me in. Lieutenant Colonel Tůma had been arrested almost the very day Father went into hiding. His place would be safer than being with the Proletarian in town, where any moment the police might search the neighborhood just to see what turned up.

"I'm going to need a bicycle," I told Štainer when he met me on the road.

"You'll have it," he said, hiding his own bike behind a bush. As always, Štainer was wearing his plain shirt and long stockings and looked as if he might have been born in one of the cottages around us. His false ID stated that he was a forest worker, and that was exactly what he appeared to be, down to his rust-colored hair and raveled diction. He had been stopped by the gendarmes many times as he went back and forth from Velké Meziříčí to Bohemia, but each time they looked at his card, looked at him, and were satisfied. No one could have imagined that he was a Czechoslovak officer and a leader of the underground.

But a leader he was, as I was reminded when Zajíček met us on the road. "Well, Franta," Štainer said, taking the young man's bike and setting it in front of me, "you will have to walk back to Meziříčí. Thanks for the wheels." To my surprise, Zajíček did not offer the least protest, yielding, as many people did, to Štainer's self-confident directives.

I traveled all day, past maybe twenty villages. The temperature was about ninety-three degrees when I finally rang Mrs. Tůma's bell. Štainer had been asked to get a message to her telling her I would be arriving. My neck and face were boiled, and I was looking forward to a cool bath and a safe bed.

"Radomír, what are you doing here? Why didn't someone tell me you were coming?" said Mrs. Tůma when she opened the door. She was expecting company the very next day. There was no possibility of my staying there. I thought about my recent letters from "Václav." Father, too, was completely exasperated with Štainer, who had the gall to tell the Proletarian that Luža was useful for getting people involved in the resistance, but he would have to be ditched later. Father, it seemed, was impractical, a plutocrat, an intellectual who wasted time learning English, that mercantile tongue, instead of Russian. He could not be trusted to lead an uprising because, according to Štainer, he did not understand guerrilla warfare and even at times read the Bible. All this from a snip of a soldier who had never seen battle, about a man who had fought the Bolshevik guerrillas in Siberia and commandeered an armored train—in fluent Russian.

Since Mrs. Tůma could not keep me, I decided to go back to Hermit, who at least would take me in. At sunrise I started out with my blistered neck and a crushing headache, back over the hills. But before I was halfway to Pánov, I began having horrible cramps. The ground swerved and rolled under me so that I could hardly pedal. I willed myself to keep moving, to reach Hermit even if I had to crawl, dragging the bike behind me. Every few minutes I stopped, my stomach locked in spasms. I vomited torrents of green juice, but even the puking failed to relieve the cramps and blinding headache. "Hold out, hold out," I told myself. But after every mile, I had to get off the bike and fight with myself to get back on. I still had Tišnov ahead of me, a busy district town. I wouldn't be able to stumble through the streets throwing up and falling down without someone noticing me. Luckily, it was Sunday, a day of little traffic. When I reached the central square, my cramps had abated. But just as I got past the town, I was again overwhelmed with spasms, and I couldn't go any more. I fell face down into a ditch near the road with the bicycle next to me. I smelled earth as my cheek sank into the grass, and I felt myself being taken into the damp soil toward a pair of eyes that were opening and closing. The eyes got closer as my boy-life receded behind me. Just before I lost consciousness, I could make out a figure around the frightening eyes, waiting for me: it was the dead man.

I came to and looked at my watch. I had been unconscious almost an hour. No one had passed in all that time. No one, apparently, had seen me. Vomit-stained and weak, I was the luckiest man in Moravia. The cramps were milder, and the hills stretched out more easily until at long last I saw the chimney of the brick factory. Hermit dropped his shovel and embraced me as I came up. Even Mrs. Hermit welcomed me with the fragment of a discussion she had apparently been having with herself. For the next three days, I rested.

The weeks of rejection ended when I contacted the Hašek family, whom I had visited with my parents in 1939 and 1940. Eduard Hašek owned an estate, Okarec, where students fulfilling a summer labor obligation could assist with the harvest and help Hašek meet the grain requisition. The two servants and five young people who were there knew me as Ladislav. I was still not registered, of course, but it did not occur to anybody that I was wanted by the Gestapo. I remained for the entire month of August 1943, one of my best periods in the underground, living semipublicly, bagging the cut grain in the fields with other youths and swimming in the pond in the evening.[1] What makes this time special for me, however, was not that I had an almost normal life, working and socializing, but that during this easeful period I became a dedicated resistance fighter. My primary goal was to defeat the Third Reich, whether I was alone in my room or enjoying a picnic with the young people. I began to live with a cemetery in my mental landscape, the graveyard of all those who had starved in the camps or died suffering in the prisons or who killed themselves in one last, great sacrifice. Despite my conversion, which must have been going on long before I fainted in the ditch, I still missed girls and friends with whom I could share intimate thoughts, and all those luxuries of free men. But when I got really lonely, I had Hitler to think about.

---

1. It was while swimming that I met Leopold Chmela, who was also staying there. Hašek must have told Chmela who I was, for he came to me privately and let me know, without saying it expressly, that he was happy to be working with Father. I later learned that he was a primary member of the Ambassador Heidrich resistance group and that Father was indeed in touch with him. Chmela wrote a book after the war summarizing Czech losses during the German occupation. He became the general director of the National Bank.

For some time I had been outlining the tenets of a new postwar republic. My program, "What We Want," was similar to other radical programs that were being hatched all over Europe in the occupied countries. It called for such measures as nationalizing our heavy industry, reducing our twenty-eight political parties to two or three, providing all citizens with free education, and finally, an idea endorsed by everybody except the Sudeten Germans: expelling the Sudeten Germans from our territory. I was as proud of my wistful program as if I had formulated the Fourteen Points. Like every resistance movement, we were plotting a revolution. This was what people could expect from us if we succeeded in defeating the German dictatorship. I thought it all through, revised my draft many times, and sent it to my father.

"Thank you very much for your program," he wrote back. "I read it and am now rereading it and I like it so much," he wrote, with his typical back-handed praise, "that I would not believe it is your work if you hadn't sent it to me." Father had no particular use for intellectuals. That I was scholarly hardly meant more to him than if I had been a champion at canasta. One of the scratches in our relationship was that he was tepid about my attending university. It was Mother who insisted I must have a higher education and encouraged my bookishness. Even now I don't understand it.

Father was doing the only work possible for him, making contacts with other resisters. Perhaps I should explain here that when I say "resisters," I generally mean people like my father who were combatants, who planned an uprising, linked groups, smuggled information to the Allies, or tried in whatever way they could to influence the outcome of the war. Somebody like Mrs. Novák, who was basically a provider and supporter, was certainly important to the resistance, even though we didn't refer to her as a resister. If the Germans discovered her actions, she would be just as dead as the fighters she helped. Moreover, people like her helped to keep the resistance alive when no active resistance was possible. No one in fact really knew where the other active people were or how many still survived. There was no club called The Resistance. We were all like weeds, springing up here and there in the cracks in the Nazi system, being rooted out, coming back again from a few seeds. "The resistance" refers to many, many large and small clusters, fragmentary and overlapping operations of varying effectiveness. Some people, such as Štainer, were part of several clusters or cells. As we had no publicity during the critical war years, we only found out who the active resisters were when they came out of hiding after the war. In the underground, Father was constantly trying to locate other leaders so that when the time came for action, they could coordinate their efforts.

In 1933 while Father and I were both recovering from bronchitis in a sanatorium in the High Tatras, we got to know an engineer, Karel Staller, who was also a patient. Staller was a technical whiz. He developed a new type of machine gun—the Bren—which he sold to the British before the war. At the sanatorium we saw him every day for a month and got to know his two sons as well. Unlike other engineers I've met, who typically had no discernible personalities, Whiz Staller's moods ranged from exuberant to manic. He'd burst in on us with kinetic news bulletins, pop around the room flailing his chubby arms, and insist on boxing or engaging me in some rough play. In 1939 he became general director of the Brno Small Arms Factory, supervising even its division of automobile production. He was as excessive in his resistance efforts as he was in everything else, willing to do anything to damage the Nazis, even though he worked under their noses as one of their essential technical experts. In addition to donating his own money to the resistance, he siphoned funds from the Small Arms enterprise and smuggled it to the Allies.[2] The Germans made the Small Arms Factory part of the Hermann Göring Konzern, one of whose directors was Hermann Göring's brother. Albert Göring stayed at Whiz Staller's apartment on his visits to Brno. Lubricated by Jägermeister and plum brandy, and probably by Staller's stimulating ebullience, Albert was wont to make jokes about other Nazis and spill a few drops of information. In 1940 he even confided to Staller the date of the German invasion of France, which Staller promptly reported to the British.

In May 1943, Father and Whiz Staller met in a forest. Being one of the few Czechs still allowed to travel to Slovakia, Staller was transporting microfilm out of the Protectorate in his shaving kit and in coins. He would take the film to Bratislava, where his son lived. From there, the Slovak resistance smuggled the film to Switzerland, using a Slovak exporter who was allowed to travel to Switzerland five times a year. From Switzerland another courier took the film to our exile government in London.[3]

2. Our particular organization never seriously lacked money, as far as I can remember. Besides Staller's contributions, there were those of Eduard Hašek, who gave us 300,000 Protectorate crowns. The Count and Countess Lichtenstein-Podstatzky gave us 560,000.

3. The courier was Rudolf Fraštacký, a Slovak sugar exporter, who carried the film in the heels of his shoes. His business transactions were ostensibly helping the Germans evade the Allied blockade. As part of his work, he regularly traveled from Bratislava to Switzerland. There he would meet the former Czechoslovak envoy to Switzerland, Jaromír Kopecký, who then sent to

At that time our first batch of transmitters had been destroyed by the Germans, and we had not yet reestablished cable contact with any of the Allies. For over a year the courier network Whiz Staller organized from the Protectorate to Slovakia to Switzerland to England was almost the only means of contact between the home resistance and President Beneš or between us and the Slovak resistance. It was not until 1944 that London was able to drop transmitters to us by parachute.

It was a touchy question whether Staller should remain in such a dangerous position, working cheek by jowl with the Germans. He was providing crucial intelligence about the levels of their industrial production and the new munitions they were developing. Father thought the risk was worth it; that is, he thought, I suppose, that the information was worth Staller's life. Whiz Staller had relatives near Brno and Velká Bíteš and could therefore go back and forth from Prague without arousing suspicion, each time giving Robotka information for Father.

The contacts with Whiz Staller are a good example of Father's difficult situation regarding Robotka and Štainer. Staller had no interest in conferring with Robotka except as General Luža's messenger. Staller and Robotka were from the same town, knew each other, and were both living legally. It made sense to use Robotka as an intermediary to avoid the danger of personal meetings between Whiz Staller and Father. But if Robotka and Štainer took it into their heads, they might simply fail to bring Father's messages, or neglect to give Father information that Staller, or someone like him, intended for Luža. Robotka would not commit such impertinence on his own, but whatever mischief Štainer conceived would spread to Robotka like bacteria, destroying his good judgment. As time went on, Štainer and Robotka increasingly took it upon themselves to decide which messages of Father's they would actually deliver.

Grňa sent a report of Father's meeting with Whiz Staller to Beneš and Ingr, letting them know through the couriers that our group was forming. The London government was asked to acknowledge receipt of the microfilm by giving a password in one of the Czech broadcasts of the BBC. At the beginning of each news broadcast there was usually a string of such coded

---

London, through transmitters or couriers, the information Fraštacký brought him. Sometimes Fraštacký took the microfilm to Istanbul, where the Czechoslovak government in exile had representatives. Fraštacký escaped Czechoslovakia in 1948 and became a banker in Toronto. I met him several times after the war.

announcements: "Erica watch. Spring is coming. Memory is watchful. The corn is green." The Germans, too, heard the communications but could not decode them, we hoped. A few weeks after the meeting with Whiz Staller, confirmation came that Beneš had received the microfilm and knew about our organization. Listening to Hermit's radio, Father heard Beneš' coded message: "Delta to the Nile."[4]

Meanwhile, Hašek found a shelter for me three or four miles away in a state experimental station for fish breeding. At the beginning of September, when all the students left to return to their gymnasia, I, too, left for the isolated station where I would stay for two months, walking in the autumn woods and talking to the manager about the habits and sex lives of fish.

It was now the fall of 1943. The Allies had landed in Sicily and were fighting their way up the Italian peninsula. All year the Soviets had been receiving prodigious quantities of American matériel and were steadily advancing toward us. Father was restive because he needed to meet with Grňa to make some plans and to stifle certain others that he had gotten wind of. Eager to make a contribution to our work, I told Father I would set up a meeting at Hašek's for October 1943.[5] I was pleased when everything seemed to go well.

"When the war is finally over, those two up there will be the ones making decisions for the whole country," Štainer commented as he and I walked a little way behind Father and Grňa. "They will run things." In the evening we all listened to the BBC. The German retreat was continuing. Štainer, who

4. It was also in 1943 that Mrs. Eliáš put Father in touch with one of the most important underground groups in Prague, that of President Beneš' former envoy, Arnošt Heidrich. Ambassador Heidrich had been close to Eliáš as well as Beneš. Eventually, he was to provide Father with a transmitter, a device that he received from the Czechs in London and smuggled into the Protectorate by way of Turkey.

5. When I volunteered to make the arrangements I was nonchalant about the difficulties of setting up a meeting between underground leaders. First, I had to find a large enough place, one that both men could get to. They could not use their own hiding places, since none of us wanted to know exactly where the others were located; at that time, even I wasn't sure where Father was living. They would need to confer about fourteen hours, so we had to be able to spend two nights. Štainer was to accompany Grňa, and the forester Rudolf Sedlák would bring my father in a cart. Though we had no ration cards with which to buy groceries, I needed food for several men and myself, six or seven meals apiece. Generous as always, Hašek took care of that by slaughtering a pig. And finally, I prepared a backup place—the fish station—in case they spent hours getting to Hašek's, only to find that some last-minute development made the meeting too risky.

was absolutely certain about everything, was certain the Allies would invade western Europe by the end of the month. "It will happen this October," he asserted, "or I am an idiot."

"I think you will have to wait five or six months, Karel," said my father, "until the spring of '44. The Americans and British are not sending their land forces into the Pacific. That's good. It means they are assigning priority to the European front. The next big development should be the spring offensive of the Red Army, and only with that, I think, will we have the Allied invasion, probably at Normandy. A seaborne attack like this on Europe is completely unprecedented. It will require massive preparations. Just think about the coastal fortifications. Even after the invasion, it will take months of hard fighting before the final surrender. Don't ever underestimate the Germans." We still had to confine ourselves, Father warned, to building only the framework of our organization. Radio Moscow had for weeks been exhorting resistance fighters in central Europe to help the Russians by starting "Partisan warfare"—guerrilla activity. Father shook his head. "We have to lie low until spring," he insisted. "We are scattered individuals being hunted down every hour by the best, most determined secret police in the world. We're in the geographic middle between the western and eastern fronts, too distant for either the Americans or the Russians to help us. Of all the occupied countries, we are the farthest from a front. We can't start any kind of partisan warfare without weapons. We can't fight tanks with revolvers."

Grňa began talking about the postwar republic. "We must formulate a clear program of social democracy. The bureaucracy must be better paid than in the past. And there is the question of individual rights versus *iusti civitatis*," he continued, warming up to his lecture mode, which enabled him to be dull in two languages. Štainer chimed in with his favorite theme, the shortcomings of our former army officers. Father argued with Štainer, and Grňa echoed Father's opinion on every point.

I was glad when I could finally go to bed, even though I had to sleep with Grňa. "Would you be so kind as to cut my hair before we turn in?" he asked. "It doesn't matter if it's not a perfect job." I had never given anyone a haircut, but as Grňa's head looked like a stork's nest, I figured I couldn't make him look worse. "I heard you were a sympathizer with the former agrarian party," he said as I snipped. "I'm happy to find out it isn't true."

I kept my distance from Father, since I didn't want to be criticized for preferring private family conferences to open discussions about our common work. But the next night Štainer and Grňa slept together, and Father and I were finally able to talk.[6]

"Grňa's a typical professor," Father said, his voice gray with disappointment, "good at airing theories. He's well-read, rational—all the things Štainer is not—honest and upright, but Heaven knows, no politician."

"He's inexperienced," I answered, "but that will change with time."

"I wish it were just that," Father said. "He doesn't have the drive, don't you see? The will to power. Power is nothing unless you know what to do with it and are willing to use it. A man like that will never be comfortable with power. He's only comfortable talking about it. Doesn't have a speck of political know-how."

"Look, Father, Grňa may not be a first-class politician," I conceded. "But there isn't anybody else. And Štainer, too. I know what you mean about him. But he's helped us through some tricky situations. If he's not intelligent, he's at least smart."

"It is quite high-minded of you to defend him, my son. I can assure you he defends you to nobody." Father was sour and frustrated. "He's a watchdog, good for sniffing and barking and rousing other dogs. But like an aggressive animal, you have to keep him on a tight leash, and there's no way I can supervise him."

The meeting resumed the next day, and I saw that Father was right about both of them. Father thought it was urgent to make contact with Colonel Theodor Lang of the Protectorate troops. The troops were set up by the Germans as a nonmilitary unit permitted to carry only light weapons, but they were ten thousand strong. Father said we should also begin trying to recruit leaders of the gendarmerie. Štainer and Grňa would not hear of our contacting any of these "collaborators." Father insisted that we had to coordinate our efforts with those of the Slovak underground, our only hope for procuring heavy weapons. Despite Slovakia's status as a fascist German satellite, many former Czechoslovak officers remained in its army, men who could make a decisive contribution to the Czech national uprising. "It's all very well for you to talk about our ideal social democracy, Grňa, and for you, Štainer, to rail against the 'comfortable bourgeois resisters,'" Father thundered. "But right now we have to defeat the Germans. To do that we need

6. Father always used cover names when discussing other resisters. He never, never divulged a comrade's true identity, even to me. However, I have substituted real names when quoting Father, out of consideration for the reader trying to remember all our cohorts.

people with military experience and people with money and anybody else who will help us." As an army officer, Father had not even been allowed to vote because he was supposed to be the defender of both the left and the right. He had no patience with partisanship.

Grňa next proposed that, as the political head of our revolutionary force, he should promote resisters from the army up to the rank of colonel. Štainer heartily seconded this idea. "Well," said Father, his face darkening, "as the military head of this so-far nonexistent revolutionary force, I must tell you I have no intention now of promoting anybody to anything. What of the people whose contributions we don't know about? Are they to be inferior to the ones recognized? Look: once the action starts, I'll appoint a special officer to gather information about those who worked in the underground. Then we can see about promotions."

The conclusion of the meeting was friendly enough, but Father was drained and depressed as we prepared to walk to the field where the forester Sedlák would pick him up for his return to Bosonohy. He told me he wanted me to work with him when we came out of hiding, as some sort of assistant or political secretary. I had no ambitions for that kind of career. I wanted to study and travel. But I made no protest, because what I wanted most at that moment was to remain near my father. How good it is now to remember that for three weeks in 1943, or maybe it was as long as a month, Father forgot to criticize me for being indifferent to sports, disliking competition, and hating exercise.

"That document you sent your father is remarkable," Professor Grňa told me in parting. "Václav, you're a lucky father to have such a serious, intelligent son."

"This big delinquent?" Father answered. "Today he became a man. This is his twenty-first birthday." His words were addressed to Grňa, but his eyes spoke to me.

"I'm not a delinquent. Just an agrarian," I said. Grňa looked confused and finally managed a smile. Father laughed. He pushed on my chin with his knuckles so that my head turned and I glanced around, just in time to see behind me, agitated and vulnerable, the face of Karel Štainer.

Milada (center) and Radomír Luža with friends, 1931

Milada Luža, 1945

Vojtěch Luža in Sokol competition, 1912, choreographed pose

General Vojtěch Luža, 1938

Slávka and Alois Eliáš, 1922

"Teta Tíni," Celestina Peschl, ca. 1914

František Jedlička

Novák house in Javůrek, Radomír Luža's first shelter

The mailman Josef Hlaváček, "The Fast One"

Jan Sec

Jan Sec and the bus that transported Vojtěch Luža

Karel Štainer's false identity photo,
1943

Professor Josef Grna

Josef and Helena Robotka, 1933

"The Hermit," Bohuslav Indra

Hermit's house in Pánov, brick factory in rear

Vojtěch Luža's dug-out hiding place under Hermit's floor

Radomír Luža recruiting a villager, 1944

Radomír Luža's false identity card, 1944

Mayor Jaroslav Kobylka and his mother, Božena Kobylka

Kobylka's house in Kadolec, where Vojtěch and Radomír Luža hid in the attic

"The Giant," Josef Ondra, at his blacksmith shop

Jan Votava in the room where the shooting took place

V

We were at the end of 1943, and the worst year of my life was about to start. In the fall, Roosevelt, Churchill, and Stalin had met in Teheran to plan the final offensives of the war. From Sicily, the Allies were progressing north-ward, while the Red Army had pushed the Germans back to the Dniester River, about six hundred miles away from us.[1] It was clear by now that Hit-ler would lose the war. What was not clear was whether we in the under-ground would live to see the surrender.

Father expected the Atlantic invasion in about six months, which meant that we might have to last another year in hiding. We hoped that Hitler would be so busy preventing the collapse of his armies that he would neglect his hateful projects in the Protectorate, but in fact his police were as fervent as ever in tracking down resisters and tyrannizing everyone else. German policy toward the Czechs did not change, and though the terror was not as barbaric in the Protectorate as in Poland, it remained far worse than in Hol-land, Belgium, or France. By now, everyone knew someone—a relative, a neighbor, a coworker—who had been arrested by the Gestapo. In 1944, ac-cording to State Minister Karl Hermann Frank, the man in charge of perse-cuting us, the Nazis were executing over one hundred people a month in

---

1. Italian forces had signed an armistice on September 3, but the Germans rushed reinforce-ments into Italy to hold the country until the bloody end. By now the submarine war in the Atlantic had been won. The previous spring, a quarter of a million men had surrendered to the Allies in Tunisia.

the Protectorate, but they were not publicizing the deaths as they had in the past. The Czechs, whose labor was vital to the war, were not to be pushed to the point of rebellion. "Only the very drastic cases are being put in the newspaper—to savor the details," Frank explained.[2] Hitler had decided in 1940 that the Czech nation would disappear. He was therefore eliminating intellectuals and military leaders just as if he were winning the war and all of central Europe were about to become German country. Even when the Allied armies were at the borders of the Third Reich and German cities were being bombed to rubble, Frank was still describing his delicious vision of exterminating Czechs. Those who survived the war, he said, as if he expected to toast the armistice, would be either Germanized, if they qualified, or annihilated.

But despite the Gestapo's merciless and imaginative correctives, the Czech resistance was resurging. New groups were appearing, and we could see that the time had finally come to plant the scattered cadres for our murderous uprising. I had to start organizing from nothing. On foot, I could get to two or three districts within a thirty-mile radius, and in every village I hoped to recruit one or two, at most three men.[3] In the beginning Hlaváček helped me by making the initial visit to someone he thought might be willing to work with us—perhaps a teacher, butcher, or innkeeper, someone like himself who came into contact with almost everybody in his community and was widely trusted.

"I'm glad you consented to meet my young friend," Hlaváček would say, using a cover name for me, or no name at all. "He represents an important secret organization. I know him well. Now I'll leave you two alone." Without mentioning that I was living underground, I began by lecturing the new conspirator on the urgency of keeping quiet about every detail of his activity. I explained that he should have in mind two or three very reliable people he could ask to help us when the time came to mobilize for an insurrection. If he was in a position to pick up information we needed, I might ask him to perform some specific task, such as watching the movement of convoys on the main road. I inquired about whether he had access to any guns, or knew of possible shelters—always a pressing necessity. We set up what we called a

2. Karl Hermann Frank, *Sudetendeutschtum in Kampf und Not: Ein Bildbericht* (Kassel-Wilhelmshöhe, 1936), 128, 64.

3. I organized in the area around Brno, including the city, suburbs, and surrounding countryside; part of the district of Tišnov; Velké Meziříčí, especially the southern part around Bíteš; and part of Rosice-Zastávka. All of the latter lay west of Brno.

"dead box," a place where we could communicate by leaving messages. A broken branch on a designated tree or a church pew with an upside down missal meant, "Meet me in our usual place; I have news." I never asked anyone to engage in propaganda or sabotage—I was afraid of such initiatives, in fact—but instructed each new member simply to report any information he learned. I asked if he usually confided in his wife and whether she was talkative. Then I exhorted him again to be secretive, warning that, for all of us, the closest and most constant danger was one's own impulse to blurt too much to friends. My last question to each man was whether he knew someone in another village who might be a potential supporter. If he provided me with a lead, I approached that person directly, using a different cover name. In that way I was soon able to dispense with Hlaváček's help and set out on my evening journeys alone.

I learned to walk everywhere. At first my trips were only from Nové Město to Brno, but eventually I could make it easily from Brno up to Bohemia without stepping on a highway or a road, moving through the rolling landscape of western Moravia. It was poor man's country, not pastoral as I want to remember it, but specked by small houses with broken porches like those you might have seen in rural communities in Michigan or Mississippi in the forties, the only difference being that in Moravia there were plaster saints instead of old cars in the ragged front yards. Unlike the United States, Moravia has no real wilderness anywhere. The forest floors were scarred with paths. People went into the woods at all hours to hunt for kindling or mushrooms or just to take a shortcut, so it was not hard for me to avoid using the roads. After dark, the hamlets were sloe-black and perilous because of the patrolling gendarmes. But during the day, there was a soothing intimacy about the run-down villages enclosed by fields or woods and buffeted by a constant, booming wind.

The more I thought about our situation on those long, cautious walks, the more impressed I was by what the Germans had almost accomplished. When I thought of the Nazis' amazing security apparatus, rooting out Jews and Communists and resisters all over occupied Europe, probing into every classroom where contraband words might be lying about, every kitchen where a few eggs might be hiding in a flour sack, and every cellar where shortwave radio signals might penetrate, I wondered that there were enough Nazis to go around, enough to carry out the policing of whole populations. In fact there were not enough Nazis. By the end of 1943 the Germans were turning their captured Czech victims into informers. In many cases these informers purchased the lives of their loved ones with their information and, though they might have had no heart for it, became productive detectives for the Gestapo. By mid-1944, entire bogus organizations were operating in the Protectorate, established by Czech spies to attract good-faith resisters. In just a few bitter months I would learn about them firsthand.

I was far younger than the men I recruited. Most were from thirty-five to sixty, old enough to understand that underground work was serious business. The resistance was not a movement of youth, nor of women, whom we rarely solicited unless they had unique access to some information. A few women were drawn into the work because of the involvement of their husbands or relatives, and they often proved to be more reliable than the men; but the resistance, like the regular army, was largely a man's world.

Oddly, I never met any Communists during those months of recruiting, except for my friend the Proletarian. The Czech Communists had been distinguished resisters in 1940 and 1941. They shifted their stand a couple of times in those years, either cooperating with the democratic resistance or attacking Beneš as a tool of the imperialists, depending on their directions from Moscow. After Germany invaded the Soviet Union, they decided that the wisest course was to join in a unified home resistance. They hoped eventually to infiltrate and subsume the democratic anti-Nazi groups. Instead, the powerful Communist underground was practically wiped out during the two periods of martial law and did not recover until very late in the war. After the Soviets dissolved the Comintern in May 1943 and demonstrated a willingness to work with the western powers, the Party began to look a little more respectable. We anticipated that the Russians would be the first Allies to reach us, and we would be part of their operational zone. In early 1944, I was ready to cooperate with Communists in the underground, if I had known any. But by this time the renascent Communist resistance networks had been permeated by Gestapo agents—usually Communists who had been arrested and had turned informers as a condition of their release. German tribunals were vicious against those Communists who refused to cooperate. Any action that indicated Communist association—donating money to the Red Relief, for example—brought an automatic death sentence. This special attention to Reds effectively thinned out the leftist population so that it was not until late in 1944 that a few Communist groups emerged—and I never ran across them.

*   *   *

When my stay at the fish station ended, Father arranged for me to return to the Nováks. I stopped for a visit with Hermit and had been with him about a week when he woke me in the middle of the night. "Come quick," he said. "Štainer brought someone to the shed. A poor devil—a Russian prisoner escaped from the Germans." Štainer at that time was hiding in a barn. Someone came to him with the news that in the Vysočina hills nearby was a man in very bad shape. He had jumped in a river to escape the Gestapo search dogs and had remained in the cold water many hours before some villagers pulled him out. He was as limp as a tissue and could not walk, so when Štainer found him, he set him as well as he could on his bicycle and brought him to Hermit.

Alexander Dmitrijev was an engineer from Smolensk. He was a first lieutenant in the Red Army when he was taken prisoner by the Germans and sent to a camp near Carlsbad. He escaped and made his way eastward, walking at night, sleeping a little in the day, and starving both day and night, since the German people refused to help him. Once he crossed the Protectorate border, Czechs gave him food, and if they couldn't shelter him, at least they didn't report him to the authorities. Some months after Štainer brought him, we learned that the Gestapo had begun using Russian prisoners as informers, releasing them and sending them as agents provocateurs into the Protectorate. But there could have been no danger of that from this wretched scrag. With his hollow face and feverish eyes, his voice almost too weak to hear, he looked exactly like what he was: an animal dying of hunger and exposure. Hermit did not dare keep him in the house. In his horrible condition, it would be absurd to try to pass him off as a workman. Nor would it do to pretend he was a relative who looked foreign and emaciated and happened not to speak a word of Czech. Instead, we made him as comfortable as we could in the shed. Father came and conversed with him in Russian, I flung my little store of Russian nouns at him, together with a few generic Slavic verbs, and Hermit grunted and nodded, which was the way he communicated with everybody, Czech or not.

I became fast friends with Alexander, my first rich contact with a Soviet citizen. He called me Vladimír; I called him Aleš. He was different from everything I had heard about Russians. He never once mentioned Communism or the Bolshevik Revolution. He never talked about any political ideology, but rather about missing his wife and parents. As my Russian improved, we were able to discuss composers and writers—Dostoyevsky, Pushkin, Gogol, Turgenev, Goncharov, Lermontov—he had read them all, and several philosophers as well, with the spectacular exception of Tolstoy.

"You haven't read *War and Peace*?" I asked incredulously.

"I read *War*," he answered. "I skipped the chapters on *Peace*." I didn't know many first lieutenants in the Czechoslovak army who had read either one. The Bolsheviks had not destroyed Russian culture; Aleš was a living representative of it. And he was as much a part of western civilization as I was. I could not fail to notice, however, that as a proud officer of the Red Army, he had a peculiar perspective. He described an incident in Kiev when a passenger pushed an army officer off a streetcar. "The soldier took out a revolver and shot the civilian on the spot," Aleš reported, satisfaction flickering for an instant on his lip, "and there were no repercussions." That was decidedly unwestern.

It was Aleš who taught us about *zemljankas,* a type of camouflaged hiding place that was to save our lives again and again up to the very end of the war. After he gained weight and looked like a human being, he built a zemljanka for himself near Hermit's. First he dug a large hole in the ground, deep enough for a man to stand, and walled it inside with wooden planks. He put in a wooden bench that could serve as a bed. Then he replaced the cranium of earth over the hole, the entire work taking him about five weeks. The entrance was in a nearby bush, concealed of course, so that once grass began growing again on the roof, the zemljanka was practically impossible to find. Aleš taught our people how to use small arms and eventually commanded a special group made up entirely of escaped Soviet war prisoners. It was quite an effective unit whose members needed no training and, in fact, trained us. Aleš made the Red Army real for me. We were not alone, listening in the dark to broadcasts and otherwise knowing nothing of the faraway struggle for our liberation. He was a messenger from the front, proving to me that the fight was real and we were a real part of it.

We never discussed Stalin. Although I was eager to talk about him, Aleš pointedly avoided the name. My attitude at that time toward the Soviet Union would be hard for an American to understand. I thought Communism was naïvely idealistic. My family and close friends were democrats and pluralists and of course did not want our country to be a unitary state under the aegis of any single party. Father himself was anti-Communist because of his experience with the Bolsheviks in the First World War. But unlike Americans, our people were not overwhelmingly hostile toward the system of the Soviet Union. The Communist Party was just another part of our country's political life.

Americans were horrified when they observed Soviet totalitarianism in practice in the 1930s. They rightly saw Communism as a threat to all democratic systems, equal to or greater than the threat posed by fascism. We, too, were shocked at the way the Soviet Union treated its own people. For us, however, there was no question that the fascists were the enemies and the Soviets were the possible deliverers. Our attitude toward the West had become deeply ambivalent. After Munich, it was always the French and English we mistrusted, not the Russians. Stalin had been Czechoslovakia's only friend during the Munich crisis, shut out of the conference like us. Without Stalin's Red Army now advancing toward us, Father and I and the people involved with us had scant hope of surviving the Nazi regime. We believed—or needed to believe—Stalin's promises at Teheran and later at Yalta that he would respect the sovereignty of the countries in eastern Europe. To western eyes, the Soviet terror and the purge trials were evidence of the viciousness not just of one leader, but of the whole Communist system. Though we in Czechoslovakia hated what was going on in the Soviet Union, we did not foresee that it would have anything to do with us. Father and I regarded Soviet Communism as one views another's religion. We neither followed it nor felt that it needed to be extirpated. Those were Communists purging Communists in Russia; the upheavals had no more to do with us than if the Pope had begun excommunicating fractious Catholics, or if Baptists had taken to drowning the people they christened. Stalin's brutal methods of industrializing the steppes, we thought, gave no forecast of what he would do if the Soviets entered our highly industrialized country.

In December 1943 President Beneš had traveled from London to Moscow to sign a friendship treaty with the Soviet Union. The treaty was quite popular in the Protectorate, where we were not supposed to know about it. It carefully stated that the Soviet Union would not interfere in the internal affairs of the Czechoslovak Republic, which would remain a sovereign state. We thought the Grand Alliance between the Soviets and the western powers would continue after the war and spur the Communist regime to undertake reforms. There would be trade and projects for joint defense and the Bolshoi Ballet touring the United States. None of us had ever heard of a cold war.

It was soon time to end my visit with Hermit and Aleš. When I got to Javůrek and walked into the small kitchen, the sun came out in Mrs. Little

Spruce's face; however, it was clear from the expressive silence of her son-in-law that I was there on sufferance. He never spoke a single word to me during my stay. As for the fearsome grandmother who considered me a disease stalking the family, we decided to tell her of my presence and confront her objections. But when the moment of truth came, Mrs. Little Spruce could not bring herself to risk Babička's chasing me out, and so we continued our daily deception, the whole house scrambling to lock doors and clear away my traces the instant we heard the drumbeat of her stubby shoes outside the back door.

I was doing my organizing in the area around Bíteš and Javůrek, near the vital road connecting Brno and Prague, when I received a notice from Father, writing from his shelter at the Secs': "Something has happened which I do not like at all. Be careful! You are going to make problems for yourself and a lot of other people." Then came a second curt letter:

> Robotka advised me to inform you immediately that you cannot leave your shelter on pain of death. I don't know the whole story, but apparently something happened while you were at Hašek's this summer. Did you tell somebody more than was necessary? I can't believe you would have done something like this to endanger yourself. I'm trying to investigate and I'll get to the bottom of it, but that won't be for another month. Until then, you are under house arrest. Naturally, I'm suspicious of any information that comes from Štainer and Robotka, who have always come to me with complaints about you, even during the summer. I think this is just a rumor, but I can't do anything until I get a precise report of the investigation.

That was just like Father, writing to me, his son, about "precise reports" and "investigations." I had no idea what they were exercised about, but I was furious. Who was supposed to carry out this death sentence? Štainer? Robotka? Who the hell were they, to threaten to kill me? Štainer claimed to have heard that I divulged my real name to a young girl when I was staying at Hašek's. That was baloney, of course. I dashed off an angry note to Father, who by this time had ascertained for himself that the whole thing was nonsense, and I got another letter in reply:

> I did not take this insult to you as calmly as you suppose. Your question as to who gave Robotka the right to threaten you was exactly what I said to him myself. Nobody gave either of them the rights they are constantly usurping. They are full of insolence against both you and me. Štainer, who was unstable to begin with, has let his work with us go to his head and he has lost all sense

of his true position. Robotka is completely under his influence when he is with him, and acts even against his own intermittent good sense. In the first place they are beside themselves with jealousy of you, especially Karel, who sees in you a young lad who is more competent than he is. In the second place, I am the real target here. They wanted to humiliate me by embarrassing you. And Štainer may have thought that if he fabricated some story about what you did at Hašek's, he could make it impossible for you to return there next summer and he could get this shelter for himself.

We have to be cool, you and I, until I am in a position to straighten these people out. Forget about the whole thing. But do stay off the roads as much as you can. They are patrolling every pathway now, especially around water mills. We form a joint society, you and I. Whatever happens to one of us involves the other, so we must both be careful. And keep your distance from Štainer and Robotka. Forget the notion that they are your friends.

They were not always Father's friends, either, despite their vital services to him in the past. They might be abashed in the presence of their general, but outside, they denigrated him. Štainer once told my mother, of all people, that the London officials pointedly indicated that they considered Grňa the pivotal person in our group. Father's impression was that Grňa was practically unknown by the Czechoslovak officials in both Prague and London. When I reported the story to him, he just couldn't believe it. Those two snipes, I thought, were graduating from petty nonsense to serious misdemeanors. I buried Father's letter, tried to bury my wrath for the time being, and went on with my recruiting.

Father was now ready to make some moves. He reached out to a Prague umbrella organization, PRNC. Whiz Staller was connected to it as a secret courier, General Novák and the remnants of ON made up another section of it, and it had lines to many of the surviving high-level bureaucrats and intellectuals.[4] More of a concatenation of resistance groups than an indepen-

4. PRNC, the Preparatory Revolutionary National Committee, claimed to be the successor to the great resistance networks destroyed by the Gestapo in 1941. Right of center, PRNC was not a body of active resisters but rather a ramulose organization that served to put several groups in loose association. The people around General Novák were among its leaders: Jaroslav Kvapil, a famous playwright; František Richter, the director of a printing enterprise and a former Russian legionnaire; Judge Emil Lány, former president of the land court for Bohemia; the great Czech poet Josef Palivec; literary critic Václav Černy; the writer Jaroslav Kratochvíl, who was also a member of the Communist underground and used his influence to get the Party to cooperate more closely with the democratic resistance. Some of PRNC's other members were Jaromír Dvořák and Josef Mainer from Pilsen and Kamil Krofta, a former minister of foreign affairs. One

dently active organization, PRNC had been recognized by President Beneš, in a cable sent to the group from London, as the official political organ of the Czechoslovak government in exile. Though Štainer dismissed this organ with his single worst word—"reactionaries"—and wanted no part of it, Father insisted on making contact. With the help of Dr. Káňa and Mr. Jedlička, he began communicating regularly with PRNC.

Mrs. Eliáš, Lešek's widow, also bravely cooperated with us, acting as our liaison to the Ambassador Heidrich group. It was discomfiting to talk to Slávka Eliáš at that time because she did not believe she was a widow. She had convinced herself that Eliáš' execution in 1942 was a lie put out by the Nazis, who were saving him to use later in some political maneuver. From time to time she remarked about projects her husband would take up after the German defeat. The end of the war thus brought her no joy—only cruel disappointment.

Father was prepared, as he had always been, for some kind of guarded involvement with other resistance leaders. Eduard Soška, an acquaintance of Štainer, got wind of an underground military organization and managed to meet a pair of its representatives, Stanislav Jizera and Viktor Ryšánek, names that even now take up a whole page when I print them in my mind. Eventually not only Soška but Štainer and Robotka made inquiries about Ryšánek and Jizera and confirmed their trustworthiness. They reported that the two were part of a sizable group, mainly officers, secretly organized around a General F., whom Father guessed was either General Fiala or General Fassati. Even Robotka, normally as even-tempered as a tree, was excited about making connections with a large, well-organized group. Shouldn't Luža, too, meet Jizera and Ryšánek, these representatives of General F.? After their infamous death threat against me, Father was in no mood to chat with Štainer and Robotka about anything, but wanting to communicate with others in the underground, he finally consented. If Ryšánek and Jizera had been carefully screened, he wrote, he would come once more to Okareč for a meeting in January. The new men were not to know exactly where he was coming from.

Thanks to Father's constant preachments, we had all been tutored in ob-

---

component of PRNC was a group led by Professors Josef Drachovský, Josef Hutter, and Růžena Vacek. Another component included representatives of the Czech Protectorate police, such as Bohdan Šefčík. Rudolf Fraštacký served, like Staller, as a courier. In addition to wanting to communicate with the people loosely attached to PRNC, Father was in contact with Ambassador Heidrich's group, which included Leopold Chmela, the legionnaire whom I had met at Hašek's.

sessive caution. When bringing information to Father, we were instructed not to share it first among ourselves. We were always to refer to each other by our cover names. Every word uttered to another person had to be weighed as if we thought our companion would be arrested by the Gestapo the next day. For the meeting with Father, Ryšánek and Jizera were put through several layers of precautions to prevent anyone from following them. Robotka met them at the railroad station in Brno and brought them to Okarec.[5] Grňa arrived with Štainer, and Father was again brought by the forester Sedlák.

Jizera was a lieutenant colonel of the cavalry, rather short despite his long legs, tanned, and slow moving. Ryšánek, a noncommissioned officer, was his aide, although he was far more intelligent and assertive than his boss. Ryšánek had a pronounced squint and tended to look past you when he talked; his llama face winking into the rear distance was hard to forget.

"Who is General F.?" Father asked them.

"Fassati," came the answer, a general who was not very active in the underground but gave his name to the organization that was largely run by Jizera, his chief of staff. Štainer's face brightened at this information. He was dying to be the chief of staff of an inactive general who would lend his name to an organization and turn him loose to run it. As the meeting progressed, Father as usual became exasperated with Štainer and Grňa because they objected to our drawing on the ten thousand Protectorate troops and the police in the countryside—the gendarmerie—for the uprising. The two new officers, however, sided with Father.

Father next brought up the necessity of making contact with the approaching Red Army. Ryšánek thought he could transport an emissary across the Protectorate border to eastern Slovakia and help him get to the front in the Ukraine. At this time several Russian officers who had been captured by the enemy and escaped had, like my friend Aleš, made their way from Germany to the Protectorate. Our members had helped some of these former prisoners. Štainer suggested that one of them, an Armenian general staff major named Iljikčan, be dispatched to cross the front and establish liaison in General Luža's name with a Soviet commander. Some weeks later

5. He gave them each a ticket good for several towns, so they did not know where they were going. In the station he told them their destination was Jihlava, but after they were on the train, he gave them new tickets, to Studenec. Once there, they had to walk two and a half miles, still not knowing where they would stop, until the three of them reached Okarec.

Ryšánek did indeed transport our emissary to Slovakia, but that was as far as he got. We waited for a message on the BBC signaling that Iljikčan had reached the Russians; it never came. We concluded that he had been unable to cross the lines. It turned out that Iljikčan had joined a band of Soviet partisans and was killed in battle somewhere near the Slovakian border.[6]

The last thing Father talked about in this meeting of endless talk was how the two groups, his and General F.'s organization, would cooperate. The two officers were ready to combine the groups, with ours being dominant in deciding policy. Ryšánek nodded toward Father. "If we can't trust Václav's judgment, then whose can we trust?" he asked, his open eye warm with admiration. Father was not eager to expose our members to people we did not know. Grňa sternly opposed the merger, setting his jaw and pushing his lower lip into his mustache until Father assured him that the two groups would retain a formal separation. Ryšánek was going to be Father's intermediary to General F.'s organization, but Father still did not want either Ryšánek or Jizera to know that his hideout was in Bosonohy.

Having constricted his temper through the meeting, Father blew up at Robotka on the way home for withholding information from him in subservience to Štainer. "I'm not going to let myself be told what to do by some captain," he said. "Štainer is not a politician or strategist but a soldier, and not a very good one at that. The two of you are Czechoslovak officers. Štainer has to obey orders or leave us. It's not for either him or you to decide whether I should know something or when." Robotka apologized, and the field was quiet after this cannonade. But Father was not through with Štainer.

"Can you imagine?" Father said, still dissipating his tirade when I met him at Hermit's. "That wobble-brain Štainer asked me again about promoting him to colonel and he even had the nerve to nominate himself as my chief of staff! All this time I've been thinking he should be court-martialed after the war for insubordination."

"Why don't you give him his promotion?" I asked. "And Robotka too.

6. Jakov Tĕvosovič Iljikčan was taken prisoner at the beginning of 1942, after suffering a severe head injury in battle. With his companion, Senior Lieutenant Nikolaj Bachmutsky, he escaped from a prison camp in central Germany. On reaching Nové Mĕsto, near the Czech-Moravian border, in November 1943, the two received help from our organization. We were never sure whether Iljikčan abandoned the mission we gave him or was simply unable to carry it out.

They would owe their ranks to you and you might get some cooperation out of them."

"I don't think I have authority to do that sort of thing in this situation. Let Grňa promote them. As the last living member of the Petition Committee, he thinks he's entitled to promote people up to the rank of archangel. He'd like to improve everybody's station in life." Father then remarked that he was considering as his future chief of staff a general from General Novák's group.

I had so much to tell Father, who knew hardly anything about what I was doing. My groups were setting up from Tišnov to Zastávka and from Brno to Křižanov and Bíteš. Soon we would have a framework that would cover Javůrek, Domašov, Říčany, Ostrovačice, Lažánky, Maršov, and more, and I was doing it all on foot. I wanted to discuss my next moves. After the Czechoslovak-Soviet treaty, broadcasts from Moscow were urging the home resistance to establish what they called national committees, local bodies of a few citizens who would represent the larger population. I thought the very idea was completely stupid. How could we meet under the eyes of the Gestapo and descant upon the general will? That was the best way I could think of to get arrested. I could hardly wait to hear Father's reaction to the broadcasts. But the Little One accompanied us from Hermit's, and we couldn't discuss anything in front of him. When we arrived at the Nováks', Malý and Mrs. Little Spruce exchanged their usual greeting, a hostile glare, and then Mrs. Little Spruce took possession of Father for the rest of the evening. The next morning he got up before me and spent the entire day talking with her. You'd think they were plotting the assassination of Hitler, so intense and exclusive was their conversation. "Why, she isn't even a member of his family!" I thought, my old anger awakening, along with my guilt for resenting a wonderful lady who every hour was saving my skin. In the evening, on a bus driven by Sec, Father returned to Bosonohy without hearing any of my great news.

By the spring of 1944 my cadres were ready. It was certainly not a network, but rather a structure for a network that could be filled in later. Not one member other than Hlaváček could have named more than two or three others. I carried records in my head and cyanide in my pocket and hoped I could get to them both if I needed them. Father sent me a volume of Hegel for my name day in March. Though he still did not know what I was doing, I considered it a congratulatory present for my efforts.

* * *

I had not seen Mother for almost two years and wasn't sure where she was. Since it was more complicated to get mail to her than to Father, we wrote each other only about three times. Part of our letters—Father's too—always dealt with the problem of how to use our clothing. The fewer garments we had, the more we seemed to discuss them. Once I made the mistake of giving a pair of my father's knickers to Štainer. Father reproached me about it so relentlessly that I finally had to ask Štainer to return them, just to get Father off my back and placate Mother, who got in the middle of the dispute.

Suddenly Mother arrived at Mrs. Little Spruce's. She had been staying with the gamekeeper Josef Pavlas, but hearing a rumor that the Gestapo was planning to make house searches in Velké Meziříčí for hidden food, she decided to leave for a few days until the danger had passed. I was astonished to see that she looked radiant. Country food had cushioned her middle, and her dress seemed rather long, but her unmade face was cheerful, and the corners of her eyes had lost their wedges of lace. Mother had been sheltered at times by the forester Sedlák near Bíteš and then by the family of Oto Homoláč, a prosperous farmer in Radoškov. In each case she posed as an aunt who had come to live with them. It was Mother who recruited Homoláč's daughter, Vlasta, one of the most effective and fearless people who ever helped us, so effective, in fact, that Grňa promoted her to Lieutenant of the Partisans, up from womanhood. After the Homoláčs', Mother's next shelter was in the valley below Javůrek with the family of a miller, Josef Hála, and then she stayed with the Pavlases. In the Pavlas house she worked from morning till night almost as a servant, but she loved it there, caring for the children, being part of the family. I wish I could have watched her, the hyacinth of officers' wives, chattering with the peasant women who came to visit Mrs. Pavlas, pretending to be steeped like them in the idiom of village life.

From time to time, both Grňa and Štainer stayed in Meziříčí, so Mother had come to know both of them well, and Robotka, too. Unlike Father and me, Mother preferred big, tousled Štainer to Robotka—it was odd how Robotka's faultless grooming could irk some people. Štainer had done his best to win her over as his ally, but even to her he criticized Father and made me out to be an imbecile.

"Štainer thinks he's Gulliver in the underground Lilliput," I said. "But I don't see how Grňa and Robotka, who respect Father and have some sense, can be Štainer's cupbearers, never confiding in Father, undermining him. That's the mystery."

"It doesn't take a soothsayer to figure it out," answered Mother, showing me her palm in a dainty gesture. "They know very well, all of them, that they are not in your father's class. If he has contact with other resistance leaders, sooner or later he'll be working with people of his own caliber. Even if he tries to be loyal to Grňa and the others, they will be pushed into lesser positions as more experienced people come in."

It was true that Father no longer had to depend as much on Štainer and Robotka. Ryšánek was taking his messages to General Novák. Dr. Káňa, Mrs. Eliáš, and our old supporter Jedlička were his connections to several groups in Prague. Even so, Štainer was trying to disparage Father. When, as the military head of our organization, Father asked Ryšánek a question about one single district of General F.'s organization, Ryšánek refused to answer him, not because of any prohibition by Jizera or General F., but because Štainer, Father's lowly subordinate captain, had forbidden him to discuss such things with General Luža. Father naturally wanted to flay Štainer, but as long as he was underground, he couldn't even demote him. "I would welcome with open arms a capable counterpart, a true politician I could work with," Father had written to me. "That's what I miss so much and am looking for. Even Grňa would do, but without Štainer, though I don't have any personal grudge against Štainer and I don't want his old sins to stretch. . . . Grňa acts in close conjunction with him, but I think he would like to form some real bond with me." When Mother complained to Robotka about his and Štainer's refusal to answer Father's questions or carry out his directions, he seemed surprised. "Why, we brought him Jizera and Ryšánek, didn't we?" he asked. "What more does he want?"

In April 1944, after two and a half years of waiting and frustration, things were finally going. General Ingr, minister of national defense in the exile government that had formed in London, sent a microfilm to Father through Zdena, the cover name of a courier connecting London, Slovakia, and the Protectorate.[7] Staller picked up the microfilm in Bratislava and removed his name from it, a routine precaution that in this case saved his life. He then

7. Zdena was Jaroslav Krátký, a major of the Czechoslovak army, who was sent by Beneš and Ingr to Slovakia to run secret transmitters connecting London with the main resistance groups there. He was also charged with getting information about the underground in the Protectorate. He arrived clandestinely from Istanbul on March 3, 1944, using the passport of a man who had just arrived in Istanbul and was to remain there. Reaching Bratislava, Zdena's first contact was Rudolf Fraštacký, who oriented him to the Slovakian resistance. Zdena was eventually caught by the Gestapo and assassinated in prison by the SS.

brought the microfilm to Father. Father charged Sec with getting it enlarged, Sec gave it to Ryšánek, and in April Father sent me one of the prints. It read:

> We welcome the important news that General Luža is alive. Offer him all possible assistance. It is urgent that he maintain contact with Zdena, while taking every security precaution, in particular because of the vital information General Luža can provide regarding the military situation in the Czech lands. . . . Luža can give extremely important reports about the possibilities for direct action in the Czech lands and about preparations for a general uprising. He can give information regarding the material and moral situation of the Czech people, and assess their will to resist. He can provide specific information about individuals, particularly in the military, who might be appointed as leaders.
>
> Gen. Ingr

"When I gave a copy of this to General Novák," Ryšánek told Father, "he asked if you can see him in Brno. He wants to go over with you the plans made so far for the uprising."

"That would be difficult," Father answered. "Where could we meet?"

"There's a merchant in Brno, Karel Paprskář, who will let Novák use his apartment." Some people in our organization already knew Paprskář. Robotka had spent the night at his apartment in January, on his way to the meeting in Okarec.

"Did General Novák propose a date?"

"What about the twenty-sixth of May?" Ryšánek asked.

"Tell him not to come in his full dress uniform," Father said archly, "and we'll meet on the twenty-sixth."

Next, Father received a communication from Slovakia, again brought by Staller. The Slovakian underground movement Flora, led by Vavro Šrobár, was considering Father as the possible commanding officer of the Slovak national uprising. General Ingr sent a cable to Slovakia requesting the closest possible cooperation with Luža. There was talk of Father going to Slovakia to establish the military center of the resistance. Father, however, had not seen this second cable from Ingr and wanted to be sure he understood the instructions. He sent a message to London asking that the BBC use the words "Peter leaves for Rome" to signal him to leave for Slovakia. We were not certain how Father and I could get across the Protectorate border to Slovakia; that was among many unsorted details. Father finally decided to dispatch Ryšánek to Slovakia to talk with his former colleague in the Slova kian army, Lieutenant Colonel Makoň. Father instructed Ryšánek to find out as much as he could about the Slovak army's plans for the uprising.

On this occasion, Ryšánek's third or fourth meeting with Father, he was admitted into Sec's house to receive his important orders. Ryšánek had obtained a bottle of slivovitz—the brandy was still relatively easy to get—which he pulled out of a briefcase stuffed with shoes. "I've been afraid lately that the Gestapo is getting close," he explained. "If they had stopped me in Bosonohy, I planned to say I was looking for a shoemaker." As Father never drank, they shared the bottle with Sec. To Sec's surprise, Ryšánek knew his real name and was acquainted with his military record, though Father had prevented Sec from engaging in any underground activity. Sec was hiding a general, and could not therefore expose himself and his charge to the routine risks of resistance work. Ryšánek finished his glass and was preparing to take his leave when suddenly he turned and asked, "How will Colonel Makoň know me? Will he surrender the plans for the Slovak uprising to someone he doesn't know?" On a scrap of paper Father then scribbled the words, "The bearer of this note is working for me, General Luža."

Perhaps Father felt some unease about the note after Ryšánek left, but then he had many other things on his mind. The end of the war, the end of our ordeal, was in sight, and he might lead us in taking our country back from the Germans. I of course knew rather little of what was going on. Father told me about his possible departure for Slovakia and he asked me to accompany him, but until I could get some concrete information, I continued my organizing, tried to stay out of the way of Mrs. Little Spruce's family, and avoided asking Štainer or Robotka for anything.

I wanted to prepare Mrs. Little Spruce for the possibility that I would be leaving. My presence there seemed to mean so much to her. I looked at the skein of brown hair at the nape of her neck, its gray threads catching the light as she bent over her work. We would miss talking with each other about books and life. She looked back at me and smiled her little smile that started on the bridge of her nose. But since I had been schooled not to offer people information that could only endanger them, I told her nothing. An hour later I was reading alone in my room, wishing I could open my window to the cool spring night, when a short letter arrived from Father, the coded words engraved in the paper from the pressure of his urgent pencil: "We are in immediate and great danger. Get ready to move fast. Don't talk to anybody. Someone close to us is a Gestapo informer."

VI

For two years I had believed we were secreted in darkness, unseen by the predator stalking us, waiting in our holes to return to a world that was waiting for us. Now I realized that our hideout was the animal's mouth, and we were crawling around on its tongue in the illusion that he was still looking for us. The Gestapo knew exactly where Father was and had been watching him for months.

It was Robotka who first found out about the informer. Dressed elegantly as usual, Robotka was in Brno on Saturday, May 20. As he crossed Freedom Square, he heard someone behind him running to catch up and turned to face a pink and anxious Paprskář. Robotka had not seen him for several months, though he was aware that Father and Novák had been offered his apartment for their coming meeting.

"I must see you, my friend," Paprskář said breathlessly. Robotka was surprised. He had met him through Ryšánek and had once slept at Paprskář's apartment, but he did not know him well. "It's important," Paprskář continued. "Come with me to my business." Robotka let himself be led to a shop in Dominican Square.

"Is it so serious?" Robotka asked, when they were settled behind the two-way mirror in the rear of the store.

"You know perhaps that the Gestapo has started using Czech agents to infiltrate resistance groups? Yes, Czechs. A man is caught harboring someone unregistered or being involved in some resistance. He's offered a reprieve for himself or maybe his family if he'll get more involved in the resistance and report on everyone he deals with. Perhaps you have heard of Erlan?" Paprskář's tone was more and more unsettling. Erlan was a business firm; Robotka thought he had heard of it.

"Erlan? The import company? What about it?"

"Erlan's front is an import company. In reality, it's the headquarters where informers come to report to the Gestapo on their contacts. Jánská Street. Number seven." Paprskář spoke deliberately and intensely, watching Robotka's eyes.

"How do you know about these things?"

"Erlan is run by the Germans," Paprskář continued. "The Gestapo has cover apartments there for agents to use as their 'homes.' There are other cover apartments, too, all over Brno. An informer can bring resisters together for meetings. Generals perhaps. Even generals living underground can meet in the so-called apartment of a Czech friend, and the Gestapo will know every syllable the generals utter." Paprskář was speaking very slowly now.

"So you are one of these Gestapo agents?" Robotka asked.

"Not just me. Ryšánek, Jizera, and Paprskář—" he said, gesturing toward himself, "work for the Gestapo. We are all part of Erlan."

Robotka took a long breath. "Why are you confessing this now?"

"I—I just. . . ." Paprskář's fingers were twitching.

"Why now? Why not when I first met you, you . . . ?"

"It was right before Luža's meeting at Okarec. I was afraid if I warned you, Luža would call off the meeting and the Gestapo would know that I had confided in you. I didn't know then what kind of movement you were, didn't know your true names. I found out from the Erlan files—'a very important organization.' After Ryšánek set up this meeting next week with Luža and Novák, the full meaning of it hit me—Ryšánek leading all these blindfolded people to—I can't go through with it. I can't deliver a man like Luža to the Gestapo." With that, he pressed his stuttering fingers into his eyes and wept.

In 1941, the Gestapo established at its two headquarters in Brno and Prague something called the Third Section, *Nachrichten Referate,* for the purpose of boring into underground organizations. The head of N. Referate picked his collection of informers, "V-persons," from the Gestapo's supply of trapped resisters. These spies extracted information from "A-persons," often genuine resisters like my father who might never find out that their confidants were under the control of the Nazis.[1] Each headquarters had a catalog of all the informers. To accommodate its increasing number of Czech agents in Brno by 1942 and 1943, the Gestapo set up the import firm Erlan with a liquor company as its official owner. Informers came there with their reports.

Ryšánek was the most productive of all N. Referate's spies. He had been in Sokol and the army. Those were excellent credentials for a resister, enough to make people trust him at once, unless they found out that the Gestapo had started routinely employing Czech informers. Jizera, with his higher rank of lieutenant colonel, was not used for day-to-day operations but for meeting important people. Jizera had the personality of a politician—forward and voluble, shaking hands readily and once discomfiting the decorous Grňa by attempting to embrace him. Ryšánek, however, was reserved, with an analytical mind and good memory. He knew how to play second fiddle, to stay in the background, always convenient and competent.

Without Paprskář's confession to Robotka, I don't know if we would have found out about the informers in time to escape arrest. But Ryšánek had aroused other people's suspicions. When he went to Slovakia to deliver Father's letter to Lieutenant Colonel Makoň, he made the mistake of introducing himself in Bratislava as a former major of the Czechoslovak army. Ryšánek had only been a sergeant major in the old army, a noncommissioned officer. The men on Makoň's staff took out their list of military officers of the First Republic and naturally could not find Ryšánek's name. "How could somebody with a squint like that have become a major?" Makoň's assistant asked his colleagues. "Interrogate him. Try to find out why he's lying."

Slovakia was still closely supervised by the Nazis in April 1944, but it was not formally part of the Reich, nor was it occupied as we were. The Slovaks, including these army officers who were secretly part of the resistance, had more leeway than the Czech officials in the Protectorate. They arrested Ryšánek on the pretext that they suspected him of anti-Nazi proclivities. But within forty-eight hours, the Gestapo brought him back to Brno, put him in

1. *Vertrauensmann* (confidant) and *Auskunftsperson* (informant). The informer system was especially effective against the Communists. So many Czech Communist resisters were captured and induced to cooperate with the Germans that the Communist underground was gradually dismantled.

jail for the sake of appearances, pretended to question him, and then released him. When the Slovak officers learned that their "resister" had been
let go, they figured out that Ryšánek must have been in contact with the
Gestapo all along. But they had no way to let Father know what they suspected.

On Sunday, May 21, 1944, the morning after seeing Paprskář, Robotka came
to Sec's house to tell Father the terrible news: Ryšánek and Jizera were Gestapo agents.

"I thought you and Soška had screened them before you brought them
to me," Father shouted at Robotka. "You told me Ryšánek was in Sokol. A
noncommissioned officer. A member of ON. General Fassati's assistant. You
mean to tell me you never checked any of that?"

"Some of it was true, Václav. He was in Sokol. And people from PRNC
told us he was a sincere nationalist. But there is no organization around
General Fassati. Apparently he has no idea how his name is being used."

Father and Sec paced up and down wildly for several minutes. "Let's wait
until Ryšánek shows up here," said Sec, "maybe together with Jizera if we
can arrange it, and we'll shoot them both, or better yet, strangle them."

That idea appealed to Father, but in a few minutes he realized that if
either of the informers disappeared, the Gestapo would swoop down immediately on Sec's house. He chewed his lip thoughtfully. "They won't do anything before the twenty-sixth. If the Gestapo is planning to take us, they'll
do it then, when they can get General Novák, me, and the plans for the
uprising all at once. So that gives us a few days to clear out. When I don't
show up for the meeting, Ryšánek will find out we've escaped. Then the
hunt will start."

"The first thing we have to do is warn General Novák not to come," Robotka said.

Father calmed down. "You and Helena and Sec and Fanynka will have to
go underground immediately. Malý, too, and his wife. We have five days.
We've got to find places. They'll make house searches of this entire area, so
we'll get as far away from Bosonohy as we can. Hašek's is out. That's where
we first met Ryšánek and Jizera. We'll have to warn Hašek." They were frantically trying to remember what information they had divulged to the informers. Father also wondered what Štainer might have revealed to them
behind his back. Ryšánek and Jizera had been quite clever at exploiting the
antagonism between Father and Štainer, "that wretch Štainer," Father called

him, "who made me so desperate for competent men that I let myself depend on two slimy traitors."

"Let's not waste time now blaming ourselves," Robotka said quietly.

"I'm not blaming ourselves; I'm blaming you!" Father thundered. "You and Štainer keeping secrets, countermanding my orders, and when I tried to put Štainer in his place, do you remember what you told me? 'We brought you Jizera and Ryšánek,'" Father quoted, emptying his voice to mimic Robotka's colorless timbre. "'What more do you want?'"

As his son, I knew that Father was painstaking when it came to assessing blame—it was almost a hobby. After any mistake or misfortune, he patiently reconstructed events, attributing precise degrees of censure as he went, taking as much time as necessary to measure out the correct amount of criticism for everyone involved at every level. It was a civil procedure I had witnessed many times and expected to see repeated in the future whenever the informers were discussed. I was sure Robotka would never, ever, live down his failure to screen Jizera and Ryšánek.

But I was wrong. He did live it down, in a way I would not have believed possible, by doing something that neither Father nor I was capable of doing. Until then, I had been disgusted by Robotka's subservience to Štainer and outraged at his threatening me with death. But on May 21, he conceived a project requiring such independence and self-control that from that day on, I considered him a hero.

"Think a minute, Václav," Robotka said. "If we all disappear, Ryšánek and Jizera will know we've found out about them. We can't get far in five days. The Gestapo will track us right away. Instead, you and your son and Sec and Malý leave tonight and go as far away as you can. Ryšánek and Jizera must not know that we're on to them and they've lost you. So I'll stay. Soška and I will keep meeting them. I'll make excuses as to why they can't see you and let them think we still trust them completely. Maybe I can stall them long enough for you to get completely out of this region."

"Rudolf," said Father, using Robotka's cover name, "It's courageous of you to offer to stand alone within their reach. But that leaves you with no protection at all if they decide to snatch you."

"It's the safest way," Robotka replied. "According to Paprskář, right now they are primarily after our transmitter codes. The Germans realize they made a mistake in the past by arresting every resister they discovered. When they smash an organization, new groups form to replace it and they have to start all over again following people, infiltrating, trying to locate the leaders.

The policy now is to watch the organizations, get into them, and milk the people for information. I'll give Ryšánek something he can take back to his bosses each time. Paprskář thinks he will be able to warn me if they decide to wipe us up. I'll be okay at least for a couple of weeks."

Father yielded uneasily to this plan and Robotka left to start a cascade of warnings to General Novák and others. Father began reviewing names the informers might have heard, faces they might have seen in connection with us, going first by alphabetical, then geographical, then chronological order. Ryšánek and Jizera were already into PRNC before they met Father; they knew Novák, Drachovský, Hutter, Lang, Lány—the whole Prague organization had apparently been infiltrated by the Gestapo and would have to be warned. Who else? Father was certain he had never mentioned Homoláč, Mrs. Little Spruce, Kravka, Jedlička, or Dr. Káňa. Ryšánek did not know either Pavlas or the Proletarian by name, but he knew that a gamekeeper in Meziříčí and a Venetian blind maker had helped arrange some meetings with Grňa. The informers knew approximately the area where Grňa was hiding in a primitive farmhouse, but Grňa would be taken care of by Štainer. Because Štainer could move about semipublicly, he had always met Ryšánek and Jizera outdoors and had not led them to his shelter. We never mentioned Hermit, but Ryšánek and Jizera had handled Iljikčan, the Red Army major, our last supposed liaison to the Soviets, who vanished at the Soviet-Slovakian border. It now seemed to us that they might have delivered Iljikčan to the Gestapo. Iljikčan had met Hermit. Could he have revealed something about him under torture?

In the midst of these lucubrations, Ryšánek presented himself at Sec's door, his potato face smiling blandly. "I have some news about the meeting with General Novák" he told Father. "Colonel Lang is going to send his plans for using the Protectorate troops in the uprising. We've arranged that Jizera will pick you up on the morning of the twenty-sixth and take you to Paprskář's by car."

My father had surprising talents, but performing was not one of them. At the sight of the loathed informer, Father marched restlessly around his bedroom, snarling laconic answers, hardly trusting himself to look at Ryšánek, lest he should lose control and decide after all to squeeze his lying throat.

"Václav is really strange today," was Ryšánek's understatement to Sec as he was going out.

"Oh, well, you know, he's been sick. His stomach. He probably has ulcers. He's been underground a long time. The stress is getting to him finally," Sec explained.

"A man like that should know how to handle his nerves," replied Ryšánek, who had mastered his own. He turned his head with the squinting side toward Father's closed door, aiming an invisible gun in his familiar mannerism. "You'd better keep an eye on him," he said.

We had to move out fast. Malý had a relative in Javůrek who would hide him and his wife. We thought Fanynka and the little boy could be placed. But when it came to putting Sec somewhere, we might as well have been concealing a movie star. Thousands of people had seen his face as they boarded the bus between Brno and Bíteš; he could never be passed off as a workman or relative who suddenly popped up, even in one of the more distant villages. As for Father, he had no place to go, no place at all. Ryšánek had a picture of me; the latest Gestapo rules required that anyone under the age of thirty-two had to have a special card, and Ryšánek, taking along my picture, had promised Father he would get me one. He was aware, too, that I had been recruiting in the area around Bíteš, but he did not know any of my contacts. I would therefore have to ask people in my organization to find immediate shelters for Sec, Fanynka, Father, and me, as far away from Bíteš as possible.

That night, Hlaváček and I started out in a heavy rain to see the three or four people I thought were most likely to help us, especially Homoláč's daughter, Vlasta. She was a young girl—nineteen—whom nobody would suspect of working for the resistance. I hoped the Homoláčs would take in Fanynka and her son. I would take Father and Sec to Pokorný, a teacher I knew in Katov, while I looked for permanent shelters. Even with my flashlight, which I normally used as sparingly as possible, Hlaváček and I could hardly see a step in front of us. Again and again we thought we were lost. My first stop was a place outside Bíteš, "Nine Crosses," so called because nine robbers were hanged there in the eighteenth century. Today Nine Crosses is a huge gas station and restaurant on the throughway between Brno and Prague, but in 1944 there was only an unprepossessing inn, run by a man I called the Turk. Hlaváček left me there; he had to return through the storm-darkened woods in time to go to work the next morning.

The trip was like tens of others during those tedious years underground. I always had to have someone from each village accompany me to the next one, lest the gendarmes hear about a lone stranger passing through and decide to investigate. Every three-hour walk was thus an eight-hour journey. The Turk was not pleased to see me, but he agreed to take me to the Homoláčs' village later in the day. Meanwhile, he brought me to a mill where I was to wait for him a few hours. Dawn broke, hours passed, and still the Turk did not return, so I made my unwelcome way back to his inn and badgered him into accompanying me. It was clear that if I had not come after him, he would have left me waiting at the mill until the end of humanity.

I had become habituated to attics and sheds and was marveling at the civility of the Homoláčs' carpet when Vlasta came in. She was a direct, confident girl, so poised that you assumed without looking closely that she was pretty, a girl who could ignore a ringing phone. Sexy but not seductive, she was accustomed to the appreciation of men, but when she flirted back they sensed that she was only practicing. She was prompt in anything that helped the resistance. The Homoláčs owned the largest farm in the area. Like many of the people who helped us—Mrs. Little Spruce, Kravka, Hašek, Hála— Vlasta and her family saw themselves as somewhat distinguished from the general community around them and considered it fitting that they would do what average people would not. Unspoiled, playful, and strong, Vlasta was the one soldier whom everybody in our organization, women and men, learned to like and trust.

I set out on a bicycle for Pokorný's school in Katov while Vlasta went to get Father. I wasn't sure she was up to so much walking—six to eight hours through dense brush—but she left with the air of someone going to fetch a doctor, her brown hair bobbing. Vlasta was an ideal liaison. Messages could travel unsuspected in her barrette; identity cards could mingle unnoticed with the mess of other papers in her bag. Even money didn't look like money when Vlasta put it in her shoulder strap; it looked like innocent rent from a tenant cottager.

The teacher, Pokorný, was markedly unenthusiastic about harboring Father, Sec, and me even for a few days, but I could not afford to withdraw politely because of his reluctance. The three of us, and Vlasta, too, the first night, stayed in the attic of the school on some straw and hay. It's not as quiet as you would think, lying on straw. There was plenty of life in those clumps—beetles, mice, mites, and gnats—but for us it was heaven because it was dry and for a few hours we felt safe. I stretched out, closed my eyes, and tried to stop my mind.

Father fished his radio out of his knapsack, and we listened to the Czech edition of the BBC news. Usually there was some commentary by a well-known Czechoslovak exile using a cover name. That evening the speaker was Prokop Drtina, secretary to President Beneš, who had been one of the leaders of the Political Center when he fled to London in 1939.[2] That voice, like all the voices from London reaching us in our rat holes, was so impersonal, so comfortable—the voice of a well-dressed man in an insulated, well-lit studio. The people abroad felt safe every night; I could tell it by listening to them. "They have no idea what we are going through," I said bitterly, "no idea of this horrible life underground. In London, they know words, words, a few passwords. Here there are dead people, more and more dead people. Soon there won't be anybody left to hear their patriotic claptrap." Drtina probably did not deserve my resentment, as he later proved to be a man of deep conscience.

The next night I left to warn Hermit that the Gestapo might know of him. "Burn all notes, everything," I advised him, "and send Aleš away, for his own sake and yours. Go underground, where at least you have a chance. Don't stay here and wait for them to come for you."

"Will your father be all right?" he asked.

"He left Bosonohy already. We are going toward the Bohemian-Moravian hills."

Hermit shook his head in a slow, thoughtful No. "I'll stay," he said, "I have trouble with my knees and prostate. I can't survive in the forest or on the run. You are strong, my son. Your life is just starting. You can outsmart them. Save yourself." I left him with a heavy heart, thinking I had seen him for the last time, for he might well be the first one arrested when Jizera drove up to Sec's house in Bosonohy and found the place deserted.

When I returned to Katov, I saw that we were now four in the attic of the school, as Vlasta had brought us Fanynka. Pokorný was appalled. I was furious with Fanynka on several counts. Vlasta's house would have been an excellent shelter for her, but she ruined it by sauntering up to Homoláč's door in splendid daylight, watched by all the field workers. Not only could she not stay there after that, but none of us dared use that shelter, either. Everybody in Radoškov now might suspect that the Homoláčs were harboring strangers. The only one who could remain with the family was the Secs' little brat, who, Vlasta said, was a handful. We thought about putting Fanynka with a relative of Pokorný, a mill owner, but Pokorný refused to make the

---

2. Using the name Pavel Svatý, Drtina became the most popular of all Czechoslovak commentators on the BBC.

arrangements. He was taking care of four people, after all, and had a right to feel that he was doing enough.

There was something else. Father gave me the bulletin that Fanynka was, of all things, pregnant. "What? How could they let this happen?" I exclaimed. "That's the last thing we need!" Father didn't answer. He wanted Fanynka near him. He liked her—God knows why—and I could see his mood lifting when he looked at her little squirrel face. All his life, Father had been a man's man, surrounded by his own kind. I think it was while he was underground that he discovered he really enjoyed women.

I contacted four more people in four different villages nearby, asking them to help us find a shelter. Each reported to me in turn that he had found nothing. Out of nervousness, Pokorný was chattering nonstop all day long, his tensity sharpened by his aunt, who referred to us (with an eloquent gesture toward the attic) as "bringers of death." Sec miraculously found a place for himself near Křižanov, but Fanynka, who would soon have to undergo an abortion, was still ours. Pokorný located a doctor in Bíteš who seemed willing to perform the operation, but it turned out he didn't know how. At the end of a futile visit, the doctor confessed that he had mentioned us to a friend of his, a gendarme. Now we all had a brand new reason to be wretched with anxiety. It seemed that things could not get much worse.

There was a legionnaire in a village ten miles away, we were told. Perhaps if we talked to him and used Father's name, he would keep us. On this slender hope, we started out at midnight, Father, Fanynka, and I, to meet one of our men, Pepek Pařil, who would then take us to the legionnaire.

Father was gnawing away on the informers. "You know, Jizera never once looked me in the eye. But Ryšánek! Such intelligence and composure! Whatever I asked, he took care of it. To think that an able military man like that could be a traitor." Ryšánek had in fact been so efficient that Grňa felt bound to promote him to captain. Then there was Štainer, an inexhaustible source of vexation, instructing our people to come directly to him with information and not to Father, making sure his insults—"stupid theoretician," "idiot"—reached Father's ears. Robotka at least proved his courage by continuing to meet with Ryšánek.

We walked and talked the whole night. When at dawn we reached the sawmill where we were to meet Pepek, Father was drained. He sat against a tree, rubbed the stubble on his chin with the heel of his hand, and fell asleep, his fingers outstretched in front of his nose. He sits there still in my memory, achingly vulnerable, his breath strong and metallic, a moist rope of dirt in the creases of his neck. He woke up as I tried to shift his head to my bunched-up jacket. "I don't need to sleep," he apologized. "Here, Son, you lie down and let me keep guard. You must be tired." But before I could refuse this offer, he fell asleep again, snoring mildly, while I watched him and waited for Pepek.

Pepek did not come. We waited the whole day but there was nobody. We had no food. We couldn't turn back to Katov, but we weren't sure how to get to Kadolec, where Pepek lived. Finally, we started out in the dark with Father's map, he going first, perspiring with his heavy knapsack, Fanynka in the middle, and I last. At dawn we huddled behind a drapery of bushes.

"I'm going to find that legionnaire," Father announced. "I'll take Fanynka with me. A man and woman together are not as noticeable." In an hour they were back, my father's face wearing an announcement that they had been turned down. The legionnaire was so frightened that he would not even give them a drink of water. Both the Gestapo and the SS were all over Křižanov, he said, making dozens of arrests. Our situation was desperate. "Well, we can't stay here indefinitely," Father asserted, re-collecting his courage. "Things may not be as dangerous as this man thinks. One of us should go to Kadolec and find the teacher Maloušek. He knows the mayor of Kadolec—Jaroslav Kobylka I think is his name. I met him once through Maloušek." From our nest in the bushes, I looked with my field glasses and could see no one, so Fanynka and I ventured out. As we neared the village, an old man appeared ahead of us, walking with his stick. I hoped his eyes were too weak to notice us, but Fanynka went straight up to him and began talking, loudly, since that was the only way he could hear her. She had recognized him as the mayor's father.

The SS, it turned out, were still on the other side of Křižanov, so for the time being, the mayor could let us stay. It was good to eat, to go to a safe attic, to be among people who were not afraid. Everyone who had taken us in since we found out about the informers had stipulated, "Only one day," or "Only if you have nowhere else to go." These people accepted us willingly. Since the previous summer, Kobylka had been helping four escaped Soviet prisoners hiding in a zemljanka. Two or three times a week he brought them food and supplies. "In the winter," he commented, "it will be hard to get to them without leaving tracks in the snow." We asked whether we couldn't use a zemljanka the Russians had abandoned, but he explained that all the dugouts eventually filled up with water. Kobylka worked all day on his farm, attended to his duties as mayor of Kadolec, and was willing to care for seven extra dependents, finding food, preparing meals, getting us blankets, all without a furrow of resentment.

"Tomorrow will be a very dangerous day," he warned us, idly stirring his tea. "People are saying the SS will sweep Křižanov. If that happens, they may decide to come on to Kadolec."

"We should go hide in the woods all day tomorrow and tomorrow night," I said. "When the crisis is past, we can come back." We were exposed in the forest, which gave little camouflage and no comfort, but if we were caught there, the Kobylkas would not automatically be condemned with us. In that spring of so much faithlessness, the weather, too, betrayed us; it was storming when we left for the woods. The rain soaked our socks, sleeves, and collars. A raw wind slapped the bushes back and forth so that it was difficult to find one with enough leafage to cover us. Father was in pain from rheumatism. He was only 53, but his joints, he said, were 150, having been left over from some past life and reused. Every four steps Fanynka complained of morning sickness, but I forgave her at once when from my hiding place I heard her retching miserably in her bush. She didn't need my compassion, however, since she had all of Father's. When the twenty-four hours ended finally. Kobylka came with the information that there had been no searches and the village was quiet. We went back to the attic, thanking God and Kobylka for every hour we could stay there.

After the war, Božena Kobylka, the mayor's mother, who was about sixty-five when we came to her house, wrote down her modest description of how she and her family saved our lives:

> One night my son brought these gentlemen—I didn't know their names— from the forest. At first I was very frightened and might have objected. But then I looked at them, at their condition, and I felt too sorry for them to say a word. I just asked God to help me and started to work. I thought, "To live such a life is a frightening thing!" I asked them how they could have lived this way underground for such a long time and I started to shed tears. They told me not to feel bad, that they were soldiers and they had to tolerate both the good and the bad without being frightened.
>
> I put them in the attic at the very end on some straw and hay. They were right above the kitchen. While I was working I listened carefully for any noise. It was so risky. If they turned over or spoke to each other up there, it could be heard. My son was a mayor. We had all kinds of visitors—gendarmes, people from the economic control—any noise at all would have given us away. When I had to bring their food to the attic, I put it alongside the wood in the wood basket, or I hid it under my apron.

The young gentleman's father stayed the whole day in the attic. Only when the house was quiet and there were no more visitors he would come down to talk with us, to find out the news. If there had been some rumor or something bad had happened, my son would bring the old gentleman to the woods where he would spend the night. Then my daughter would wait for an opportunity to bring him food. When things seemed safe again, my son brought him back. The older man was extremely cautious. Only once during his entire stay did he go out into the yard and enjoy the sun.

By 1944 we were again able to send cables abroad through transmitters, so on June 5, Štainer sent an urgent message to the Czech military center in London: "Lieutenant Colonel Jizera from the Price Control Office in Brno is a Gestapo agent. Please warn. Ryšánek, living under the name of Vejvoda, with a Brno address, cover name Pavel, squints, wears glasses, pretends to be working in the name of General Luža—is a Gestapo agent."

We heard the message broadcast twice on the BBC, but Robotka was still meeting Ryšánek as if nothing had happened. "I told him we didn't believe the announcement," Robotka reported, "that we figured there had been some misinformation. If he and Jizera were informers, I said, then we would all be arrested by now, especially Luža." In fact, even when it was public knowledge that Ryšánek was accused of working for the Gestapo, he and Jizera were able to continue operating because most people simply could not believe the charges. Many resisters had been confiding in Ryšánek for almost four years and remained unharmed; their organizations were intact. Of course, hundreds of individuals had been arrested in Moravia, some of whom he knew, but others he could easily have fingered were still free. That seemed proof that he was not reporting to the Germans.

Eventually, we were able to confirm that not one arrest was caused by our disclosures to Ryšánek and Jizera; neither Father, Robotka, Štainer, nor Grňa told them the name of any resister they didn't already know about. Moreover, the Gestapo never learned that it was Paprskář who had exposed the informers. He became a double agent, helping us avoid capture. He told Robotka about other Czech informers and alerted him when he thought the Gestapo was about to change its tactics. If the Germans decided to arrest Robotka, Paprskář was sure he would find out about it in time to warn him. At some point during the summer, Ryšánek realized that Luža had slipped out of his sights, but by then he was trying to convince everyone in the underground that he was not a Gestapo spy. It was the wrong time to arrest Robotka, who was thus able to continue his game with the informers until the middle of September. In the fall of 1944, the war was coming closer, and the resistance was becoming more active. It seemed likely that the Nazis would revert to mass arrests, so Robotka at last went into hiding.

Ryšánek remained active and treacherous.[3] I saw him for the first time after the war when I attended his trial, and I was struck, as everyone was, by his intelligence and self-possession. He was a different breed from the other Czech spies, the scenters on leashes, helplessly trying to appease the masters at their backs. The Nazis had provided Ryšánek with a salaried job, a free apartment, and bonuses for leading them to choice quarry such as Father, but I doubt that material rewards were what motivated him to become the Gestapo's champion mastiff. He was a type, I think, a quiet, compulsive competitor whose satisfaction was not merely in having his victims captured but in knowing he had won against them in an insidious battle of wits. I couldn't discern from watching him in the dock what his true feelings had been toward the Nazis or his Czech prey. Because of him, many people died horribly.

In Kobylka's attic, we still had to arrange an abortion for Fanynka. Vlasta, Mrs. Homoláč, and Mrs. Little Spruce were all trying to find someone to do it, but the four doctors they approached either could not or would not perform the operation. By this time Vlasta was teasing me about being a responsible young man who always stood by his girlfriends when he got them in trouble, even if it meant turning Moravia upside down. Fanynka meanwhile did not endear herself to me with her blabbing (she told Vlasta exactly where I was hiding!) and she became even less dear when I found out she was always carping about me behind my back. God did answer some prayers, however, despite the wartime backlog. A midwife in Bíteš finally performed the abortion. Sec located a refuge for his family, but not before Fanynka and the boy had been chased out of two other places I found for them.

It was in the dark of Kobylka's attic that Father and I heard about the Normandy invasion in a BBC broadcast that was like the first lights of Christmas. Peace was in sight. The Germans could not possibly win the war. We only had to hold out and the nightmare would be over. The invasion was taking place just as Father predicted. First, the Allies established a

3. The parachute group Carbon, which was dropped into the Protectorate in 1944, walked straight into his web when it sought shelter with an A-person, one of his unwitting informants.

bridgehead and were building ports to accommodate a supply of men and matériel. Then would come a great offensive—the breakthrough. Father, however, thought that the main front was still in the east because the bulk of the German army was being drawn there.

Even now, the Germans squandered themselves hunting down internal enemies. We were rejoicing over D day when news arrived that almost the entire PRNC organization had been wiped out by the Gestapo. General Novák had been living legally. He was warned that the Germans were about to arrest him, but by fleeing he would have abandoned his family to the Gestapo's revenge. He decided to wait for them rather than go underground. Arrested during the night of June 22, 1944, Novák was tortured but was not executed and managed to stay alive in the Gestapo prison until the end of the war. Along with Novák, Colonel Lang and many others were taken. Richter committed suicide.[4] Since April, the Ambassador Heidrich organization had been joined to Father's, at least in the sense that they formally endorsed close cooperation with our group. They, too, were hit. Leopold Chmela was arrested on June 6, followed soon afterward by Heidrich himself.[5]

As the Allies were closing in on the Germans, the Germans seemed to be closing in on us. This was something of an illusion because, though we didn't realize it, resistance networks were popping up toward the end of the war faster than the Nazis could smother them. Just the same, Robotka was turned down more than twenty times as he tried to find a place we could go if we had to leave Kobylka's attic.

The Prague arrests were nearly simultaneous with another devastation, this time involving Štainer and some paratroopers who were bringing in transmitters from outside. In the Protectorate we were separated from our

4. The Prague N. Referate, always jealous of the superior efficiency of its counterpart in Brno, wanted credit for the PRNC arrests. There was a confrontation in which both the Brno and Prague groups claimed to have penetrated the Revolutionary National Committee. General Novák's successor as head of PRNC was General František Bláha, who was arrested in the fall of 1944. Bláha's successor was General František Slunečko, who had been living underground since 1940 in eastern Bohemia.

5. I talked with Heidrich in Washington, D.C., where he resided after he escaped from Prague in 1948. He was Secretary General of the Czechoslovak ministry of foreign affairs. He described how Father's contact man, Robotka, met Heidrich's aide, the writer and diplomat Zdeněk Němeček. Mrs. Eliáš also provided liaison between the groups. Heidrich's narrative of this period can be found in the Heidrich Papers, Hoover Institution Archives, Stanford University.

political leaders in London by a thousand miles. Without communication with us, the leaders could not credibly represent themselves abroad as the voice of Czechoslovakia. Nor could the resistance at home claim to have any true authority without links to our exiled government. We had to have cable contact. The Germans knew it and had dedicated great effort to locating and smashing our secret transmitters. First there had been the Sparta network with eleven transmitters, which provided the Allies with some twenty thousand intelligence messages until it was destroyed in 1941. Then the Czechoslovak army abroad trained special volunteers whom the British dropped into the Protectorate. These paratroopers restored communication and succeeded in assassinating Heydrich, but by the beginning of 1943 they, too, had been hunted down. Throughout that year we could only use couriers, people smuggling messages in their clothing and passing them to other carriers, who took the missives through Sweden or Slovakia to the London government. But the slow courier system became impractical as the tempo of the war intensified. Beneš, Ingr, and František Moravec, the head of military intelligence abroad, decided to try to reestablish transmitter contact with us. In April 1944, therefore, they began dispatching new teams of paratroopers, fourteen in all, charged with gathering intelligence on their own and getting information to and from the home resistance.[6] Each team of two, three, or four men included at least one wireless operator with a transmitter.

It was difficult enough for these paratroopers to land in the Protectorate and find groups to help them—the resisters were, after all, hiding. Once a team got set up somewhere, the transmitting itself was dangerous. Each station required at least two people, a radio operator and an officer to code and decode the messages. The operator had to be careful not to transmit too long at any one time, since he had to keep the transmitter open long enough to receive incoming responses, too. The transmitters had to be moved frequently, lest the Germans follow the radio waves and track them down. Even when the transmitters were diligently lugged around the hills to ever-changing stations, the Gestapo usually located them within a few months. The machines were about the size and weight of phonographs. It was hard to conceal them on a bicycle, the most sophisticated means of transport at our disposal. And it was harder still to find shelters that could be used as transmitting stations.

6. It was Czechoslovak paratroopers from the army abroad who first reported that the Germans were producing the V2 rockets with which they bombed Great Britain in 1944.

The first wave of paratroopers were lucky. Our people managed to make contact with two of their transmitter teams, Calcium and Barium, before they had endured any great hardship. The paratroopers were supposed to be left in zones where they could likely find support and were given names of individuals who might feed or hide them. But these addresses were old, and because any drop might be drastically affected by weather conditions, the teams often landed far away from their targets and had to live as best they could. All of them had received excellent training from the British in marksmanship and outdoor survival, as well as in coding and transmitting, but some fared better in the underground than others. It was a shock coming from the free world to a situation where every step, every word required preparation and secrecy.

The four members of Calcium knew on landing that our organization was in the Bohemian-Moravian hills, and they were looking for us when Štainer got word that they were down. Unlike Robotka, who was supposed to be working all day, every business day, Štainer had no job and could devote all his time to the resistance. And unlike Father or me, he could travel. Men in their twenties had all been mobilized into labor divisions; when I went anywhere, I was as conspicuous as a child wandering the roads in the middle of a school day. But a "forest worker" did not have to hide from the gendarmes or the various patrols. Consequently, it was Karel Štainer who found the paratroopers, helped them locate a shelter, and brought them supplies. The Calcium group was dependent on him. When he asked them to transmit messages for our organization, they never hesitated, and though nearly everyone in both Calcium and Barium came to despise Štainer, they never thought twice about handing him cables they received from London that were addressed to our organization.

The Calcium paratroopers had announced their landing in late May through their transmitter, which was called Milada: "Established contact with organized, illegal revolutionary committee named Spring, headed by uncompromised politicians and military. You have already received some reports from this organization." Štainer sent this cable, though it was worded and coded by the Milada operators. Another cable informed the London government of our partisan strength, "a few hundred men headed by the military, who form the core . . . active in the Bohemian-Moravian hills." London had apparently answered the first cable with a request for information about Ingr's Adolf—the code name for Father. Štainer reassured London: "Ingr's Adolf is with us."

To send a cable, we had to first get word to Štainer, the only one of us who knew where Calcium's transmitter was hidden. Because all of us, especially the transmitter operators, were moving from day to day wherever we found shelter, it could take Štainer several days to deliver a message, even when he was trying. Nevertheless, this was much simpler than communicating with our government through couriers, waiting for a dispatch to make its uncertain way across the continent and back again.

However, on May 23, the Nazis struck Calcium. Its leader was at a pond expecting to meet his teammate when he was surprised by the Gestapo and received the Hitler Kiss: he was shot dead on the spot.[7] The other paratrooper, on his way to the meeting place, was a mile away and heard the shots. Completely by chance, a different group of Gestapo stopped him. He thrust up his hands in a gesture of surrender. "Come closer," they ordered him. When he was about twelve steps from the two Germans, he pulled a blur of metal from his holster, shot twice at each target, as the British had trained him to do, and hit both the Gestapo men. One of them managed to return fire and the paratrooper was wounded, but he nevertheless escaped. A third Calcium member, along with Štainer, had been in the woods approaching the pond, heard the shooting, and also got away. However, the Gestapo now had one of the two bicycles the paratroopers had been riding. Did they have the bike with no connection to us? Or did the Germans now have a bike registered to the blacksmith we called the Giant, who just a few nights before had opened his home to my father? Father had several frightened days before he learned that the Germans had the other bicycle, with no connection to him. But as the pond was under the care of the gamekeeper Pavlas, the entire Pavlas family—the people who had previously sheltered my mother—now had to go underground.

All of these arrests and deaths left me knotted in fear, yet it was during this moil of violence that Father insisted he had to become more active. The D day invasion was his signal to draw in all the resistance organizations he could reach to prepare the explosion—the coordinated military uprising. He therefore set out over my objections to meet some leaders of the Bohemian underground. Pepek, though he was asthmatic, neurasthenic, and easily panicked, walked with him all night to his first appointment, about twenty-five miles away. "He made it fine," Pepek reported the next day. "He guided

---

7. A young woman who lived nearby was a Gestapo informer, inexplicably, since her husband was active in the Czechoslovak army abroad.

us with a map. When we arrived, a number of men were there. Your father talked to them all and then he left with one. Don't worry."

Alone in Kobylka's dark attic, I did worry. Father's identity papers were good enough to get by a Czech gendarme, but if a German patrol stopped him, that was something different. My fretting was cut short, however, by the warning of another search. Faced with going again to the woods, I decided to ask Kobylka's other resisters, the four Soviets, if they would take me into their zemljanka until the latest alarm had passed.

Living underground, in a hole carved out of mud, the Soviets looked like a colony of Cro-Magnons, or rather, Cro-Magnon skeletons. Nikolaj Bachmutsky, one of the two officers and the leader of the group, was a fighter pilot who had been shot down at the Leningrad front. Though wounded, he had escaped with Iljikčan from their German prison camp, made his way into the Protectorate, and was found by our organization. I didn't dream that he would become one of the closest friends of my life. When I saw him in the weird light of the zemljanka's oil lamp, I had to fight down a spasm of nausea. His skin was a yellow varnish over jagged shoulders and a back in which the knob of every vertebra was visible. His mouth was a grinning scab, his hair moldy straw clinging to his skull. But despite his appearance, Nikolaj's spirit was undamaged. If he ever got out of the zemljanka, he had two immediate goals: killing Germans—all he needed for a battle, he said, was a pistol and some Germans to kill—and enjoying *děvočky*—girls—or more precisely, female comfort. Sasha was a Ukranian and a teacher in civilian life. He, too, looked like a decaying corpse and had a weakness for děvočky. Maxim was a good-hearted Tartar. Misha, the fourth man, had been a member of a kolkhoz, a Soviet agricultural cooperative. Though he, too, was hardly more than a male core with femurs and humeri sticking out, he longed for open spaces. He and the others were cheerful, however, while confined like animals in the air-starved zemljanka; confinement in the German camp had been unspeakably worse. None of the men weighed more than eighty pounds. All cherished a special hatred of the Nazis.

Each of us had a piece of a cup which we used for eating, cutting, washing, everything. We were hungry most of the day, for we cooked in the middle of the night, filling the catacomb with smoke. Our food was water boiled with a piece of fat for flavoring, an unsalted placenta which we devoured greedily from one single pot. We talked constantly that week, the Soviets blasting away like trumpets, as if there were an auditorium between us instead of just four feet. Our number one topic was not Communism, as I had hoped, but water. Our zemljanka was big but porous; when it rained out-side, as it did often that June, it rained in the zemljanka, too. I never heard a socialist word from any of them, though I understood from the tenor of their comments that they admired Stalin and considered him responsible for the Soviet successes in the war. They were all bright men—I was reminded that Russia was not the primitive society of hulking Bolsheviks that I had imagined. But I was bored to death there without any contact with the out-side world and glad when we finally lay down on our wooden beds about four in the morning with a blanket and some hay.

If I had to characterize life underground in a couple of words, I would say we hurtled between boredom and terror. After a week, there having been no searches, I returned to the attic. I was retraining my body to be motionless when Kobylka, glancing out of a downstairs window, spied a black sedan going to Maloušek's school. Since almost all cars on the road belonged to the Germans in those days of gas rationing, that could only mean one thing. Soon Kobylka burst through the hatch with the terrible news: Maloušek and Moravanský had both been arrested by the Gestapo. Maloušek was the civil-ian leader of the Meziříčí resistance group; Moravanský was its military commander—the man Father had met in a ditch. In the past year, we had approached Maloušek only through cutouts; therefore, though his school was just two hundred yards away from the mayor's house, he did not know that Father or I had been staying in Kobylka's attic. But he did know our past connection to Kobylka. He knew about the Soviets now living in the zemljanka. He knew about many things. It could only be a matter of hours before that knowledge was extracted from him.

I had to get the Soviets out of their trap in the zemljanka. Pokorný in Katov agreed to supply them with food if they stayed in the forest, but with the misfortune of his fellow teacher fresh in his memory, he would not keep them in his school. Hermit, too, turned me down. "I apologize. You know that Iljikčan could have divulged my name. That was close. I just cannot do it." Vlasta and I finally brought the Soviets to her parents' beehive, a large cottage which was far too open and exposed to be a real shelter, but it was all I could do in this emergency. The worst of it was that the Soviets were incapable of talking in a low voice. Even Vlasta was nervous. The crisis had a horrible climax and was soon over, for Maloušek was tortured to death without revealing anything. I heard again his words, uttered with so much fervor, as he had led me down the hill from the estate where I was refused shelter: "This very minute people are suffering under torture."

There was a schedule of emotions when our compatriots died, and I awaited it. First came shock and outrage so deep and keen that it would harrow up your insides if you gave in to it. Then a wash of relief, because a confidant's death meant he could no longer endanger us. Relief was followed by guilt, the guilt of a survivor, guilt that I knew would be implacable in the case of this brave teacher who had stored in his head so much information about all of us and died hideously because of his determination to keep it there. Finally would come the long, quiet grieving for a dead comrade. Those were the waves that had swept me in the past and that I thought would now break over me at the news of Maloušek's excruciating murder. But the truth is that in my dry, deep, numb fatigue, I only felt relief. The more effort and hardship it cost us to stay alive, the cheaper everyone else's life became.

Though the end of the war was in sight, both of us, Father in the hills and I in Kadolec, were scrambling from one semishelter to another, glad to get any temporary hole that we would have considered too insecure in former times. If we were going to last even another month, we needed identity cards that would allow us to move around. Vlasta recruited a printer, Jan Ročejdl. With money I raised for supplies, eventually about 25,000 crowns, he made expertly forged masterpieces from several districts, along with rubber stamps—enough for our entire organization.[8] Vlasta delivered a whole sack to me during a thunderstorm; her hair and clothes were wet as seaweed, but she had managed to keep our crisp, new identities completely dry.

The center of Father's operations had now moved from the suburbs of Brno to Nové Město, near the Moravian-Bohemian border, where he found two commanders with sizable clandestine groups of their own in the districts bordering Prague.[9] The first was a former lieutenant colonel, Josef Sva-

8. Ročejdl's cards were so precise that even an expert might have trouble distinguishing them from authentic Protectorate cards. After the war his printing devices were displayed in a resistance exhibition in Brno and at the Military Museum in Prague.

9. No one was sure of the exact number of people in our organization at any one time. We did not keep lists and for safety's sake deliberately avoided sharing information. Moreover, "organization" was a loose term. A person was a member of an organization if he was recruited to fight in the projected uprising or if, like Hermit, he was someone who could be relied on to try to help the organization. Maloušek was thus a member of the Moravanský group, but he was also part of our organization and perhaps some others.

toň. Long underground, he headed a well-defined organization on the Bohemian side of the hills. Since he had been something of an expert in guerrilla warfare when in the military, I referred to him as the Partisan.[10] Partisan Svatoň adhered to Father like a disciple. He was indignant that Štainer and Robotka tried to isolate and undermine the one person who had some appreciation of what lay ahead of us.

The second man who gravitated to Father that summer, Josef Císař, was still living legally in Prague and had a regular job. In his secret work, he was the leader of an extremely important underground group, Avala, which included the association of Czech volunteer firemen in its membership. There was a firemen's organization in every large community in the Protectorate, men who could mobilize at a minute's notice and who were connected to all the other fire departments across the country. Firemen were the only people in the Protectorate who had at their disposal both gasoline and vehicles—fire engines. The Gestapo from time to time quashed the leaders of the firemen's resistance, but in wartime, firefighters were too badly needed not to leave the associations intact. Císař Fireman, as I called him, was therefore an invaluable ally. Besides the fire brigades, he had organized the Czech hunting societies. Hunters meant guns—they were among the few people allowed to carry firearms and ammunition, and they, too, were represented in every district of the Protectorate. In 1948 when I escaped from the Communists, Císař Fireman came with me. We became good friends, and it was he who later gave me much information about Father's activities during this period on the Bohemian border.

Grňa wanted to reconfigure our organization to include the new groups that were coming in, especially Císař's, and to change the name from Spring to the Council of Three.[11] R3 would have Father and Grňa as its military and political leaders, as before, with Císař Fireman as the third voice. Beneath this triumvirate there would be an executive committee and then a broader layer of fifty or sixty people. Only those who had been active in the resistance could lead the national revolution. Father was cool to these suggestions when Grňa presented them to him in their conference chambers behind a tree. "An army can only have one leader," he told Grňa. "And Council of Three sounds a little pretentious, don't you think? That automat-

10. Svatoň's organization, I found out later, spread from Vysoké Mýto to Moravia; he had also gathered to him the remnants of ON in eastern Bohemia.

11. *Rada tří* in Czech, hence the abbreviation R3.

ically locks in power with just three people. What if we want to take others aboard? Do we call it Council of Four? Then Council of Five?" What Father did not say then was that he cringed at the thought of Grňa as pilot of the republic.

"When you put together Císař, Štainer, Robotka, Grňa," he told me in Kobylka's attic, "all of them together don't make up a political force that you'd trust to lead a shouting match, much less a life-or-death revolt. What we do in this transitional period is important," he continued, "because the people who are still standing after the insurrection will be the ones who fill the postwar political offices. This will be a revolutionary situation where there is not such a clear division of civilian and military power as you have in a stable, established government. Grňa has qualities, but he is not the man to wield great authority or to break new ground."

Grňa's latest faux pas had been to ask Svatoň, a lieutenant colonel, to disengage himself from Luža and join Grňa's political staff. Partisan Svatoň was both amused and irritated by Grňa. He showed Father a meddlesome letter Grňa sent him full of detailed, clumsy military instructions which, he remarked, "even an officer trainee would be embarrassed to sign."

"Grňa wants to co-sign all of my military orders," Father complained. "He insisted on it."

"What did you say to that?" asked Svatoň.

"Nothing. I'll issue orders as I see fit, and he can go fly a kite."

Father was exacting and fretful, temperamental and trying. Whatever he was, he was not easygoing. But there was a transparency in his personality that allowed people to see through his moods. He was a born leader, unassuming but compelling, who had no need for the upholstery of rank. At one point he was hidden in Krásné by a blacksmith we called the Giant because he was about six feet five inches. The Giant was acting as a courier for the people around Father, in addition to his regular work, and he had a new baby who kept him and his wife awake all night. He was exhausted most of the time. Thinking he had heard a cry, he got up one dawn to find Father walking the baby, crooning to it softly. "You sleep at night from now on," Father said, putting the infant down and reaching for a diaper. "I can nap during the day. There's no reason why I can't get up with this little person." And thenceforth he did. It was one of the anecdotes told after the war that contributed to the transubstantiation of Vojtěch the Hardhead into Luža the Hero. The Giant joined a large society of people who would have followed Father to the ends of the earth.

* * *

Calcium had resumed transmitting after the incident at the pond. In August, Štainer, using his own words and his own delusions of authority, sent another special cable describing our group as "led by Professor Dr. Grňa, Ingr's Adolf, and a third man. . . . The Council of Three includes all the important underground organizations. The Communists are cooperating, but are not part of the organization because they do not have any center here."

In answer to this cable, London replied, "Ingr's Adolf we know. But who are Dr. Grňa and the third man?"

Štainer was shameless in exploiting his monopoly of the transmitter contacts. When Father gave him reports to send to London, he brought the wireless operator only those he considered worthwhile. Likewise, when messages arrived from the London government for our organization, he would manage not to tell Father their contents. He did not hesitate to send reports himself in the name of Father's organization but without letting Father approve the text. Each time Father discovered Štainer's insubordination, there was a long tirade until, exhausted, Father would sigh, "The man has an infection in his brain. It doesn't do any good to talk to him. He needs trepanning!"

In one instance, General Ingr sent a message: "We ask Ingr's Adolf to give a concise report immediately on the situation and potential of the military." Štainer never gave Father the request. Other cables did not reach Father. Maybe Štainer withheld them or maybe not—given the difficulties of reaching the transmitter, we could never be sure how much information he was intentionally losing. Without the text of the cables from London, Father could not even be sure that the exile government had confirmed him as supreme military commander of the national uprising.

Others had even less patience with Štainer's complexes. The Czechoslovak officers operating Milada were soon fed up with Štainer's trying to subordinate them. They had not undertaken their intricate and perilous mission so that they could take orders from some unknown captain. Father ranted that he was waiting for the day when he could set up a military tribunal to court-martial Štainer. But I knew when that day came, Father would weigh his contributions to the cause and forgive the miscreant.

Father expected to have his own transmitting station—two to four operators, either Barium or some other group—for his exclusive use during the national uprising so that he could maintain constant contact with London.[12] The main action during the insurrection would be at home. As the military commander, he would be responsible for directing it. The risk in this plan was that if Father and his close associates were captured, there would be no insurrection. The London military had the idea that they would direct the uprising by transmitter. Our organization would indeed have a separate line to London and would report to them. If Father wanted to issue an order, he would send it to the military officials in London, who would in turn communicate it to the leader of each group at home, a method Štainer hotly defended. That would allow the exiles to run the whole show from abroad. They argued, plausibly, that this would be safer because no one leader at home would know all the plans for the uprising and therefore could not reveal them even if arrested.

Safer or not, Father was having none of it. Communication would be awkward and unreliable; one could never be sure that all the groups had actually received the instructions. Most important, the revolution would be directed by the self-serving exiles that, except for Beneš, Ingr, and a few others, Father and Grňa held in utter contempt. Even during their lapses into lucidity, Father said, the politicians surrounding Beneš were not competent to fight a revolution. Father knew that the home resistance must direct the uprising, get credit for its success, and organize the provisional government which would follow. In Slovakia, Poland, France, and elsewhere, Father's system of central control was the one that prevailed.

As the uprising took shape in his mind, Father looked for men in the Bohemian-Moravian hills who could be part of his future staff. To my surprise, he was planning to offer a position to Eduard Soška, despite Soška's having been one of those who exposed him to the informer Ryšánek. "He's intelligent and dependable," Father remarked several times. I was not much impressed with Soška. He showed the sort of fatuous cynicism that one finds in young people before they realize this is the only world that will be offered to them and they may as well make the best of it. I did, however, like another of Father's cohorts, Rastislav Váhala, a lawyer from Prague, who was clear sighted, blunt spoken, and steady as brick.

12. The group Barium was led by Captain Josef Šandera; Barium also had some dealings with Štainer and disliked him. Identified by an informer, Šandera was captured by the Gestapo on January 16, 1945, and committed suicide at the moment of his arrest. A second member arrested with him hanged himself in Pankrác prison. The third man in the group was absent from the hideout when the Gestapo closed in. He survived the war.

During this early part of July 1944, Father was hidden by Cyril Musil, who also sheltered Soška, Partisan Svatoň, and the paratrooper who had been wounded in the shootout. They stayed in a hayloft, where they held endless colloquia, joined by Karel Štainer. When Štainer and Luža were together, Musil could hear them shouting fifty feet away. "Once when I brought them food," Musil later wrote, "General Luža was explaining that it would take the Allies a good two months to enlarge the base in Normandy; only then could they start their attack against Paris. Štainer insisted they would be in Paris in a week. 'We have to be prepared to stay underground another winter,' General Luža said, 'and for us it will be the worst winter. It will take that long to defeat the Germans.'" Musil noted that Luža was clearly the knowledgeable authority in these debates, the one who had thought deeply about the impending events. "We must have a revolution," Father had stated in a letter to me, "even if such an insurrection is not necessary from a military standpoint to defeat the Germans. Without a revolution, the political field will be dominated by desiccated party people who will return from abroad. They'll shuffle off the plane and utter a few platitudes; someone will drive them to their old offices. And that will be the end of all significant change—everything. What is not done during this brief revolutionary beginning will never be done later on."

Father above all wanted a revolution, but he didn't want to incite a revolution with the likes of Grňa or Štainer, men who were in no way capable of dealing with its aftermath. Nor did Father underestimate the value of guerrillas as an adjunct to the regular army. He knew, however, that an undersupplied guerrilla army could never stand up against the Wehrmacht. Father planned to start the revolution by seizing arms stored in an SS training camp near Benešov, south of Prague. There were enough weapons, including some heavy weapons, to arm ten thousand men. The insurgency would next move to an ammunition factory in Vlaším. Benešov and Vlaším would be the Lexington and Concord of our revolution. In addition to weapons dropped by the British, Father was hoping also for an arms shipment from the Red Army.[13]

The uprising depended on weapons. Father sent one of his very few cables to General Ingr on September 9, 1944, pleading for arms:

13. Much of this information was given to me by Váhala in the 1970s during our secret meetings in Vienna and in Ljubljana, Yugoslavia. Váhala was allowed out of Czechoslovakia for ostensible visits to relatives, but the purpose of his trips was to meet me.

We have consolidated the home resistance under a unified leadership and have for a long time done everything we can to carry on our fight. To be effective in this critical period of the war, we need weapons. We made an urgent request about two months ago; you promised arms within two weeks but nothing happened. I am very resentful of this situation because ours is one of the most active groups, led by possibly the most dedicated soldiers of the republic. For the sake of these men, I ask you to intervene immediately and fulfill your commitment to send us arms. Please, Brother General, explain why we have not received the weapons and do everything you can to insure their delivery. It is difficult to imagine all the obstacles and hardships we are facing every moment. I urge you to take my words as seriously as they are meant.

Father's demand for weapons was futile. Ingr and the other Czechs abroad wanted to arm us. But in the British view the Protectorate was part of the Soviet war zone; the Soviets were therefore responsible for supplying any anti-German insurgency. The British realized that any weapons they dropped might eventually fall into the hands of the Communist Allies, with whom they were increasingly disillusioned. As for the Soviets, having marched over a thousand miles, they did not want to set things up so as to congratulate the Czechs on liberating themselves. Nor were they eager to take over a country with an independent army that looked to its own leaders for direction.

On August 29, 1944, Slovakia erupted in revolution, led by military men who were in the resistance. The uprising was supported by both democrats and Communists.[14] We did not yet know what direction the Red Army, now standing at the Slovakian border, would take, and we had no way of judging whether the advance would be a matter of two or three months or only a few weeks, but we were confident the Soviets would soon be in Moravia, abetted by Slovakian insurgents. Now we were bombarded with broadcasts from Moscow exhorting us to take inspiration from our Slovak brothers and begin our own insurrection. Father was adamant that we were not going to begin anything without adequate weapons. But on the assumption that we would get them, he was ready to find a hideout in the Prague area, staff his future headquarters, and make preparations for the fight.

It was over one hundred degrees in Kobylka's attic when Father and I

14. Father, the only Czech who would have been acceptable to the Slovaks, was pleased to have been considered for the leadership of this uprising. But the London government decided in April 1944 to appoint a Slovak, Lieutenant Colonel Ján Golian, who was the head of a Slovak underground military organization.

talked about what we hoped would be his last underground journey, the trip to Prague. "Get things ready here so that you can join me when I send you word," he said. "You will be part of my staff. Bring Sec and Malý with you." We conferred about where to place the men's wives when we left, what clothes to bring, and all the other exigencies that we usually discussed before one of our secret trips.

Then, our proximate business out of the way, we talked about a dozen things—politics and history, and whether we should take the word *socialist* out of our socialist program for the postwar society.[15] Father described for me the meeting between President Beneš and his generals in that fateful September of 1938, when Beneš decided to accede to the Munich Pact. "He's surrounded now by dead wood," Father said of Beneš.

> Most of them are ambitious mediocrities. Munich will haunt Beneš. People will forget his real significance. During the First World War, it was Beneš who ran the government. Masaryk set general policy, but Beneš, the chief of staff, was doing the black work, the administrative chores. He's honest, dedicated, and even now he has a lot of initiative. It was because of his political maneuvers that we were recognized as a war power and became part of the Allied coalition earlier than Poland, which was a state before we were. He is the best possible choice to lead us into the peace conference.[16]

15. Father's idea of social democracy was close to that of the anti-Marxist leftist Josef Macek, who had been a former member of the right wing of the Social Democratic Party and editor of the review *Our Time*, of which Father was an avid reader. Macek's theories would place him today in the right wing of Britain's Labor Party or in the center of the Democratic Party of the United States. Father admired him so much that he asked Hermit to write to him, not using Luža's name. Macek was unpopular in the postwar climate of Czechoslovakia. After 1948 he escaped to the United States, where he became active in the exile movement against the Communists.

16. In a letter written early in 1944, Father wrote: "I would like to tell you how I see Beneš today. . . . [S]olely because of him, his political leadership . . . we are in as good, if not better, position than at the end of the last war. We have our ducks all lined up with every great power that will have a decisive word at the peace conference, particularly the Soviet Union. I have to recognize that Beneš is our best statesman, someone with European standing. He knows what he wants and he goes after it relentlessly, undaunted by enormous obstacles. He recognizes the reality of power. He hates it when it's used against the principles of humanity, but he can always be counted on to be in any room where great decisions will be made. He tries to hang on to his philosophical principles but mostly in theory. I think he keeps coming up against the practical truth that he can only spend his store of prestige on those humanitarian ideas that further the welfare of Czechoslovakia. As the companion, collaborator, and successor to President Masaryk, he constantly invokes the ghost of the great man, implying some sort of spiritual union between them. He knows how to use Masaryk's moral prestige to enhance his own position.

"Today it's clear that our prewar foreign policy was the one that always correctly assessed the

As usual, Father left before I was ready to let him go. When Partisan Svatoň came for him, it was about ten in the evening and foggy. I had my usual anxieties whenever I saw him go off, and I had to fight down my superstition that September and October were unlucky. I gave him the little work of art I had been saving—his new identity card, perfect in every detail. He was going to fill it in with "Musil," the surname of our skier friend and perhaps hundreds of other Czechs. "I always wanted to be an athlete," he said. "This is my chance." Father was in a good mood. I can see him now, handsome in his hat and weatherproof Hubertus, smiling and joking with his comrades. Between him and his next uncertain bed was a muddy obstacle course of barking dogs, wrong directions, and the probing flashlights of killers. He shook my shoulder one last time and set off.

In the next days I saw Hlaváček, Kravka, Hermit, and the printer, as Father had instructed. In Nové Město I prepared Partisan Svatoň to take over my organization in my absence and, if need be, look after my mother. Svatoň showed me photos of his wife and children, who were in an internment camp. He seemed to me a warm fellow with sincere respect for Father. "He *knows* so much," Svatoň asserted, "one must defer to him, even though one or two of his opinions are a little daft."

"Such as?" I asked.

"Oh, well, you know . . . it doesn't take away from his overall brilliance . . . he thinks the war is going to last till 1945."

Word finally came back from Father that he had made it to the area below Prague and was being looked after by Císař Fireman's group. He was still moving from pillar to post, sheltered for only a night at a time or not at all. By the time I heard from him, he had gathered a staff of five close supporters. Josef Ouředník was a leader of an organization south of Prague called Sázava, after the name of a nearby river. The second man was Císař Fireman. The third, Staff Captain Jiříkovský, was a part of Ouředník's group, a man Císař and Štainer had known for a long time. The fourth was Váhala. Finally, there was young Josef Koreš, formerly a lieutenant in the reserve, who served as Father's adjutant and accompanied him to all his meetings.

---

international situation and understood the regimes of Mussolini and Hitler. Our country never wavered in its commitments, and never went through the total diplomatic conversions experienced by the Poles, Yugoslavs, Rumanians, and even the French and British who pushed the Russians aside in 1938. . . . There are leaders of other occupied countries living abroad, trying to get the ear of the Allies, but they don't have the massive support at home that Beneš enjoys."

I developed a great affection for the lawyer Váhala, who served as my contact to Father. Váhala was young—in his thirties—well educated and polished. Although I never knew whether he was married or where he had lived during his life, I felt I knew him like a childhood friend. He seemed unaware of the dangers surrounding us and was almost cavalier about them without going so far as to expose any of us to peril. He was too earnest for jokes and too pragmatic for the bouts of despondency the rest of us suffered. Bright, direct, and cool headed, he made you feel you could spend your life around him without finding him wearisome.

Father was trying now to subsume all the underground groups in the Czech lands under his leadership, though they were to remain functionally independent. Their names were just another list to me then, more data to be cataloged in my head. But eventually I was able to see that these groups were important elements in the Czech resistance; they comprised large potential forces. Besides Ouředník's organization, Sázava, and Císař's networks of firefighters and hunters, there were the remnants of ON and PRNC, clusters of intellectuals in Prague, the fragments of Ambassador Heidrich's group, a large area under Svatoň's control, and other groups under the Council of Three spread from Domažlice to the Slovakian border, embracing a large part of the Protectorate. Also in Prague was an association of trade unions already engaged in illegal activities under the forward-looking name Revolutionary Trade Unions. Through Váhala, who was quite leftist, Father was in contact with both these trade unions and the few surviving leaders of the Czechoslovak Communist Party. We were no longer an organization of a few hundred, but a federation of scattered thousands. By September 11, 1944, when Father had a staff meeting, all these significant groups had signaled their acceptance of Luža as the leader of the uprising. Partisan Svatoň told me that his people—and there were hundreds of them—would not accept orders from anybody else. The Prague organization was for the first time publishing several thousand copies of an underground journal, the *Czechoslovak Resistance,* with some articles by Father.

When the western Allies were at the Rhine and the eastern front was moving, Father issued his first military order as Supreme Commander of the Home Resistance, signed in his true name, which each district leader of the resistance was supposed to distribute to his cadres. The order explained how to mobilize military units and warned that any former officer who refused to participate in the uprising would not later be allowed to rejoin the regular army. Father decreed, moreover, that any officer who allowed himself to be arrested by the Nazis would be put to court-martial after the war. This was a heartless ukase, if ever I heard one, and naïve, besides. If a man were not scared into killing himself by the threat of German capture, he wouldn't be driven to it, in the last weeks of the war, by the fear of a court-martial, either.

But Father did not ask for my opinion. His affairs in order, he sent for me to come to him and I started out. I was bringing him three sets of new underwear, his eyeglasses, some street shoes he could wear in Prague, since all he had with him were his hiking boots, some forged Rembrandts, as I called our new identity cards, and Sec and Malý—the heaviest burdens of all. I couldn't understand why Father wanted to take Malý with him to Prague, except to show his loyalty to the Little One. After the Ryšánek debacle, both Malý and Sec ceased to be the men I had known. Malý was always nervous now and depressed. Both he and Sec had been bold when they were attached to Father, but going underground somehow disoriented them and made them passive. Malý especially was a pain in the neck.

We were going to Nové Město to wait for a contact man who would bring us to Father. Soška came to escort our caravan to the next stop, a one-room hunting cottage in Bohdalov, where he had arranged for us to stay for a day. All night long we chased shadows, unable to find the cottage, while I grew increasingly desperate and angry, since it was only Soška and I who were really looking; Sec and Malý just followed along grumpily until dawn, when we finally came upon it. The owner, a man named Jan Pliczka, was an official in the Protectorate bureaucracy, an eye-catching figure in an impeccable hunting costume, complete with a matching hat that he never took off and a shirt whose monogram he lovingly stroked in one of the cottage's four mirrors. Each time he addressed one of us, Pliczka pulled himself up to his full height, erect as a sea horse, but every part of his face, including his ears, moved ceaselessly. His eyebrows worked furiously while we exchanged small talk. His nostrils waved like antennae. His pursed lips agitated in big semicircles over his teeth. When he was finished talking, he bit the air noiselessly and aired his molars while listening to the reply.

Pliczka's cottage stands out in my memory as the symbol of a miserable period in the underground. For over a week we waited, Soška, Malý, Sec, and I, for the contact man who would bring us to Father. We did not dare make a fire, for the little building was supposed to be uninhabited. During the nights, we stayed in its single room with one of us keeping guard in the freezing darkness. Every morning about five we had to go to the forest and freeze outdoors for the rest of the day. Finally, Váhala came from Prague with an alarming explanation as to why Father had left us stranded at the cottage.

"You can't go to Prague," Váhala said. "Stay put until your father can figure out the next move. Some terrible things are happening."

Father had held his September 11 staff meeting with his four associates: the Sázava men—Ouředník and Jiříkovský, Císař Fireman, and Koreš, along with a fifth man, Váhala himself. Two days later the Gestapo killed Ouředník and arrested Jiříkovský. It happened this way: The Gestapo had gone to Císař Fireman's apartment to arrest him, but instead of their intended victim they found Ouředník, who happened to arrive there at the same time. The Germans shot and killed Ouředník, whom they could not immediately identify. Finding his address in his pockets, they went to search his quarters. There, again fortuitously, they collided with Jiříkovský, who was coming to Ouředník's house with some messages. Jiříkovský managed to swallow some of the messages before his capture, but not the one mentioning Rast'a, who was of course Rastislav Váhala, Father's liaison to the Communist Party and trade unionists—the sober, composed man before me.

"Jiříkovský is being tortured," Váhala reported grimly, "but so far he hasn't told them who 'Rast'a' is."[17]

Císař Fireman had gone underground—we found out later that he escaped capture only for another month. All the safe houses Father had used, the places I was headed for as I followed his tracks to Prague, were now dangerous traps because Jiříkovský, who knew about them, was still in the hands of the Gestapo. The entire Prague section of our organization was shattered, but Father was still, as the Germans phrased it, "at large."

"I talked to him only a few days ago in the woods," Váhala assured me. "He's being guarded every moment."

That night I stood watch near the window, searching the emptiness, trying to think beyond the wild, soundless percussion in my temples and chest. We could do nothing now but wait. But not in the cottage. It was only a matter of time before one of us would be spotted.

"My days are numbered, my boy," Pliczka said as we left, reaching his tongue toward an imaginary fly. "The Gestapo may be looking for me every

17. Jiříkovský never revealed Váhala's identity and managed to survive in prison until the end of the war. He later became staff captain for state public security and joined the Communist Party.

hour. I must be wary. They know men like me are the backbone of the resistance." So that Father's next courier could send us a message, I gave Pliczka the address of a gamekeeper who had been bringing us food. To my amazement, he wrote down the address in a little book which he kept in his overcoat along with his recent letters, all the while grimacing madly and expatiating on the likelihood that he would be captured. Pliczka later claimed he had served as a reserve intelligence officer in the army, though the only intelligence he was ever trusted with, so far as I know, was this address. "Don't ask me my real name," he said in parting. "Though I don't want to be rude, one can't be too careful." But he had forgotten that the day I met him he pulled out a letter from the file in his overcoat that showed his full name, even his middle name, and his address, along with Váhala's true name, which otherwise I would not have known.

Father meanwhile was making his dangerous way back toward me. Having nowhere to sleep near Prague after all the arrests, he was trying to get back to the Bohemian-Moravian hills with his aide, Koreš. Here, I supposed, we would continue waiting together for the weapons drop.

I was hoping to stay in Krásné with the Giant, whom Soška was to contact, but somehow the Giant never received our password. I stood in his blacksmith shop, describing Soška every way I could think of without using his name, saying, "Surely you must have met him." No matter what I said, the Giant would answer flatly, "There's some mistake." When I despaired and was turning away, he looked at me appraisingly from the corner of his eye and said, "You can stay." As for Sec, he took him at once, waving me off with the assurance that he had an excellent shelter for him and would give him the best care he could ever hope for.

I left Malý in Křižanov, where he gravely informed me that he would pass up the opportunity to join Father and would return instead to his original shelter. "I'm so sorry we won't be working together," I said, my heart suddenly lighter. We were not fond of each other, but we had always been courteous. When I returned to the Giant, an irate message was waiting for me from Sec. Perhaps he, too, might decide to go off by himself. The "excellent" shelter had turned out to be a wet zemljanka with our friends the Soviets.

In the Giant's storage room, I settled down on a pallet next to a cradle the baby had outgrown. It calmed my nerves to rock the cradle with my toe and count the casualties of the last months while I waited for some word from Father.

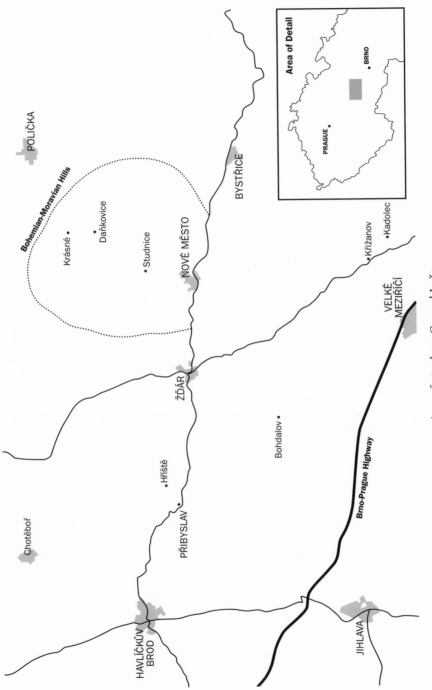

Area of attack on General Luža

VII

The mild, hesitant September had turned into the worst October anyone could remember. From a distance, the rain seemed a blue-gray mist hanging day after day over the low Moravian hills, but in fact it was a stinging, almost freezing downpour that by five o'clock buried the forest paths in black night and numbed the faces and legs of the two travelers. The men appeared to be a father and son, well-dressed, by the village standards of Hříště, though it was hard to tell because their pants and sleeves were drenched and sticking to them. They must have come a long way with their large briefcases and knapsacks. In spite of the cold whipping their backs, their steps were deliberate and weary as they opened the door to Jan Votava's tavern, trying not to let their shoes soil the clean wooden floor.

"Good evening," the young man greeted Votava. "The mayor told us this might be a good place to stop and dry off. We came from Chotěboř and we're completely soaked."

"Certainly, Gentlemen," said Votava, glad to break the loneliness of the afternoon. "I'll light the oven and warm it up in here. You can stay as long as you like. I have a room if you want to spend the night, but only one. If you need a room each, you and your father should have stopped in Přibyslav."

The two guests looked at each other, pleasantly amused that someone should take them for blood relatives.

"Would you like to see our identity cards?" the young man asked.

Votava raised his palm in a casual gesture of refusal. "Just put your wet things on these hangers and sit here next to the stove," he said. "My daughter will make you some tea."

Marie Němcová lived above the one-room tavern with her father and her young son. Her husband was somewhere in a Gestapo prison. The two arrivals were grateful for the tea. They took off their shoes and drained the water out of them. The older man put his boots and wet Hubertus next to the heater and wrung out his socks. He took out a map as he sipped the tea. "We are looking for the best way to Olešná," he said.

At the municipal hall not far away, Jaroslav Honza, the mayor of Hříště, was also ending a monotonous day when he spotted an acquaintance, Josef Navrátil, a Czech gendarme from Přibyslav who had come to Hříště to buy some black market milk.

"What's new with you, Honza?" the gendarme asked.

"Absolutely nothing. All this rain keeps things quiet. Two travelers stopped in to ask where they could go to get dry. That was the total of my new things today."

"Strangers? Where?"

"I sent them to Votava. But I checked their identity cards. They're all right."

"I'll go have a look at their cards, anyway," Navrátil replied. "The Germans are always complaining that we don't do enough. I want to show them a little activity." He started out, but in a little while he was back.

"Let me use your phone," he said. "Since there are two of them there, maybe I ought to call the station in Přibyslav and get some fellows to go with me."

At Votava's tavern, the young man had spread his pullover and shirt on the back of his chair and set the chair against the chimney. The older man put his bare feet on a wooden bench that had absorbed the heat. "This is such good tea. Could we possibly trouble you for another cup?" Then, glancing at Marie, he said, "We feel almost at home here, my friend. Please excuse us for relaxing this way. We've had a long trip."

Seeing that it was still raining steadily, the visitors inquired about spending the night, but then they said, "Well, no. We'd really like to get to Olešná this evening. Our things are almost dry. We'll just go on." They chatted a few more minutes with Votava, who sat with them in front of the stove while they finished their second cups. The room was by now warm and cheerful. The young man waved his shirt in the air to dry it a little more before buttoning it over his white ribs.

Only Votava saw the tavern door burst open. As if the gust that followed had blown them in, three gendarmes were suddenly inside, their pistols pointing at the strangers.

"Welcome, Gentlemen," said Votava reflexively, not yet appreciating that the men were holding guns.

"Hands up!" one of them barked. The gendarmes bounded across the room, making the floorboards squeal. The young man froze in astonishment. The older man, his back to the door, seemed not to have heard.

"HANDS UP!" the gendarme roared, only about four feet now from the men. Votava sprang back from his chair and instinctively retreated to the side wall. The older man's eyes opened wide, but he did not look behind him. Then he jumped up and turned in one agile movement, his right hand coming out of his pocket at the same instant with a Browning. He fired at the gendarmes and would have shot a second time when the revolver jammed. But it was already too late, for even as he lunged toward his targets, poppy-colored splotches were appearing on his shirt. "Jesus! Mary! What's happening?" Votava shouted. But no one heard him. The bullets from three guns tattooed the man's big body—eight, nine, ten deafening shots. He fell heavily on the chair Votava had just left, pushing it aside as he crashed to the floor. The three gendarmes, their guns lowered, then stood motionless and a little awestruck, looking through the smoke at the fountain of bright arterial blood spurting from one of the holes in the man's chest. After perhaps a full minute of spell-like silence, one of the gendarmes moved to check the body. It was then that the sound of the man's last breath reached Votava through the smoke—a deep, untroubled sigh of letting go.

No one saw the younger man run out. Though he, too, had been shot twice, he made it across the road and took out through a field. He somehow got over a high wire fence but, once on the other side, stood in a puddle of his blood and could go no farther. He looked one last time at the starless sky with its indifferent rain, jammed his revolver firmly into one side of his head, and fired so that the explosion blew his brains and part of his skull out the other side. His pursuers were met in the road by a villager breathlessly reporting that a man had shot himself in the field. The gendarmes soon saw that they were to be deprived the satisfaction of a capture, being able only to take possession of the man's body and the useless mess that was his head.

The police doctor came from Přibyslav to examine the bodies, and two Gestapo arrived from Jihlava, none of them taking much notice of Votava, who remained in the room, staring mutely at the runnels of blood staining the floor from the stove to the door. The corpses were taken out and brought to the fire station. The doctor gave a Gestapo officer a sack and a list of the effects: the young man had three or four hundred crowns with him, an identity card, and an army-issue gun. The older man had been carrying seven thousand crowns; two pistols; a notebook with an entry that did not make much sense to the doctor; the beginning of an essay in which the dead man had written, "Life without freedom has no meaning"; a French book about guerrilla warfare, some hundred pages of which the man had translated in a neat binder; and a copy of the *Czechoslovak Resistance.* There was an identity card, too, with the name signed in small, precise script: Václav Musil.

One of the Gestapo men went through the things carefully, then packed them up and drove away. But a few minutes later, when Votava and his daughter were cleaning up the floor, the door opened again. The Gestapo man returned to the stove and with a pleased expression picked up the mountain boots that were still not entirely dry. "I think I can wear these," he said to no one in particular as he left. Nothing then remained of the strangers except a green Hubertus heaped in the corner of the empty room.

Because there was company for lunch at the Hálas' house, a few baked apples had been added to the rabbit. "Aunt," whispered Hála's young daughter to the woman putting turnips in the plates, "remember." The woman sent the little girl a knowing wink and, sliding her turnip spoon under an apple, deftly slipped it on the child's dish in place of a turnip. Mrs. Hála would not have reproved the aunt and, anyway, she was too busy listening to her guests to notice. "I pray every night that they'll get here soon," the lady visitor was saying. "So many searches. Every day. Every little town—someone arrested or shot."

"You know, they got General Luža," said the man.

The name came to her slowly, as if it had risen from her own thoughts, and she believed for a moment that she herself had placed her husband's name on the visitor's lips. "Somewhere near the Bohemian border," the man continued. "Or that's what I heard. You know how these things are—

you can't be sure. What they're saying is that some Czech gendarmes—collaborators—cornered him in an inn and just blasted him away," he said, gesturing lightly with his fork. "I guess that's better than turning a man like that over to the Gestapo to be skinned like this rabbit."

The aunt looked down and saw that she had dropped the turnip spoon into the pitcher of tea where it was trailing a tiny stream of oil. She fished it out and began circling the table with the pitcher, filling glasses. Mercifully, no one seemed to be paying any attention to her. Though she could not feel the cold pitcher in her hands, she was not spilling the drink. She realized that she must be in some sort of shock. She wondered if the blessed trance would last until she had finished serving the meal and could leave the room without attracting notice.

For over a week, I could not be certain that the man shot in Hříště was Father. Váhala came to me on October 6 with the news that the Gestapo reported Koreš and a man carrying the identity card of Václav Musil had been killed. "There has been no positive identification of Luža," Váhala said. "You don't know for sure until you know. It wouldn't be the first time your father's death was reported falsely." But I did not let myself hope. I received the confirmation around the eleventh. The bodies of Koreš and Father had been loaded on a truck and taken to Gestapo headquarters in Brno. While Váhala was telling me about the shooting, Father was already being cremated and his ashes put into the Gestapo's storage.

I later pieced together what had happened. When Father was staying near Prague, nobody knew his hideout except his adjutant, Josef Koreš, and a man called Karel Müller who was the contact man between Father and the others in the organization. With no direct communication, it took some time before Father learned that Ouředník had been killed on September 13 and Jiříkovský had been arrested. The Germans did not know that Luža was in the vicinity of Říčany and, in fact, believed he was hiding somewhere in Moravia or Slovakia. But they were increasing their activities in the border area, making many searches, watching some of Father's collaborators. To make matters worse, a Gestapo informant visited Mrs. Ouředník, and a day or so later the widow was arrested—this was the meaning of the note in Father's diary that the police doctor had not understood. So Father decided to get out of the area at once and head back toward Bohdalov, where I was waiting. Father, together with Koreš and Müller, started out at midnight on September 29. About two in the morning they stopped in a village where

Koreš had been promised a safe house, but as the government patrols were all around, Koreš was refused the shelter. They continued to the next village, where Koreš had a friend. This man, too, was frightened because of the searches and increased danger from the Gestapo. He reluctantly allowed the three men to stay only one night in his stable, gave them something to eat, and sent them on their way. They next went to Kácov, a small town where Koreš had been promised still another shelter in a farmhouse. First Müller went to talk to the farmer while Koreš and Father waited in the forest; he was turned down. Then Koreš went to explain to the farmer that their situation was desperate and they would only stay two or three days. Finally, Father joined the discussion, telling the farmer that a refusal might mean death for one or all of them. The farmer—who knew only Koreš' name, not Father's—put them in a hay shed, gave them some bread and milk, and told them they could rest a few hours and then would have to leave. At this point, Müller decided to return to Říčany to see Váhala and others and perhaps find out where there might be some other shelters. Father and Koreš continued on foot to try to reach the Bohemian-Moravian hills.

It had been raining several days when they reached Přibyslav, in the foothills. As the town had a gendarmerie station, they did not think it wise to stop there but continued another two or three miles to Hříště. By this time, they had walked some fifty miles. They had no contacts in Hříště, but since their identity cards were good, they thought they could risk going to an inn. They were now about eighty miles from Prague, out in the more lax countryside. As they made up their minds about where to go, they saw the municipal hall and decided to ask for directions.

It was apparently their bad luck that the mayor they spoke to later happened to see a gendarme from Přibyslav, a station which had a reputation for its eagerness to serve the Germans. The mayor, Honza, in the first place should not have mentioned the presence of travelers to any gendarmes, even informally. Gendarmes were obliged to see that the identities of strangers were checked, else they were vulnerable to some terrible reprimand. In this case, the two men's cards had been checked, and that was all that was required from either the mayor or the gendarmes. The fault for the assassination of course lay with the three Czech gendarmes, Josef Navrátil, Stanislav Kunderka, and Bohuslav Mečíř, who were eager to exercise the authority delegated to them by their German masters. No thoughtful Czech patriot in those last months of the war, or any time for that matter, would go out of his way on a rainy night to double-check the identities of men who had already been inspected by the mayor and who gave no cause for suspicion. Finally, I have no explanation as to why the gendarmes burst into the tavern with their guns ready. Neither they nor the Gestapo who were called after the shooting were aware that the barefoot man in front of the stove was General Luža—that was ascertained only when the photo files in Brno were consulted. The normal procedure would have been for the gendarmes to greet Votava, approach the travelers courteously and ask to see their papers. Since Father and Koreš had perfectly acceptable identity cards, they would readily have yielded them for inspection, and that would have been the end of it. The gendarmes might have stopped to have a cup of tea themselves and commiserate with the strangers about the dismal weather before going home to supper with their families.

The three gendarmes and the mayor received rewards from the Germans ranging from two to three thousand crowns apiece. Realizing the unpopularity of their feat among their fellow Czechs, they gave the money to charity. They also got a letter of thanks from the commanding officer of gendarmerie in Nové Město, who noted their extraordinary achievement in acting against "the enemies of the Reich."

On April 10, 1945, the Brno office of the Gestapo received orders from Berlin to dump Father's ashes somewhere on a road. In a few days the Gestapo headquarters would be liquidated and Brno would be occupied by the Red Army. Nevertheless, the Gestapo dutifully filled two paper bags with Father's ashes, drove out to a road where they dropped them, and returned the empty urn to storage, as if they had nothing more pressing to do in these final hours before the German defeat. I would hardly believe this detail had I not seen documented copies of the Gestapo's bizarre order and a subsequent report that the assignment was carried out by two officers whose names are mentioned. After the war, we received the hollow urn.

When it was clear that Father was dead, I reported the news to Svatoň, who was staying in nearby Proseč with Soška and Grňa.

"I want to kill the Přibyslav gendarmes," I told Svatoň, "not just for Father's sake, but as a warning to all the other lickspittles who are so quick to do the Germans' bidding."

Svatoň nodded. "Every member of that station. And the quisling mayor Honza as well. I'll write out the order. You'll be the commanding officer of the execution party."

Father and Grňa had generally opposed this sort of exemplary mass assassination in the past. The resistance, Father thought, was not supposed to be in the business of terrorism but was instead a force against terrorism. Nevertheless, both Grňa and Štainer were all for wiping out the Přibyslav gendarmerie. I wanted Nikolaj Bachmutsky with me on the strike. Father had appointed him partisan commander of all the Soviet war prisoners in the Bohemian-Moravian hills. He had been a fervent admirer of Father and wanted to avenge his murder. And most important, he was my best friend and I trusted him completely. If Nikolaj were with us, we could carry the whole thing off. He thus gathered a group of eight Soviets for the action, including all the comrades in the zemljanka who knew my father, and a medic in case some of us were wounded. To this group we added four Czechs: myself, Sec, the Gypsy, and Adolf Šedý. We were twelve stout-hearted men, but we had practically no weapons. All of us together had only a few pistols and a handful of bullets, whereas the gendarmes were armed with carbines. We would have to avoid any sort of shootout at all costs and count on seizing the guns of the gendarmes for the trip back.

As we began thinking through the logistics of the strike, our immediate problem was that none of us had ever been to Přibyslav. We didn't have the slightest notion of where to find the gendarmes. We asked the Giant, who had never been there either, to explore the town on his bicycle, since he was still living legally and able to move about. He made a map for us showing the location of both the mayor's house and the gendarmerie. Thus we set out from the village of Daňkovice at about 10 P.M. on October 25. We had thirty miles to go. Around midnight, we encountered our first citizens' patrol, fortunately only a couple of kids. "Who are you? Why are you out here?" they asked. I started shouting at them in my Czech-accented German, hoping they would assume we were some sort of authorities and not report that they had seen a strange, small army near the hills. We continued on our way until about five in the morning, when we stopped near the edge of the woods at Račín. The Soviets were booming like fieldpieces as usual, shouting back and forth in Russian as they went through the sleeping forest. I reminded them a dozen times of the patrols all around. Under no circumstances would I try to keep going during the day when we were sure to be noticed. The twelve of us together looked like some pan-Slavic volleyball team roving the backwoods. So we waited in the forest the whole day, nibbling our rations, too excited and uncomfortable to sleep. It was cold, so cold that I urinated only blood.

As we approached Přibyslav the next day, I sent Sec and Adolf ahead to scout our path. So long as we could surprise them at the gendarmerie, we had a chance. If they managed to call for other gendarmes or, God forbid, the German police from Jihlava, then we were lost because we had nothing to fight with. At about 7 P.M., Sec and Adolf reported that the gendarme station was in the town square, and as was the custom in Czechoslovakia, the whole population was out promenading before dinner. We would have to stay put until the street cleared. Svatoň's order stated that Nikolaj and I would execute Mayor Honza while the rest of our party killed the gendarmes. I liked having military orders to follow, even if the military was somewhat makeshift. But the Gypsy and I realized that as soon as the mayor was hit in Hřiště, there would be calls for help to the Přibyslav gendarme station, putting the whole area on alert. We decided our main mission was to get the gendarmes, and we would shoot the mayor afterward if we had time.

The station was located in a house, identified only by a piece of paper taped above the bell with "Gendarmerie" scrawled in ink. One of us would have to go alone to knock on the door. As we debated who would do it, shifting our weight back and forth on our suddenly colder feet, Nikolaj crossed the square and rang the bell. A clock somewhere was chiming eight. The owner of the house lived with his family on the first floor; the gendarmerie station was upstairs. When the landlord opened the door, he was confronted with Nikolaj's pistol. Two of the Russians stayed outside to stand guard. The rest of us went in, a few at a time, and ordered the owner to take us to the station above. We knew that the station was locked and only one gendarme—his name turned out to be Jiří Hörner—was inside, for we had seen Kunderka and another member of the station go out on patrol. As luck would have it, my main target, Navrátil, had already gone home.

"Who is it?" Hörner called when we knocked.

"Vokurka," came the answer. Hörner opened the door and faced our three pistols. Sec cut the phone lines, and the others tied Hörner's hands while I talked to the landlord.

"Gendarmes from this station killed two Czechs for no reason and without any orders to do so, merely in the hope of pleasing their German bosses. Now we are going to kill them, but nothing will happen to you if you follow my instructions. Go in your apartment and stay there with your family, no matter what you hear. Don't open your door. Don't come near us or we'll shoot you, too. If you report anything after we leave, we'll send our people after you." Then, taking his key, I locked him and his son in their apartment.

I went to check on the Russians standing guard, to see if anyone had tried to enter. An off-duty gendarme from some other town, a visitor, was strolling about with his dog. I avoided his glance, but the fool accosted me anyway. "What are you people doing here?" he asked. "What is your business here?"

Many Czech gendarmes did everything in their limited power to soften the occupation. But the members of the Přibyslav gendarmerie and the man before me were of another type: stolid, obtuse, and arrogant creatures of the provincial bureaucracy, much impressed by authority, both that which they were obliged to follow and the authority that they themselves were singularly entitled to exercise as part of the German security apparatus. This man—his name, I found out, was Karel Sojka—was quite pleased with himself as he stood inspecting me with his chin stuck out. I moved close to him and pressed my revolver into his stomach. "Thanks to your officious meddling," I said, "you'll have to come inside and see for yourself what we are doing."

So far we had apprehended only two people, neither of whom was one of the assassins, and time was flying. Mečíř, the head of the station and one of Father's killers, lived nearby, so we brought Hörner to his house. "If you signal him in any way," we warned Hörner, "we'll empty our guns into both your ears." Hörner rang the bell as he was instructed, and when Mečíř opened a second-story window, Hörner shouted to him, "You'd better come down to the station right away. Some Germans have come from Jihlava."

When Mečíř arrived and saw that he had walked into a trap, he pressed his lips together and stared ahead of him impassively.

"You know why we're here, don't you?" I asked him.

"I'm a good Czech," he answered coldly. "I've always been a good Czech."

Just then, Kunderka returned from his patrol. I was taken aback by his youth. "We're here to avenge the killing of the two patriots," I said. "Were you one of those who did the shooting?"

"Why, yes," he answered insolently and then looked at me with a smirk, as if to say, "What are you going to do about it?"

I thought I was prepared to deal with someone pleading for his life or lying to escape blame. But I had not expected the truculent, dismissive attitude exhibited by all of the gendarmes except Mečíř. The smug little twits thought nothing could possibly happen to them, that they had been anointed by the Nazis. Sojka, the man I had brought in from outside, even boasted that he used to be a member of an extreme rightist party. They all denied getting any reward from the Nazis. Not one expressed the least remorse, even fake remorse, and all of them put the blame for the killing on Honza, saying that when Honza reported the presence of travelers, they had no choice but to go and check them out.

"So why didn't you check them out?" I asked. "Their cards were OK. If you had asked to see them, that would have been the end of it." They only shrugged in reply.

"Do you know what's awaiting you?" I asked Mečíř.

"I know," he replied. "Just get on with it."

There was nothing left for us to do but execute them all, even the three who had not been at Votava's tavern. If we left anyone behind, he would call to report us, and within one hour every gendarme station in the Bohemian-Moravian hills would be alerted that a gang of assassins was retreating from Přibyslav. Up until the last, none of the gendarmes except Mečíř expected that he would be shot. The men were so used to being the local authorities that they continued to talk to us with their supercilious tone even while the Gypsy and Nikolaj lined them up facing the cellar stairs where they would fall down the steps and into a niche in the corner.

We had given some thought to the operation. We had to kill each one with a single shot, to minimize the noise. As I did not relish the idea of being their personal executioner, I was relieved that Nikolaj and the Gypsy had the balls to do the actual shooting. The Gypsy held each one by the shoulders, I think, while Nikolaj, a swatch of hair falling over his forehead, pointed the muzzle of his gun at the base of each skull and fired, sending the four men crashing one by one down the cellar stairs—Hitler's Kisses, but not, for once, from Hitler's men. "Fast, fast, fast," I urged, as the medic went down to shoot each of them once more in the head, just to be sure the thing was done.

I was the last one to leave the station. Before I closed the door, I grabbed a piece of paper from the desk and wrote a parting message: THIS IS WHAT HAPPENS TO THOSE WHO FIGHT AGAINST OUR RESISTANCE. THESE PEOPLE KILLED RESISTERS AND SUFFERED A JUST PUNISHMENT. The same distant clock was chiming nine as I ran down the stairs and sprinted past the landlord's still-locked door.

Our plan had been to get the mayor next, but the Gypsy and I thought better of it. The bodies in the gendarme station would be discovered as soon as someone came to investigate the severed telephone connection. All the gendarmes from there to Nové Město and beyond would be alerted, and the Gestapo might even send search parties radiating out from Přibyslav. We had to get as far away as we could in a hurry. If we killed the mayor in Hříště, the Gestapo would know the direction of our retreat. The Soviets were warming to their task and wanted by all means to kill the mayor, but after much excited argument, I prevailed. We went in the opposite direction from Hříště, back to Račín, and then took an indirect route through the forest, going as fast as we could in order to cover the thirty miles before daylight.

When we got to Dářsko, an artificial lake in Moravia, we ran into two men robbing a tobacco shop. "We know who you are," I lied. "If you say one single word to anyone about meeting us, we will come back and kill you. And give us some cigarettes—some of these men are smokers." We made it back in about seven hours, congratulated each other, and parted company, thinking ourselves very lucky. The whole sixty-mile trip had taken us thirty-two hours.

We didn't realize until much later how fortunate we had been, for there was a witness who saw every one of the shootings and was going over and over the details with the Gestapo at the very moment when I returned to my shelter and fell exhausted into bed. Hörner, the gendarme who had not been among Father's assassins, survived Nikolaj's bullet and the fall down to the cellar. That is not surprising, considering that Nikolaj and the Gypsy were both amateur assassins who winced, their lower teeth protruding, as the gun was fired. Hörner must have felt himself truly shielded by God when the second bullet, fired by the medic, missed him altogether. After we all left, he rose like Rasputin from the cellar, his hands still bound, and began a futile racket at the window to get the attention of passersby. He next went to the landlord's door and there, too, banged away relentlessly, but the owner remained under our injunction to ignore everything and so refused to answer. He was discovered within the hour, however. Just as we predicted, the Gestapo then telegraphed all the surrounding gendarme stations, ordering the officials to launch an intense search in their areas for a dangerous band of armed murderers. But by this time it was after 10 P.M., considered the dead of night in the countryside, when many stations far in the hills were manned by only one person. The gendarmes who read the telegrams double-checked their station doors to make sure they were locked, and that was the extent of their antiguerrilla activity for the night. No one—no one—carried out the search order.

I slept for twenty-four hours when I returned, a deep, righteous sleep, for when one is young, all questions of justice and wrong and whether or not one should have acted are easily settled. "Up in heaven, Václav must be in a good mood, seeing how you revenged him," Sec told me. In the torture of my grief, I felt a plaintive moment of accomplishment. I had discharged my duty to Father. In my Hamlet visions, I imagined him looking down on me, smiling as he had smiled when he held my shoulders for the last time in Kadolec, happy to have such a son. The fantasy gave me a weak throb of satisfaction to throw against the tide of longing for him. Father's death had flooded me with the purest pain I would ever know, a pain that did not subside for decades.

Navrátil, the gendarme who escaped my revenge, met his end in April 1945, when the Allies bombed the Tišnov station just as he was about to take a train. Honza was put on trial after the war for providing his unsolicited report about the travelers to the Přibyslav gendarme. He was found guilty but was not given any sentence. In 1990, one of Honza's descendants, a granddaughter, I think, sought me out when I visited Přibyslav; she wanted to explain that Honza had not meant to bring harm to my father. She was just a young girl who, I see now, was trying to reconcile events. But I was taken aback by the unexpected meeting and was not responsive to her sincere gesture.

In later years I was harshly criticized in some circles for what was characterized as the indiscriminate murder of Czechs who bore varying responsibility or no responsibility for what happened to Luža and Koreš. I vigorously pointed out the exigencies of our situation when we carried out our mission, and I noted that we indirectly saved many lives in those last months of the war by putting a stop to the cooperation the Germans were getting from Czech gendarmes. In the press, in the gemots of postwar resistance gatherings, and in the wider court of public morality, I think I acquitted myself and my comrades.

There remain, however, periodic inspections of the lonely prison of my conscience, my own Spandau, where I am both the security guard and the only prisoner of an echoing fortress. When I look into the section reserved for the gendarmes, I am reassured that I don't have to deal with Hörner. He limped out, trailing drops of blood. Nor is Mayor Honza in my precincts, since I never went near him. Any time I check the rooms for the two men who gunned down my father, Kunderka and Mečíř, I can always report that the space there is perfectly clear. The sons of bitches deserved what they got, and I only wish Navrátil had shared their punishment. They might have been shooting innocent wayfarers that night in the tavern for all they knew, might have repeated the performance somewhere else if they had lived, and I have no apologies to make to them. Only Sojka, the officious visiting gendarme, shows up in Spandau from time to time, reminding me that he, too, was someone's father, forcing me to explain to him again and again that I could not have left him alive to sound the alarm.

"Why didn't you take me with you?" he asks.

"Take you with me where? How could I take a gendarme to our hideout? You were acting like a typical collaborator. Why did you boast about your fascist sympathies?"

"I didn't dream you were going to kill me," he answers.

At one time, people might have understood the anguish of these interior disputes, but they make less and less sense now, even to me. Outside is a world of people eating ice cream cones, driving in traffic, or doing homework, a world where the sight of two dogs snarling and straining at their leashes terrifies no one and means nothing in particular. The long night of the war is receding, its intimate fears and fevers of remorse yielding to the sane, restorative daylight.

News of the Přibyslav executions spread throughout the Protectorate. From this time on, the Germans could no longer depend on the gendarmerie to be their local police. The gendarmes began actively protecting resisters in many places, so that we in the underground no longer had to fear their identity checks, their patrols, their reports to the Germans on houses that seemed suspicious. Přibyslav was the first action in what became, after an initial lull, a campaign by underground fighters to capture weapons. As the Allies came closer to us, partisan strikes increased, and the gendarme stations eventually had to turn into little fortresses to protect themselves. The Přibyslav strike, which was planned solely to avenge my father, thus marked the beginning of the Czech guerrilla war that lasted until the German surrender to the Allies.

VIII

Věra was unaccustomed to walking through the forest without a path, and Vlasta, eyeing her thoughtfully, had to stop twice to let her catch up. Behind my shield of rhododendron, I saw Vlasta leave her at the clearing we designated for the meeting. More than two years had passed since the midnight when I had parted from Věra to go underground. How often in those first months, shivering under an embankment or alone in some filthy shed, I had dozed in the warmth of Věra's smile, in the softness of her thighs and breasts. My fantasies of her faded but so gradually that I hardly noticed her absence from my thoughts. Suddenly, her tense smile was real and her body under her wool coat was real, but by bringing her close to me I realized the distance that now separated us. Since being with her, I had had deeply fond experiences that left me still innocent, but not virginal. Whereas even though I avoided her searching eyes, I knew at once that Věra had been saving every part of herself for me. But that was only one small thing, one detail. I had sent for her to take a message to someone in Brno. I didn't have the insight then to realize that the assignment was a pretext for drawing her into my life, my new life. But not only my surroundings and activities had changed during our separation. A crevasse had opened up between us. To her, September 1942 had been only a moment ago; I had stroked her ear in our familiar parting caress, and now I would rush to greet her. She looked at me and saw the Radomír she thought she knew—conventional, too sensitive to hook a fish or turn aside an unwanted invitation—talking with bewildering coolness about things that hardly concerned her. She did not see that I was already a citizen of a foreign region, thinking in a private language known only to other resisters, grieving for people, dozens of people, she had never known, forgetting things I thought I would never forget, numb to scenes that would horrify her, relishing excitements the other Radomír could not have even watched. Nor could she know as we stood in the deepening, cold shadows that under my impersonal talk, I was dismayed by a tangle of emotions. A whimpering nostalgia pulled at me, tempting me with reflections of the gentle years of dinnertimes and Father and one's own pillow and her. But each fragile image splintered before I could possess it, striking against the fierce clarity of yesterday's hanging or this morning's transport of starving prisoners.

"You've changed," she said, when she could stand no more of my prattle.

"I've changed," I replied, and left it there. Even as I said it, I had a fleeting longing to press my mouth to the little triangle where her knotted scarf met the brown hair falling on her neck, for the fragrance of her. But the impulse was over before it had quite formed.

I was ready for Věra to go when Vlasta came for her, the two girls repeating their mutual exercise of sizing up. Ducking under a branch, Vlasta looked back at me, sending me an arch, patronizing, but somehow welcoming little smirk as the last visible part of her in the dusk. I left the Ostrovačice Forest deep in thought, pretending to be surprised that Věra and I had not exchanged a single word of love.

That entire autumn of 1944, in fact, was a time of letting go. By heartsinking degrees we were realizing that there would be no national insurrection. Impulsive, disjointed revolts might break out—suicidal rebellions of poorly equipped and scattered groups. But the organized, massive deathblow was a chimera. Not only were the Allies withholding heavy weapons, but by November we had already lost the only military leaders who could have used them effectively—Novák, Father, the other generals. In our own organization, Josef Císař had been captured a few weeks after Father's assassination. Now two members of the Council of Three were gone—the organization that was supposed to spearhead a revolution. When we lost a leader, we lost all his contacts, too, hundreds of supporters, suppliers, and fighters known to him alone. Císař, with his huge organization of firefighters, had been crucial in planning the insurrection, which was counting on the illegal trade unions and the Communist underground as well. The Nazi counteroffensive had thus destroyed the leadership of R3 and also dismembered the front that had coalesced around it. Every week we got further away from any national coordination of the resistance, even while we continued to talk constantly about an uprising of the whole country.

We had been overjoyed to find out that the Polish resistance was carrying out a revolt. The Warsaw Uprising began on August 1, just as the Red Army approached the Polish capital—an insurrection waged much the same as the one we were planning. I followed it for two months, my back teeth grinding during each broadcast, not understanding quite why it was failing, until its frightful conclusion on October 1, 1944, the day before Father's death. Neither the BBC nor Radio Moscow, our only news sources, reported that the Red Army coming upon Warsaw stopped its advance just across the Vistula River and watched with interest as the Nazis massacred the insurgent Poles. The Red Army refused to lift a finger to help the resisters. Only when the Soviets were satisfied that the Nazis had wiped out the insurrection did they cross the river, go into Warsaw, and start killing Germans. What did the Red Army want, after all, with a bunch of armed, probably anti-Communist fighters, following their independent leaders, who would think they owed no obedience to the Reds?

Meanwhile, right next to the Protectorate, the Slovakian uprising had begun, well organized and directed by Lieutenant Colonel Ján Golian from a military center in central Slovakia. Golian had planned to start the uprising when the Soviets reached eastern Slovakia, where he would have two divisions at hand to open up the Carpathian passes for them. However, Golian was never able to coordinate his plans with the Red Army, which changed its timetable and its point of entry into Slovakia without his knowledge. Then, weeks ahead of Golian's schedule for military action, the Germans reacted to a premature partisan strike—the Russians had been calling urgently for guerrilla actions—by ending Slovakia's puppet autonomy and occupying the country directly. To resist the German occupation, the Slovakian resistance was forced to launch the uprising on August 29, 1944, weeks ahead of time, without sufficient preparation and without Red Army support. The western Allies were sympathetic to the uprising, but as it did not take place within their zone of operation, the British and Americans refused in the end to make a significant response to the insurgents' desperate plea for arms. The Soviets were again indifferent to the fate of the rebels. Though they were pleased with the military advantage provided to them by the insurrection, they declined to send decisive help to a resistance movement whose leadership was divided between Communists and democrats.

By the end of October, the army of the Slovak National Uprising, under-equipped and hopelessly outnumbered by the Germans, had crumbled into partisan groups that continued their desperate, futile struggle until the end of the war. Golian was captured and executed.

We knew nothing then about the policies of the Allies which doomed the uprising, nor could we know that the Slovaks would sacrifice ten thousand people in that blood-drenched struggle, a campaign that damaged the Germans but certainly did not destroy their power over the country. I saw, however, that these uprisings failed, dwindling in the end into guerrilla skirmishes which, in the large scheme of the war, had little military effect.

I threw myself into resistance work, nevertheless, for in quiet hours my mind was a prison of grief. I often wondered how Mother was managing, surrounded by children and the mild company of country people. When I finally saw her for the first time after Father's death, I found her dignified, harder, and somewhat withdrawn, her energy spent in battling the pain within. Grňa had entrusted me with a sympathy letter for her. "Despite any talk of disagreements between us, Václav and I shared the same deep ideals," Grňa wrote. "He was a great man." Svatoň, too, handed me a letter, saying nothing, but delicately clearing his lieutenant colonel's throat. He had been vain about his position and attentive to his uniform when in the army. I therefore expected a short, correct eulogy, with clichés standing tall and straight inside their margins. Instead, he wrote such a full-souled expression of mourning that I mourn for Svatoň when I reread it.

After Father's death, Grňa had appointed Svatoň the military commander of the Council of Three. Svatoň in turn made the command a kind of collective military committee consisting of himself, Štainer, Robotka, and, unofficially, Soška, who was Svatoň's partner in everything—almost his alter ego. It was commonly said underground that Soška was the brain behind Svatoň, a judgment I tended to believe. Soška was certainly the smarter one, though I was put off by his charm. Svatoň was steady, a typical field commander with a high opinion of himself, but a reliable man. On October 31, 1944, I gave him a formal report about the Přibyslav action; then we discussed what everyone in our organization was talking about, the weapons we hoped to get from the Western Allies.

"Now you are General Luža," I told him. "I hope to God you are careful and use cutouts for everything."

"There was only one General Luža," Svatoň replied, staring for a moment at a scene I could not see. "Don't worry; we're being careful." Svatoň and

Soška were living near a forest outside Proseč, sheltered by a postal worker. "There's a chance the Gestapo knows about this place," he continued, "so we're going to the Iron Mountains to wait for the weapons drop. Everything is ready for the big battle."

But Svatoň's last battle was a little one, short and decisive. The next day, just as he and Soška were set to go, eight Germans with machine guns surrounded their isolated cottage. Both resisters made a run for it. Soška, who was young and athletic, broke through the circle of fire and had covered two hundred yards to the relative safety of the woods when he realized Svatoň was hit. Though he must have known it was suicide, Soška—the man I thought was callow—went back for his friend, and they were both killed.

I had come to the Bohemian border to be part of Father's staff. With both Father and Svatoň gone, there was no point in my remaining in the hills, among people who thought of me as Little Luža. In Bíteš, only Hermit, Mrs. Little Spruce, and a few others knew my real name. I was liked or disliked, tolerated or resented, but not because my father had been an important man. I discussed my plans with my smiling Cossack, Nikolaj Bachmutsky.

"I'm going back to pick up the remnants of my organization, Nick. You keep going here with your group."

He smiled. "Too bad you not finish class."

To relieve the deadening boredom of the zemljanka, Nikolaj had been offering an institute on overcoming frigidity and chastity in women, lecturing in a promiscuous jumble of Russian and Czech. The previous evening he had described, for the benefit of four of us students, the advanced Crimean technique of cunnilingus. The patient was a pear cut in half, no longer young, having lain around the zemljanka in an unaroused condition for several days. "Seed fall out is too hard," he explained, closing his eyes and concentrating on his task. "Seed have to stay in whole time." Too tall for the zemljanka, Nikolaj hunkered in a way that gave the whole demonstration a curious verisimilitude. "Hear that?" he had asked us, holding the pear up to his ear. "Pear want we get married. She having a big organism."

I was going to miss the Soviets, and promised to send Nikolaj machine guns and a girlfriend as soon as possible. I was as good as my word, for the next day in the forest near Nové Město, I heard someone whispering in Russian and saw before me a line of Soviet paratroopers—six or seven men and a girl, a medic named Rufina Krasavinova—Red Army partisans who had just been dropped. Unlike the pitiful prison escapees, they were fresh and confident in new field uniforms and carried automatic weapons, sleeping bags, and all sorts of outdoor gear. The girl's short, straight hair was slicked back from her pink forehead, and her eyes were bright, unlike the grimy, mottled faces of most of our partisans. The paratroopers were an advance detachment of the Soviet army that was on its way. As always when we had contact with the outside, I was ecstatic. I brought the paratroopers to Niko-laj, and he took them into his own zemljanka. There, without fresh air, sanitation, or privacy, where procuring an absorbent or a bit of shampoo required foresight and time, Nikolaj, jilting the pear, fell madly in love with Rufa.

Four main Soviet groups floated down to the Protectorate that fall—sixty people in all—and some were near enough to work with us. Their task was to harass the retreating Germans, slow them down, force them to tie up more and more men to protect themselves. The parachute groups gave themselves the names of their favorite Czech heroes, such as Jan Hus, or in the case of Rufa's group, Miroslav Tyrš, the founder of Sokol; but they took their orders from the Red Army and maintained communication with their commander at the front. Though I didn't realize it then, partisan activity assisted by these paratroopers—gnawing the enemy at the margins of the front—and not a massive uprising, would become the main form of the Czech resistance from November 1944 until the war's end the following May. Even as I became more and more involved in guerrilla activities, I was increasingly aware of the insufficiency of that kind of action without a coordinated attack by well-equipped military. Partisan warfare was no replacement for an armed insurrection, a truth that was eventually proved by the hapless Poles, the Slovaks, Tito's partisans in Yugoslavia, and even the Maquis in France, who were fighting under much more favorable conditions than we were.

Sec and I had been living near Proseč with a kindly old couple, pious Seventh-Day Adventists. Their diet—and ours—consisted of turnips, potatoes, and milk and cheese from their goat. For Sec, vegetarianism was famine. He was not entirely distraught, therefore, when the old man, hearing of German searches in nearby villages, asked us to leave. "You can even take the goat," he offered, "if you'll just go this minute."

Our trip back to the east was a slow hegira for, though we left the goat, Pliczka and his twitches attached himself to us along the way. "I promised your father I would take care of you as if you were my own son. From now on, you are my son," he announced, his eyes bulging emphatically for an instant before they subsided under the oscillating bluffs of his eyebrows.

"My assistant Václav and I will accompany you to Kadolec, since it is so dangerous just now in these hills, especially for a man like me who is central to the resistance. We'll take our time going. After we are all settled in safe houses, I'll be able to keep an eye on you." I would have to find the safe houses, of course.

It was a great comfort to get back to familiar landscape. My little caravan finally limped into Mayor Kobylka's house, and I found a place to unload Pliczka. Eventually, he formed an underground group with Pepek near Bohdalov. By that time, to my great relief, Pliczka had forgotten that I was his son. Václav, however, remained with the Kobylkas, smitten with the mayor's sister Božena. I stood in their wedding after the war, and I ate so many koláče that I was almost sick.

I was on my way to Hermit's, going through the valley west of Pánov, when my thoughts turned to the dozens of escaped Russian war prisoners who were literally buried in the dense woods around me, living in zemljankas along the five miles of White Creek that stretched toward Javůrek. It would be a great place for an elite partisan group, since it could not be easily surrounded. The Soviet war prisoners were already trained fighters who had seen battle on the front. Their commander could be Aleš Dmitrijev, the Russian whom Štainer had fished out of the river and brought to Hermit. Within a few weeks, Aleš and I organized ten Soviets into what I called PAM 5, a group that began carrying out partisan assignments. By April, PAM 5 numbered over sixty fighters.

As for Hermit himself, I found him righteous and private as ever behind his huge moss beard—Leonardo in corduroy. "I want you to command my entire organization," I said, "if you'll get rid of that jungle on your face. Whoever heard of an underground leader that everybody in the district could describe if they glanced at him even once?" He protested this idea with his usual semaphoric terseness.

"Don't know your set up," he said, throwing his arm up to cut off the discussion. "You're the leader. You've done all the organizing." The only recruiting work Hermit had ever done was in his native city in the Sudetenland, where Czechs were a minority. Father had asked him to gather the Czechs he could reach into an underground group.

"I'm too young," I argued. "They won't take me seriously—twenty-two with no military experience. If they believe you're in back of me, they'll follow me without thinking too much about my age. I'll be your deputy, and I'll explain where all the units are." Hermit's military background was not impressive. He had no subtlety and talked to me with such directness and simplicity that I was sometimes not sure whether he was addressing me or Rek, his cherished dog. But he and I loved each other. He hated making decisions and was no leader when it came to initiative, yet men trusted him because they could see that he was good-hearted and honest. We named our organization "General Luža" and made our headquarters in a hut we built in the woods. We were relatively safe there because the local ranger would warn us of any impending danger, and we had sentries and patrols guarding us as well. Soon I was in touch with everyone: Kravka, Hlaváček, Mrs. Little Spruce—who still put me up whenever I was in Javůrek—Hála the miller, our old doctor, and the gendarme Weingart, who had warned Father that the Germans were about to search Mrs. Little Spruce's neighborhood.

In a tunnel near Tišnov, the Germans had built a new plant for making airplane engines. Called the Diana factory, it was staffed by slave laborers the Germans had mobilized from the occupied countries. With our help, twenty Yugoslavs escaped from this plant and joined General Luža, followed by some Czechs, Slovaks, Estonians, and a Belgian. If we ever received the hoped-for arms, our full membership could come together out of the surrounding villages and form quite an army.

Meanwhile, Nikolaj and the Red Army paratroopers in the Bohemian-Moravian hills had also begun making isolated partisan attacks. He settled his band of about thirty in a place crisscrossed by gendarme stations—a sort of no-man's-land, since each of the three stationmasters assumed that the area was being watched by one of the others. Without rifles, grenades, or machine guns, the Czechs among them were at first armed only with hatred of the Nazis. There were more Nazis than ever—fifty thousand German troops in the Protectorate at the end of 1944, retreating from the Allies. Nikolaj started by attacking their transports. German cars were fueled by alcohol distilled from potatoes. It was quick work to get into the distilleries and empty the storage tanks. Practically all the motor vehicles on the roads were German—everyone else walked or rode bicycles. The Russians laid steel nails on the highways, a trick they taught all of us. Or they'd wait near a road and place a stolen steel cable across it when they saw a truck coming. The truck—invariably a German transport—had to stop, whereupon the attackers killed the occupants and took their weapons. The partisans in the hills were also raiding all the gendarme stations they could get to, so that soon they had a good store of small arms and ammunition—not sufficient fire power to risk any sort of confrontation with machine guns, but fine for

going after a group of two or three Germans on the road, a ranger station
where there might be hunting weapons, or a larger gendarme station. At first
the terrified Czech gendarmes raised their elbows high away from their side
arms as soon as they saw the partisans and began reciting the ages of their
children and the names of their relatives whom we might know. But when
they learned that we only wanted their guns, they began handing them over
without hesitation and went on their way. The Germans finally had to take
away their carbines so they wouldn't lose them to the resistance.

We took blankets, shoes, and supplies wherever we could get them, and
sometimes we found ourselves with strange booty. Once in the Zhoře wood-
land we killed a few German soldiers and came into a dismaying inheritance:
sixteen horses, forty-seven cows, fifteen oxen, and no less than two hundred
sheep, all hungry, all nervous because of the shooting, and making a din you
could hear in Vienna. The Germans had brought this livestock battalion
with them as they retreated from Slovakia and were marching the animals
through Moravia, presumably to the German border. As our querulous prisoners were turning the forest into a barnyard, we distributed them to the
villagers with the understanding that they would slaughter some of the cows
and provide us with meat.

By December 1944, one month after I had returned from the hills, my
group controlled the countryside between Křižanov and Brno—the area of
Křižanov, Domašov, Velká Bíteš, and Tišnov, down to Říčany and Zastávka.
Still, I continued organizing, and by the spring of 1945, when we were engaged in all-out guerrilla fighting, General Luža had 856 active members,
not counting the hundreds of people such as the forest ranger near my headquarters who assisted us with food, shelter, supplies, or silence, without nec-
essarily being attached to a group.

General Luža was one group within the Council of Three, the organization founded by Father. R3's headquarters were in a forest house east of
Velká Bíteš. Until November 1944, the largest R3 group numerically had
been Svatoň's, covering both sides of the Bohemian-Moravian hills; but as
Svatoň kept his membership lists in his head, we were never able to reorga-
nize his people after his death. My group, General Luža, then became the
largest and most important element of the Council of Three. We were the
best situated, our center being the region from Křižanov to Brno, just where
we expected the Russians to come through. Other groups attached to the
Council of Three were contiguous to mine and sometimes overlapped. We

could not communicate with each other by radio and were trying to be secretive; therefore, none of us had a clear idea of what the others were doing.

If General Luža was the most important element in the Council of Three
by the beginning of 1945, R3 in turn was both the largest and most significant organization in the Czech resistance. In trying to describe that resistance and place us within it, a simplistic image comes to mind of a map
of the Czech lands spread over with trees—anti-Nazi trees. They grew up
spontaneously, offshoots of bigger trees or remnants of forests that the Germans had destroyed early in the occupation. At first these saplings were in-
significant, but as the war continued, they grew and multiplied, becoming
as formidable as the original clusters they replaced. We learned only after
the war how many trees there really were: 7,500 active resistance fighters
engaged in military or quasi-military activities, each one using or having at
his disposal a personal weapon.[1] The men were distributed in 120 groups.
In addition to these fighters, there were thousands of supporters such as
Mrs. Little Spruce who were outside of any structure.

The Council of Three, we may say, represented all the conifers, reaching
from the Slovakian border far into Bohemia, touching the Austrian border
in the south and reaching to the German borders in the north and west, but
thickest in the area from Brno to Prague. Not only could R3 summon more
fighters than any other resistance structure, but it was recognized by Beneš
as the leading element of the home resistance. By virtue of having sheltered
several parachute groups who were dropped with transmitters, it had regular
communication with London. And it was in a crucial geographic position in
the path of the advancing Red Army.

Just as every conifer is a spruce, fir, hemlock, or what have you, everyone
in R3 was part of some subgroup—General Luža, Tau, Delta—any one of
ten groups. Though Štainer and Robotka were the military leaders of the
Council of Three, they themselves had no army and led no fighters. Their
job was to represent and coordinate, insofar as any coordination was possible, the member organizations gathered and commanded by people like
Hermit and me.

To carry our tree metaphor a little further, we can say that General Luža
represented the pines, the most numerous conifers, covering the countryside
around Brno, the secondary roads, and all those communities in the path of

1. After the war, each person who could prove his contribution to the resistance was registered as eligible for certain emoluments. My figures come from this postwar counting.

the Soviets. Just as there are white pines, longleaf pines, etc., General Luža was eventually organized into twelve detachments, each with a leader under my command. Kobylka, for example, was the head of a detachment, Owl, centered at Kadolec; there was another detachment in Brno headed by Gustav Kristek, another near Pánov, and nine others, spread over forty-eight localities.

By far my most efficient detachment was Aleš' PAM 5, the group of Soviets holed up in White Creek Valley. Unlike the farmers and working men in my organization who were told to remain invisible in their villages and go on with their normal lives until the call came for mobilization, the PAM fighters in their zemljankas had nothing to do all day. They loved planning and carrying out any sort of action, and they approached these projects not only fearlessly but gleefully. Taking care of these sixty partisans took up most of my time. I had to find cigarettes for them, control their natural rowdiness, and keep them busy, for having been away from their regular army units for two or three years, they had become unaccustomed to discipline. They ran me ragged.

Feeding the Soviets was always a problem. The villagers cooked most of their meals, but it was up to the organization to get the provisions. The zemljankas had no refrigeration and no storage space. Food that we could procure tended to come in bulk quantities, but we couldn't feed them the same thing every day for a month until the bulk was used up. The Soviets were intense eaters. One of our suppliers was a large grocery cooperative called B's, on the edge of Tišnov. On one trip there, according to my notebook, we took away 150 kilos of sugar (about 300 pounds), 25 kilos of noodles, a quantity of flour, lentils, and potatoes. I signed for these staples with my cover name at the time, Jáchim, promising that payment would be forthcoming after the war. I remember that the owner was quite pleased to help the partisans and kept urging me to take things I would not have requested—cookies and canned fruit. "You don't sign for these," he said. "They're gifts for your boys. God bless you." The days were over when people around Tišnov were afraid to give a lone resister even a drink of water.

The Soviets were not supposed to move from their zemljankas during the daylight hours, but it was hard to keep them out of the village at night. They were young fellows, full of vitality, and wanted to spend their energy. In a different time or place they would have been taping pinups to a factory locker or joyriding on motorbikes. I preached to them constantly to use

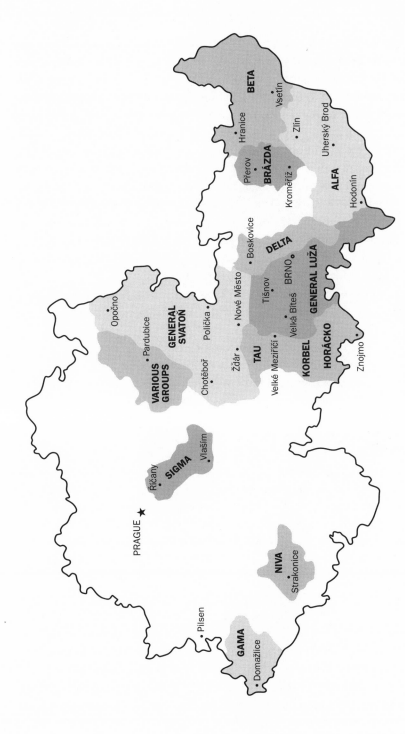

Areas in which R3 was active

judgment and discretion. One Soviet in Loňka's group, a former Soviet secret service lieutenant named Ivan, was incorrigibly reckless—visiting his
girlfriend in broad daylight, drinking in bars, coming back alone to the zemljanka in the middle of the night, and making sure despite all our warnings
that everyone he talked to knew that he was a Russian living with other Russians. How long could it be before his zemljanka was raided? Finally, Loňka
had to order his execution. It was not so much that he was endangering his
comrades. To trap such a large group, the Germans would have been obliged
to send a detachment, a conspicuous party that the villagers would notice in
time to warn the Russians. The population supporting them would have
been the real victims. Dozens of Czech men, women, and children who had
supplied them or had simply known about them would be tortured and executed because of this fool.

"Where is Ivan?" I asked a few days after the order.

"Sergej gave him the Hitler Kiss," Loňka answered. "Clean job," he observed, raising his forefinger and firing it at an imaginary neck.

Just as Aleš and Loňka were Russian commanders, the Kristek brothers were
my main Czech foremen. Karel was about thirty, young for a resister, but
already the owner of a sawmill in Ludvíkov, near Bíteš. His brother Gustav,
an architect, headed a group of resisters in Brno, all former Czech soldiers
and experienced fighters we could count on if we launched an insurrection.
He had 175 men, an impressive force—except that only 16 had weapons. It
was understood that if we got arms from abroad, Gustav would bring his
men to fight with us. The Kristeks worked as one, though their personalities
were as different as sea and desert. Despite having a wife and small children,
Karel was never slowed by fear. He was generous, lighthearted, and spontaneous, but the only thing we could absolutely rely on him for was good intentions. Gustav was more intelligent and quite dependable—a bit of a
fretter. He was constantly mulling over a marital problem that everyone else
thought was simple: his wife didn't love him.

The Kristek brothers were the backbone of my organization, connecting
me to a network of ready assistance. One of their fellows in Bíteš could offer
a safe house. Through that man, I found someone else with a couple of
trucks for transporting materials. This man in turn knew locksmiths in Domašov who would help us, and so on. I became acquainted with the Kristeks' hunchback cousin, Loucký, whom they despised, and who hated them,
along with the rest of humanity. Loucký escaped from a Grimm's fairy tale.

His jealousy of the Kristeks involved them all in a continuing cycle of petty family quarrels.

One of the Kristeks' men, a smart mouth called Sandy, was mechanical and resourceful and could make equipment work. Sandy had taken shelter with Karel Kristek, hiding not from the Germans at first, but from his wife and the job he left in a Brno cement factory. In the beginning he wasn't fond of me because I was a student, a member of the intelligentsia, and he thought we were supposed to be class enemies. I respected his skills and invited him to join us. Though there was mild tension underlying our relationship, I was eventually able to call him my friend and to depend on him routinely.

By late spring, the guerrillas in our area controlled the countryside—though not the towns—so that the Germans could not travel except in large units. When they did venture out in smaller groups, they were so nervous that even a feigned attack would send them scattering. There was, for example, an incident in Bíteš where the Germans called for the local people to surrender their horses. The conscripted horses and their owners—bewildered peasants—were all gathered in the town square with a few German military guards, waiting for the selections to be made. Suddenly someone started to shoot. "Partisans!" everyone shouted, going in all directions. In the commotion, the German commission took off. Aleš and a few of his men ran through the middle of the melee and released the horses, which were later rounded up by their rightful owners. The day Aleš saved the horses became part of the local partisan lore.

It sounds so easy, forcing a car to stop, converging on the occupants, dodging their puny attempts to protect themselves, shooting them before they were even sure what or who had attacked them—the stuff of comic books and adventure novels. The first time I saw a German dying, his chest, shoulder, and right arm obliterated, his haggard eyes watching with something like curiosity as his soft inner parts kept gushing out in spasms onto the grass, I thought I might die, too, from horror at what I had instigated. "Finish him off!" I shouted to one of the partisans, in a voice choked with urgency. The Soviet gave a grunt, the Russian equivalent of "Sure," and blasted the writhing head. The Soviets, who had seen and suffered so much more than I had, did not need to remind themselves before each attack that these bodies had either themselves tortured innocent men, women, and children, or exulted when they saw or heard about some savage act against civilians. The latest Gestapo vogue was not to arrest those sheltering a resister, but to lock the whole family in the house and then set fire to it. Still, the people we attacked were not all Gestapo; some were just young Germans who had never given an order for anyone's torture.

"You don't mind killing, do you, Nick?" I once asked Bachmutsky when he reported that he had stopped a German car and "elemented" its occupants. He stopped humming—a melancholy Cossack song I had heard him sing many times that still plays in the background of my war memories. He pointed to our new metal rattrap in the corner of the zemljanka.

"You mind to kill?" he asked. "Brother, I am soldier and officer. A soldier's job is kill, with bombs, with guns, with hands, with starve—we kill them, we win. They kill us more, they win. I am good officer; I love to kill Nazi. I protect my people."

"What about after the war? Maybe there will come a time when we'll no longer hate the Germans. Will we look back and think about the men we've liquidated?"

"I will look back and keep hate," he answered firmly, touching my elbow to reinforce his words. "No good officer think except how to kill better." He puffed up his chest, suddenly pompous. "Officer say, 'We must destroy unit, liquify traitors.' Nice words. Same shoot in brains. In peace, good officer plan for war, hope for war, pretend he hate war. What is war? War is kill Nazi. No kill, no war."

"The ones that bother me," I said, "are the Czechs forced to cooperate with Germans. A captured man whose parents or children are threatened doesn't really choose the German side when he becomes an informant. In that situation there are no really good choices."

"Right. They no choice. You no choice," he said with a shrug in his voice. "You must to kill them."

When I was not in our hut in the forest, I stayed primarily with the Homoláčs, being careful that no one, not even Hermit, knew they were sheltering me. As the autumn of 1944 hardened into winter and I hardened into the kind of leader I thought Father would value, one surprise hit above all others obsessed me. Gustav Kristek had discovered that living near him in his Brno suburb was none other than Ryšánek. Kristek conceived a delectable plan to kidnap the informer and keep him tied up in a zemljanka for the rest of the war. Having watched Ryšánek's comings and goings for several weeks, we knew his schedule for visiting his girlfriend, shopping, reporting to the Gestapo, doing his laundry. Kristek and I, together with a few aides, were prepared to hustle him into a car and put an end to his illustrious career. The kidnapping was set for March 8. This, however, was to be one of the few times after Father's death that Štainer interfered with me. "What a childish idea!" he exclaimed, when I told him and Robotka about the plan. "Ryšánek has already reported the names of people around here who are aiding the resistance. The Gestapo knows your supporters here. If they no longer have to protect his cover, they'll arrest everybody he's told them about. They'll swoop down on this area just as we are expecting the weapons drop, and the very place we have designated for the drop will be crawling with Germans." I had to admit that, for once in his life, Štainer was completely right. I called off the kidnapping.

For two people who couldn't stand each other, Štainer and I got along pretty well in the six or eight months before the end of the war. He was in the highest position he would ever have as one of the leaders of the major resistance group in the Protectorate. Štainer and Robotka had indeed inherited R3's military direction—Štainer on the western end of our forces, in Bohemia, Robotka primarily in Moravia. Both of them together were not worth Father's left foot, but they had to fill his shoes simply because there was no one else. Svatoň, Soška, Císař—men who themselves had not been equal to Father—were gone. I was too young and knew too little about the military to direct paramilitary groups. Štainer had control of several transmitters, and in the feudal ethos of the underground, where all power was decentralized, where no one could supervise anyone else and each commander required days to send a message to any other commander, whoever had any sort of advantage took control and found that others readily yielded. It seemed normal that the man who could speak for us to our government in London was our leader, and I accepted him.

We were in a revolution. A young fellow like me could declare himself "in charge" and have older veterans follow voluntarily, even though they could as easily have told me to go to the devil. With our constant burden of secrets, we all missed the security of procedure and authority, of someone else sharing responsibility, which is perhaps why we took seriously our homemade rankings and promotions. Every chain of command could be ruptured by a Gestapo raid, and in the ensuing chaos, people low in the hierarchy were pushed to the top. I was not bothered much by either Štainer or Robotka. Since their orders took weeks to reach us, they sent no more than two or three in all those months. I needed Štainer and his transmitters if I were to get weapons, and he needed me if he were to have fighters to use them. I did not know that even then Štainer was waging a subtle campaign to discredit my father.

The weeks rolled by, measured in motorcycles and cars coming down the highway from Brno. We could hear them before we could see them, and we learned to identify the Steyr, Auto Union, or Mercedes engines as they decelerated around the curves where we would be waiting. Signs began appearing on the roads in the hills: *"Achtung! Banden!"*—Attention! Partisan bands! Soon there were no more Germans driving singly or in pairs except the rare straggler from a convoy speeding terrified around the curves, a comet tail of dust and gravel in his wake.

The German response to the increased guerrilla activity was two-fold and, as usual, effective. When he realized the Nazis were losing control of the countryside, Karl Hermann Frank began frantically reorganizing the German police force, detaching special units to fight the partisans. By December 1944, even the small towns in every district had a cluster of so-called Jagd-kommandos, whose name derived from the German word for hunting, *Jagd.* As these were not large units at first, they could only control the main roads. But within a few months, towns the size of Křižanov or Bíteš had units numbering fifty. The Jagdkommandos could not stop us from attacking an isolated gendarme station or a lone supply truck; in those instances, we struck and disappeared before they knew what had happened. And they could not patrol the back roads, which remained ours. But the Jagdkommandos did keep the towns and the main transportation routes relatively safe for the German army. Moreover, because they generally had inside information, they could learn exactly where the partisans were. They were brutal when they made a raid, incinerating people who had only been marginal helpers, shooting and hanging partisans on the spot.

An even greater nuisance for us were the Vlasov troops. Stalin had his internal enemies just as Hitler did. When taken prisoner by the Germans, a Soviet could earn his release by volunteering to work as an anti-Bolshevik activist. By 1944, these renegades formed an army of some 100,000. Under the leadership of a former Soviet general, Andrei Vlasov, they fought at the side of the Germans for Russia's liberation from Stalin. Some of the Vlasovs combed the Czech villages on horseback in groups of six or eight, rooting out partisans. Others were informants helping the Jagdkommandos by posing as escaped Soviet prisoners on the Allied side. They still had their Red Army uniforms, which they made sure were filthy and torn, and they had in truth been incarcerated in German camps, so it was impossible for the Czech population to tell them apart from the Soviet ex-prisoners who were true partisans. The Gestapo might even capture them in a raid along with genuine resisters and later let them go. By the winter of 1944 the Vlasovs were all over our area. They were deadly. How could we turn away someone we thought was a starving, perhaps dying, Soviet war prisoner? But if the macerated creature we took in was a Vlasov, we were sure to be repaid with a Jagdkommando raid. At the end of the war some of the Vlasovs had a fraudulent change of heart and fought on the side of the Czechs in the Prague uprising, but that was only to ingratiate themselves with the Allies after it became evident that the German cause was lost.

None of us was immune to informers. One day I received a report from my men near Okarec, where Hašek was active. They said a woman had turned up. She was a Czech, rather young, looking for a connection to the General Luža group. She came from some distance, where another group called Hybeš was situated. Before I could respond to that information, I learned that the Soviets had taken her into their zemljanka—a serious disregard of security and an all-around idiotic move for which I angrily reproached them. We couldn't leave her there in the midst of our operation without finding out whether she was a Gestapo agent.

We had an SS uniform that Gustav Kristek had stolen from a German in Brno. I decided to stage a Gestapo raid to see what our Czech "resister" would do when confronted by a German "officer." I warned the men in the zemljanka. "Now, don't forget it's only a phony raid; don't start shooting," I told them. "Whatever we do, there can't be any shooting." The SS uniform was so tight, I could feel my face getting red as Loňka led us to the zemljanka (without a guide, I could never have found it). I made a signal to the sentry, opened the entrance to the hideout, and shouted in my best German, "All of you! Hands up! Don't touch your weapons. Come up slowly." I was making German-sounding phatic noises and trying to think of other things to say when the woman emerged. She was a pretty little thing, only about twenty-two, a girl who should have been living in a college dormitory instead of a burrow. Under the coarse material of her dress one could see high, round breasts and a nice behind. I understood why the Soviets took her into their hideout. She had cleverly told them she was carrying a child, knowing that the Russians would never harass an expectant mother; but from my vast inexperience, I judged that she was not pregnant. "Show me your identity," I said in German.

"Wait, please," she said, and calmly produced a piece of paper.

"Here is the telephone number. Please call this extension and ask for Gestapo Commissar Kren. He will explain my mission."

I unbuttoned my coat just as it was about to unbutton itself, took a deep breath, and replied in Czech, "I think I already know your mission. And as we are Czech partisans and not the SS, our mission is to root out informers like you." Even today I am astonished that such a primitive trick worked. If I had been older, I never would have tried it. If she had been older, she never would have fallen for it. I had her walk ahead of me until we were out of earshot of the Soviets and in a relatively concealed position—about a forty-five minute walk. When she turned to face me, she was still erect, but her voice was shaking.

"You didn't shoot me on the path," she said. I got out of her that she was working with another man, but she would not give me any further information. I wasn't even certain that she had been forced to become an informer. She did assure me that she had not sent any report since going into the zemljanka; therefore, if she were to be believed, the Gestapo still knew nothing of our hideout there. According to her identity card, she had the same name as my grandmother, Marta Večeřa.

She was dangerous. If she escaped, she would bring the Gestapo down on us, a big unit of machine guns swarming over the center of our operations. We all agreed she had to be executed, but nobody was rushing to get it over with. When I returned two days later, I found her still alive and lovely, enjoying her last sunshine outside the zemljanka with the sentry. She raised her eyes to mine with a brave, knowing look.

"I told Yuri to take her out and give her the Hitler Kiss," Aleš explained.

"But?"

"But he crumbled like dried up horseshit. They took a little walk, chatted—and he came back with her."

Since the Soviets had stupidly brought her into their zemljanka, I was determined that they would be the ones to deal with her. They finally shot her on the wayside between Bíteš and Tišnov, where German troops could be seen retreating in the distance. In death, she looked thirteen. Her corpse was left in the middle of the road, a piece of paper pinned to it with the penciled warning, "This is the fate awaiting all Czech traitors."

We abandoned the zemljanka she had seen, just in case she had reported it. I found out Commissar Kren indeed worked in the Gestapo in Brno; he was executed after the war. Marta, whose real name was not Večeřa but Raková, had started out as a true resister, but when she and her husband were captured by the Germans, they were forced to work as agents for the Gestapo. She had caused the deaths of scores of people, and I had to be satisfied that in putting her out of business, we had saved scores of others.

We resented the German soldiers who surrendered instead of fighting to the death, because then we had to figure out what to do with them. We would start by keeping them guarded in our shelters. Sooner or later we would be obliged to shoot them, since we had no prison camps in which to store them until the end of the war. But none of us could bring ourselves to dispatch in cold blood men who had shared our bucket in the zemljanka. If we let them go, they could lead the SS back to the area. Even if we were gone by that time, the villagers around us would bear the merciless vengeance—and at this time, the Nazis were more sadistic than ever with people who helped the partisans.

I spent a few days in a zemljanka with a captured German, a conscripted soldier from the Rhineland, not a Nazi, who proudly showed me photos of his family. He was a decent fellow. I wanted to let him go, but even if he promised never to give us away, I reasoned, he couldn't just show up again in the Wehrmacht without an explanation of where he had been. It was my duty to shoot him. After three difficult days, I made a decision. I brought him to the main highway leading to Jihlava and pointed with my pistol at his ear. "Stay on this road, but watch out for other partisans," I said. "I'm taking a big risk in trusting you not to report us. A big risk."

Though he had never failed to thank me even for the cups I handed him, this time, seeing me contemplating the risk, he merely nodded as if in a daze and moved off quickly. He stared back at the gun as he lurched down the road, perhaps expecting me to shoot him from behind. I was in a torment of anxiety for the next seventy-two hours, wondering if I had done the right thing, but when no Jagdkommandos came to exterminate us, I gradually relaxed. I was far from pleased with myself. My humane act put all the people around us in danger of being hanged, set on fire, drowned, or any of the other reprisals the Nazis were using. It turned out, however, that I was not the only partisan in PAM 5 with such a guilty conscience. None of our German prisoners was ever shot. Every last one of them was marched out for execution but was instead abandoned far from the zemljanka, so far, from the sound of the reports, that even I could not have found my way back.

In my area of Bíteš we were limited by our lack of weapons. But Nikolaj, who was in the favorable terrain of the Bohemian-Moravian hills, could be much more active with his Soviets, especially since he had four or five machine guns brought by the paratroopers. With few villages, poor roads, and slow communication through the hills, his men could strike the Germans in a populated area and then vanish into the refuge of the forests. Nikolaj was a graduate of a Soviet air force academy and, at twenty-seven, an experienced, unflinching fighter, having been shot down in 1941 at the Leningrad front. He was always in a good mood, singing when he wasn't talking, his black hair falling over his eyes as he ended long notes with an operatic snap of his head, joined in the finale by the zemljanka chorus, who had heard his repertoire of folk ballads and marching songs so often that they knew it by heart. Considering that he was my good friend, I didn't often see him; but then, we were close enough that we didn't need propinquity. I imagined us corresponding after the war in our customary salad of Russian, Czech, and German, long chatty letters incoherent to anyone with a respect for syntax.

Like so many hopes, that one was destroyed before the end of the war. In December 1944, Nikolaj was trapped by a Jagdkommando informant. Nikolaj had been going into the villages near his shelter every two or three days to get food for his group. There in a forgotten part of the hills he was approached by an informer claiming to be a needy resister. Nikolaj's hideout was a house, where—carelessly, witlessly—he brought the man and fed him. I wonder if he felt the mistake in his bones as the man went off. A few days later, a large Jagdkommando detachment surrounded the house, with Nikolaj and seven or eight comrades inside. Nikolaj covered one of the exits with a machine gun so that a few of his men actually succeeded in escaping. He was the last one to go through the door, and it was in the doorway that he was shot down—a heroic end for a true hero of the resistance. Rufa, his love, was pregnant, living in a shed in Koníkov provided by Zelený—a place my father had also stayed. On February 8, 1945, her shelter, too, was attacked by Jagdkommandos, and she was seriously wounded. Rather than allowing herself to be captured by the Germans, she committed suicide by running from the shed into their fire.

Vlasta—Dušan was her cover name, Lieutenant Dušan, after Grňa's promotion—was still the most versatile cutout we had. I saw to it that no one in our group knew her identity or home village. The Gestapo, I eventually discovered, knew that a woman was very active with the underground. They had a good description of Vlasta in their files, but they did not know her name, and they placed her residence in a Moravian town far from Bíteš. Vlasta was my liaison to Mother, Dr. Káňa, Mrs. Richter, Jedlička, and several others. She loved any bold assignment, the more daring, the better. It was through Vlasta that the Council of Three was able to transmit to London the exact site where the new German V-2 missiles were being produced, a major piece of intelligence. Hitler had pinned great hopes on V-1, a small pilotless jet plane that could be loaded with explosives and automatically steered to targets in England. The Germans started using it in June 1944, the day after the Allies landed in France. Then, later in the summer, they launched the even more frightening V-2, a high-flying rocket-bomb so fast that, unlike the V-1, British planes could not shoot it down in the air. Though these weapons failed to turn the tide of the war, they did terrible damage. Thousands of Londoners were killed by the V-1 and V-2 bombs during the last year of the war.

Jedlička received information from his son-in-law pinpointing the place where the weapons were being made, two tunnels near Nordhausen, Germany. From Jedlička, the information went to Mrs. Richter, who gave it to Vlasta, who passed it to us. Štainer cabled it to London through his transmitter, and within a few weeks after Jedlička got the locations, the Allies were bombing.[2]

Jedlička was a handsome, burly man of about fifty, intensely masculine and carefully attired from his straight brown hair to his polished brown shoes. The first time we sent Vlasta to contact him, he thought she was a double agent. The letter she was carrying for him was in my mother's familiar handwriting, but eyeing Vlasta, he decided that Mother had been forced by the Gestapo to pen the note. Vlasta looked like a country girl only from her tanned neck up. Jedlička was the director of a clothing cooperative. He sized up her elegant tailor-made suit—Vlasta always dressed like a model—noted her spurious city manners, and judged her to be an informer posing as farm girl. To test her, he gave her a message to deliver—to Bohemia, which she could only reach by taking several trains. He got on the train, too, and followed her through the hills, staying one car behind her, watching to

---

2. Ludmila Richter had come to visit Mother and me when we were released from prison. In 1939, when her own husband was arrested and about to be put to death in Berlin, Jedlička brought food to him and other prisoners, meanwhile supporting Mrs. Richter. She therefore readily assisted Jedlička in any of his endeavors. Jedlička's son-in-law had a German acquaintance who worked as a delivery truck driver in Nordhausen. The German driver supplied descriptions of the missiles and pinpointed the tunnels. In 1949 in London, I met President Beneš' former chancellor, Jaromír Smutný, who told me that the British considered this intelligence provided by the home resistance of the utmost significance.

see if she got off at any station before her assigned destination. Only when he had followed her entire trip and was sure she had reported to no one did he begin to trust her.

Our next contribution to the larger war effort was to give the Red Army the German plans for fortifying Brno against the Allied advance. Mrs. Richter got a copy of the fortifications from a German friend, a countess, I believe, who was a secretary to the commanding officer of the Brno garrison. At about the same time, Gustav Kristek came to know an engineer who was being forced to work on the city's military defense. Independently, Kristek got another set of the fortification plans and found that the two projections matched almost perfectly. Still, before we could pass along the intelligence, we had to make sure the plans were in their final form. The Germans kept revising them, trying to adapt the fortifications to natural formations. In March, I received what we thought was the last version, and I began trying to get them to the Red Army. I dropped everything, however, when I learned some terrible news: In January 1945, the Gestapo came for Jedlička.

He was taken to the Kounic Student Home and systematically tortured. For hours on end, the Gestapo used the infamous ice torture, which meant, as he sketchily described it, that he was repeatedly submerged in a bathtub of ice and water, nearly drowned each time, prior to being kicked or subjected to some more violent treatment. He never broke, even after months of such brutality as pulling out all of his nails. The Germans would have shipped him off to a concentration camp for liquidation except for the intervention of a man who had once been his employee, a Brno Gestapo member, Franz Prudky. Without going so far as to be an informer for us, this man had given Jedlička information from time to time, telling him, for example, that the Gestapo mistakenly thought my father was hiding near the Slovakian border. It was František, as we called him, who reported to us the contents of the Gestapo file on Vlasta. František could not secure Jedlička's release, but by keeping him from being sent to the camps, he saved his life. We began planning immediately to attack the Kounic Home and rescue Jedlička. But as we worked out the details of the action, I saw that I would be leading my men into a suicide mission that would fail even to liberate Jedlička and might precipitate his execution. The plan had to be abandoned. After the war, he emerged from prison suddenly old, a frail ghost of Jedlička, walking with a cane.

Massive arms for an organized insurrection would never be sent to us. But we could get some weapons for our guerrilla activities, it seemed, through Czechoslovak parachute groups that were being sent into the Protectorate to establish contact with us. Beginning in April 1944, the Americans had been dropping a few of our soldiers at a time, men who had gone into exile at the beginning of the occupation and were now coming back to join the impending fight. The men in the first team, Barium, had been captured in northeastern Bohemia because of an informer. Another group, Calcium, was the one that had refused to let Štainer subordinate its members. Each team had a specific assignment. Tungsten, a group dropped in the winter of 1944, was charged with smoothing relations between Calcium and the Council of Three—that is to say, between Calcium and Štainer. Next came the four members of Platinum, led by Jaromír Nechanský, followed by Bauxite, with intelligence and communications assignments. Because of these groups in our area, R3 for all practical purposes had four transmitting stations by the end of the war with which to communicate with London. Of all the groups, Nechanský's Platinum, which landed in February 1945, proved the most important for us, for Platinum's assignment was to arrange to have weapons dropped to the Council of Three—not the tanks and massive arms infusions we dreamed of, but arms at least for our guerrilla fighters.

First I received through Štainer an English catalog describing various kinds of containers. The arms were to be pushed out of a supply plane in metal containers, each attached to a small parachute. According to the catalog, container No. 6 would have in it three machine guns; if I wanted fifteen machine guns, I had to order five No. 6 containers. Another number designation would contain twelve revolvers, another some plastic explosives. There were rifles, grenades, bombs, pistols, and food. Before placing the order, I discussed the selections with Aleš and Hermit, to make sure we were choosing weapons we knew how to use effectively and could store.

Without ground connections, no plane could locate our dropping zone; therefore, Platinum next brought instruments—transmitters and radar apparatus. Štainer asked me to find a shelter for both the ground crew and the equipment. The best person to keep the paratroopers, I decided, was Kristek's cousin Loucký in Ludvíkov. Loucký's main qualification was that Kristek wouldn't speak to him, though they lived near each other. Just as with every underground operation, my main priority was to keep any one person or group from knowing the names, whereabouts, or actions of anyone else. Aleš Dmitrijev knew only the names of his PAM 5 fighters, and only their cover names at that. Kristek didn't know our people in Domašov, Pánov, Javůrek, or Tišnov. Nikolaj Bachmutsky in Nové Město had been cut off from the people outside his area. Even Štainer did not know where the para-troopers would stay.

Every air drop to the Protectorate—there were twelve of them in all, in April 1945—was enormously complicated.[3] The mission had to be approved first by the Czechoslovak minister of defense in London, then by the Anglo-American Headquarters in southern Italy, and finally by Allied officials in the particular airport in Italy from which the plane would take off. For our operation the scouts were dropped first. They were two energetic chaps, Nechanský and Jaroslav Klemeš, and they brought a shortwave radar trans-mitter with a range of sixty miles. The scouts got busy at once installing an antenna in Loucký's attic.

We had staked out a meadow in Svatoslav, near Tišnov, for the drop zone. When an American "Liberator" aircraft was ready to leave from Italy, the Allies would send a message at one o'clock over the BBC: "The forest murmurs." The same murmuring at six o'clock meant that the plane was in the air. A final repetition at nine o'clock signified that the flight was going well and the drop would come that very night. But it was not simple. The B-24 had to cross the highest mountains in Europe, the Alps, where there was always some weather disturbance. The crew was likely to be Polish, ig-norant of Czech geography and easily lost. If snow or fog blanketed the Pro-tectorate, there could be no drop. It sometimes happened that resisters expecting a drop received the first and second messages but not the third; the weather or the Germans got in the way.

Our drop was to occur within a ten-day period. "Stop everything," I told our men. "No activity at all right now. Catch up on your reading." The last thing we needed was to have a Gestapo patrol fanning through the area to punish some partisan raid. But as day after day passed without any word of the drop, it got increasingly harder to control the Russians who, like any guerrilla fighters, wanted to see some action. For ten days I stayed near the drop zone waiting for the signal. Finally, in despair, I went to the Homoláčs' to take a bath. I was shaving, set up with a radio near me, when I heard "The forest murmurs." It was so quick and matter-of-fact. Had I really heard it? I put down my things and ran to get Aleš and Sandy. Hála and the Turk were notified—they were to bring a cart and horses so that we could take the weapons away from the drop zone. Karel Kristek had promised to lend

3. Drops to the Protectorate were all carried out by the U.S. Army Air Force 2641st Special Group, stationed near Livorno. These twelve flights were among sixty operational flights the group made that month.

us a car, a Czech Praga Baby. He had removed its wheels to keep the Germans from confiscating it. Now, because it had been sitting unused, he couldn't get it started. He and the car were still at his sawmill in Ludvíkov at six o'clock when we received the second message. We had to get to the drop zone to lay out the lights for the pilot, and we had to bring "Eureka," the ground transmitter. The aircraft had a receiving device, "Rebecca." To guide the plane to the drop zone, Eureka's beams would cross the transmitter beams of the airplane and lock into its radar. There was only one problem: without transportation, we couldn't get Eureka to the drop zone. It was nine o'clock. We had heard the third and final message assuring us of the plane's arrival, but still neither Praga Baby nor driver appeared. Kristek had given up trying to fix the car and was frantically working to get another vehicle. At 9:15, in response to my urgent message, one of our men who owned a trucking company arrived from Bíteš with the only wheels he could find, a five-ton truck without a muffler. Roaring down the road, we certainly might be stopped on the way to the dropping area, but we made up our minds to speed past any patrol, shooting our way through if necessary.

Surprisingly, we rumbled into the meadow without incident and met our own patrols, who were on guard to make sure we were not ambushed while we waited for the plane. Thirty to forty of us were gathered for the drop—too many for the Germans to attack without bringing a sizable force, we told ourselves. We had chosen a spot that the pilot would be able to see, but as it was visible from all sides, the Germans could see it, too, especially with our lights set up. A little before midnight we heard the Liberator approaching. Nearer it came and nearer, crashing into the night silence with the tremendous thunder of four engines. Despite the blackout, lights came on in the villages around us. The pilot signaled us that he saw our flares. But instead of landing, he kept going, while all of us stood with our hands at our sides and our mouths open to the sky, mystified. In a minute a second Liberator appeared in the distance, flying very low, again with a volcanic roar of engines. We heard some antiaircraft artillery above Tišnov. The Germans could follow the Liberators on their radar as long as the planes were above three thousand feet. It was easy, therefore, for the enemy to figure out the drop area. All he had to do was track the aircraft to the spot where it slipped below radar and then note the location where the plane, its mission completed, regained sufficient altitude to be picked up on radar again. The second plane passed us up. By this time, the racket had awakened every person in every village around us. "I don't understand it," said Nechanský. We heard more antiaircraft. Then came a third plane, this one brilliantly lit up.

"What the hell is going on?" Nechanský exclaimed. "They're not supposed to have all these lights. They're behind enemy lines, for Christ's sake."

"I don't like it. This may be a German plane," I answered.

The plane was circling now, going down and down. It was the largest plane I had ever seen. We thought the noise would leave us deaf, yet each minute it got even louder. The whole meadow was bathed in light, and I could see Aleš' hair blown straight back in the wind and the excitement in Nechanský's eyes. Above our heads, a door of the plane opened and a silhouette greeted us with a raised right hand. He began pushing containers out into the night sky, each attached to a parachute—perhaps twenty or twenty-five of them—which floated down to the meadow like a flock of nocturnal white birds. The plane, the lights, the parachutes—it was all frighteningly beautiful. "Look, Father," my mind said to its constant companion, "Just look at it!" The dark figure pushed the last container out of the open door and waved a final greeting before the plane rose and disappeared, leaving the meadow and all the villages around us in dumfounded silence.

The containers weighed about 300 pounds each, so we had to divide the bounty up then and there before we took it away. I insisted that the Russians should get first-class weapons. Half of the guns and ammunition therefore went to Aleš' group and half to my headquarters. Aleš took his weapons away on the five-ton truck. Nechanský and Klemeš came with us as we loaded the rest of the supplies onto all of our carts and horses. In our hut in the forest we unsealed the packages that very night, burying the floor in layers of brown paper wrappings. We did not get what we ordered because the plane carrying our supplies had been shot down in Tišnov—that was the antiaircraft artillery we heard.[4] But we did receive twenty-seven Sten guns,

4. The Liberator was shot down. The crew of eight was forced to bail out; the men were helped by R3 guerrillas when they landed. General Luža's group took five to Nihov and sheltered them for twenty-three days. They were hidden in a hunting cabin in the woods, though "hidden" is not quite the right word, since everyone in the area knew they were there. Sometimes they helped us in our partisan strikes. Their commander was First Lieutenant Thomas McCarthy of the U.S. Army Air Force, the nephew of Franklin D. Roosevelt. The crewmen were somewhat anxious about letting the incoming Cossack division know that a detachment of American fliers was in the Soviet zone of occupation, but as it turned out, the Cossack commander invited them to an elaborate victory celebration and treated them well. We, too, were quite hospitable, even giving some dances for them. Gustav Kristek made attendance compulsory for all young ladies in the village—not that the girls needed coercion to come dance with the dashing Americans. When news of V-E day reached us, the fliers wanted to get back to their units, but the Communist authorities kept putting up obstacles to their departure. As President Beneš was in Brno on his way to Prague, our members went to him to ask him to intercede with the Soviets to let the

one machine gun, forty-five revolvers, some hand grenades and small bombs, and plastic explosives of undetermined potential. We had not ordered any food, but there were some packages of that, too, mainly coffee and tea, which Nechanský seized, flatly remarking, "That's for us." I didn't drink coffee, but among us were people who did, and had not smelled it since 1939. These paratroopers had had it two months ago, yet they didn't even offer any to my men. I was irked, but of course I couldn't start a row over something that was small in comparison to the important service the two had rendered us. I never mentioned my irritation to anybody.

The next day, their mission to organize our drop having been completed, Nechanský and Klemeš left. They moved to the area covered by our contiguous group in the Council of Three, Delta, to organize another drop that also proved successful. Various groups within R3 received ten drops in all from the Allies in 1945, supplying weapons to sustain our guerrilla fighting, but certainly not the heavy weapons we craved. Loucký packed a lunch for Nechanský, and Kristek and I took them to their destination in the Praga Baby, which this time started right up.

Loucký, putting aside his normally sour attitude, considered it the honor of his life to help the paratroopers. He and Nechanský had become close, close friends during our mission, and they remained in touch after the war. Following the Communist takeover in 1948, they formed an underground organization, were arrested together, and went on trial together. Loucký was sentenced to twenty-five years in prison for anti-Communist activities. Nechanský, trained originally by the British, had worked for the Communists as an informer. But by 1948, he was in contact with American intelligence agents and had thus become a double agent. He was convicted of treason by the Communists and executed in 1950. Jaroslav Klemeš was eventually thrown out of the army by the Communists and spent three years in prison. He was rehabilitated after the 1989 Velvet Revolution, promoted to the rank of colonel, and has continued to live in the Czech Republic.

Americans leave for Prague. They had just begun their explanation when Beneš motioned them to be silent; the president would not let them speak until they had accompanied him to the garden, where they could not be overheard. Beneš did see to it that the fliers were brought to Prague. The incident revealed that even in those first days after the war, the president of the republic had to act surreptitiously to ensure the safety of some American allies. The Soviet military was generally friendly to us, but they had no authority to influence political affairs, being controlled themselves by the KGB.

Nikolaj Bachmutsky and the paratrooper Rufa Krasavinova, 1944

Radomír Luža and Vlasta Homoláč surrounded by men of the General Luža group

Parade of resistance fighters: Vlasta, Hermit, "Sandy" Cikrle, Císař Fireman, Arnošt Vostrejš, Radomír Luža, and Jan Pliczka

Hermit (left) with Fanynka and Jan Sec, 1945

President Beneš (far left), Milada Luža, and Hermit on her left, 1946

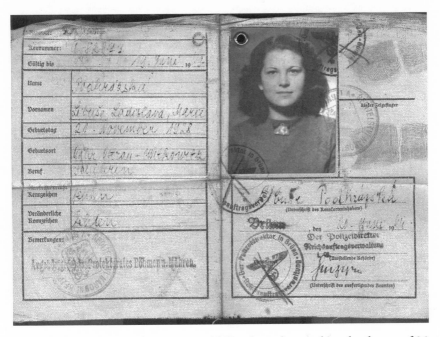

Libuše Luža's identity card, 1944, a special Kennkarte for people under the age of 26

Libuše Luža and Radomír Luža, ca. 1948

Rasťa Váhala (left) and Karel Štainer, 1986

Vlasta Homoláč, 1995

Radomír Luža, 1984

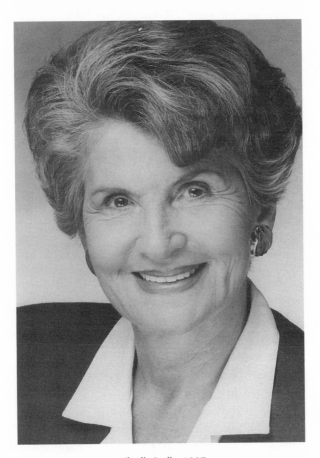

Libuše Luža, 1997

IX

The new weapons made us a real brigade. Gustav Kristek brought nineteen members from Brno, all hot for action, to join us. The Turk and Kravka brought the men from their groups. In the forest I distributed guns and gave a little talk outlining the strikes we would be able to carry out and the missions we should not attempt. I was giving some guidelines about protecting the villagers when suddenly I saw Slávek Konečný, one of my old friends. Our mothers had been close since childhood. His father, an army major and leader of ON, arrested in 1940, was serving a long sentence in a German prison. "Well, well," said Slávek, pounding me on the back as if I had been coughing. "My shy old pal turns out to be 'Jáchim,' partisan scourge of the Nazis. How are you, Old Buddy? Your father—you know, it's a blow for all of us. As far as I know, my father's still alive. I try to keep my mind off him. Did they send you any Scotch in the drop, or do they expect us to have a good time with just these guns?"

"We're lucky to get the guns. The plane with the supplies for our group was shot down over Tišnov."

Since the weapons we received were somewhat different from those we had ordered, we weren't quite sure how to use them. The plastic explosives, we found out, were fine for blowing up a storage house from the inside and killing one or two guards, but they were too weak even for the small bridge on the highway between Brno and Prague—Sandy and I wasted an afternoon trying to destroy it. Gustav and I spent another evening waiting to ambush a German freight train at the Rapotice railroad station. Hour after hour passed with no Germans and no supplies in sight, so that we finally had to content ourselves with cutting the station's telephone lines. Nevertheless, in that first week after receiving arms, General Luža turned up everywhere in the countryside around Brno—between Brno and Bíteš, between Brno and Tišnov, Náměšt', Křižanov. No sooner had my men taken the weapons than reports started coming in. General Luža had seized four military motorcycles. Or our men killed eleven German soldiers and got two German trucks. Or we destroyed an electrical tower and thus cut off the energy to a plant where the Germans were making aircraft engines. Local people helped us set up the raids and often joined in the attacks. For example, the Germans had stored supplies in temporary warehouses all along the route of their retreat. The residents, who knew everything about the movements of these retreating soldiers, knew exactly when the warehouse guards wandered away from their posts to visit the local tavern. A few of our men got into one of these storehouses and took 37,000 pieces of ammunition; unfortunately, we couldn't use German bullets in our guns.

In the beginning we were relatively inexperienced in partisan warfare, but then, so were the Germans, who were accustomed to commanding the routes and thought nothing of trundling down some godforsaken back road in a horse cart. But before the end of the war, we had become crack guerrilla fighters, as skilled as our Russian tutors. We descended on a German camp in Tišnov and liberated fifty skeletons that first week, the three German sentries having locked them down and gone off to warm themselves with a glass of slivovitz. Such a flagrant partisan action would have been unthinkable three months earlier.

Some of the German troops were clearly more lax now as they saw themselves marching to surrender. Others were merely in a hurry to reach the Americans, wherever they were, to capitulate to the U.S. forces rather than the Red Army. But others retreated in the same disciplined way as they had advanced, notwithstanding tens of thousands of loyal Aryan civilians trudging along behind them. A fifth of the Brno population had been German even before the war. When it was apparent that the Red Army was about to launch a major attack on the city, these Germans left, joining the exodus of Germans from Hungary, Poland, and Slovakia, all fleeing the Soviets. Many of them stopped for a while in Velká Bíteš, but most of them, especially those who had been conspicuous collaborators or had particular reason to fear the Russians, moved steadily toward Jihlava or other towns, following "their" army in hopes of reaching the Reich.

Though we partisans were not its foremost concern, the German army did not stand aside deferentially while we carried out our attacks. There were some close calls, one involving two German women whom Sandy and I encountered on the road. It was Sandy's habit to search through the belongings of any Germans we met and take whatever he wanted, sometimes with practical results. Sandy's rummaging had yielded forty-five pairs of shoes for our Russian men who had been wrapping rags on their feet. So I couldn't in good conscience forbid the confiscations. On April 22, he and I saw the women on the main road between Prague and Brno, apparently a mother and daughter. "What are you doing here?" I asked them. "Where are you going?"

"Our destination is undecided," the daughter answered with that correctness that is the subtlest form of haughtiness. "We will get out of the line of fighting."

Sandy had meanwhile been rooting in their rucksacks, as was his wont. I had no taste for taking people's personal things. As paramilitary personnel, it was one thing for us to seize uniforms and guns that had been issued by the German army. It was another thing to confiscate their combs and brassieres. But Sandy wanted anything conceivably useful—if not for him, then for his family and friends, or if not for them, then for their friends. The women didn't have much beyond a few necessities but Sandy, knowing that I would let them pass, was determined to take something. I fidgeted, waiting for him to finish.

Suddenly, down the road came an open German truck with two mounted machine guns, one covering the northern side of the road and one the southern, manned by two soldiers. Though the patrol was going about sixty miles an hour, they could see us clearly. To all appearances, we were about to be shredded by machine gun fire. The two German women, exchanging a wild glance, at once sprinted forward and lunged into the roadway fifty feet in front of us. But instead of stopping for the women, the soldiers sped past without shooting, thinking perhaps that we were part of a larger group and they would make an easy target of themselves if they stopped. Now I was furious with the two women and with myself for allowing Sandy to "make an inspection," as he called it, practically in the open. I wasn't angry enough to shoot the women, as Sandy wanted to do, but I no longer had any qualms about letting him take everything they had.

We could not hope to fight regular battles with our light weapons, and so the Germans continued to have tight control over the towns and virtually all the main roads and rails leading into them. But they no longer had the resources to wipe out every small partisan group as they did in 1943, and PAM 5 was gradually taking over more of the back roads.[1] In addition to knocking out oil and alcohol depots and burning warehouses, we attacked small groups of soldiers and short columns of German cars, usually by blocking the road and then throwing hand grenades into the stopped vehicles. Within days of the weapons drop, the Germans had to use convoys to move on the country roads.

It is an odd fact that, although the Soviets formed the core of my resistance group, practically no native Communists were active in our area. Sandy and a few other fellows had been party members in the old republic, but there was never any distinct Communist group in the underground near us. I had heard about the Communist underground in Brno and was eager to get in touch with the resisters, just as I would have wanted to contact a group of Benthamites or Luddites, if they were anti-Hitler activists. Through Gustav Kristek, I eventually met a representative of a Communist youth organization, a fellow named Lenc, whose group had members in the arms factories in Brno and in Rosice. In our two meetings I promised to share some arms with him, but before we got them, Lenc was arrested by the Gestapo; eventually we lost any connection to his group. I remember it now only because it was my first and only contact with a Communist organization.[2] The Communists claimed after the war that they had been the backbone and brains of the resistance. If that boast was true anywhere, it certainly was not so in our area. I knew only one other party member during the war, Jaroslav Volf, whom I had met when Štainer asked me to find a safe house for him. Volf was supposed to be the liaison between R3 and the Communist underground in Prague. I took good care of him, but whenever I asked him to do something, he always found an excuse. He was a skittish creature who was never embarrassed about keeping himself safe. "Please do not go forward with this plan," he would tell us. "My hideout is close by

1. Even as guerrillas, we received a negligible quantity of arms compared with the generous assistance the Allies gave to the French, Norwegian, Polish, Dutch, Danish, and Italian resistance.

2. I encountered Lenc after the war when he was an aide to a great enemy of mine, Otto Šling, who spent the war in exile. As secretary of the regional committee of the Communist Party in Brno, Šling decided the affairs of everyone in and around the city—until about 1949 when the Communists arrested, tortured, and executed him during the Slánský trial.

and it will put me in danger." I was relieved when he left us to live, as I heard, in the Prague Zoo. Hermit and I speculated on whether Volf found shelter with the deer or the sheep.

At that time Hermit and I had no more antipathy toward Communists than toward any other party. We understood that the Communists wanted to function as a distinct political entity and not to be merged—an important point, since we were fervently advocating the streamlining of our party system. Like the new French arrangement, we wanted to have large right, center, and left parties, with the Communists perhaps making up a fourth group. Czechoslovakia had had no less than sixteen parties in the National Assembly before the war, all fighting each other and none confronting the country's serious problems. Each government was a weak coalition of many parties forced to make all sorts of concessions and compromises in order to survive. If a man from, let us say, the leftist Social Democratic Party were given a portfolio, the cabinet then had to be balanced by taking on an agrarian or other rightist, even if there were no qualified rightist for the available post. Party affiliation had been much more important than individual capability. That was what we wanted to eradicate. Our other goals involved expelling the resident Germans from Czechoslovakia—every Czech seemed to be in favor of that—and getting rid of our creaking old bureaucracy and the entire administrative system. Lord, how Father and all of us had talked it over and over—the civil service reforms, what would be nationalized, how we would balance capitalism and socialism. No one that I knew, not even far-leftists like Sandy, wanted or expected that our Czechoslovak republic would be sovietized. We accepted the reality that, as the Soviets would seize control from the Germans, Communists would be prominent in any new government that was established. But we had no idea they planned from the beginning to monopolize power.

The broadcasts we received from the BBC—our exiled government's commentary and explication of Soviet ideas—assured us that the Soviets favored a democratic system in Czechoslovakia. The majority of people at home believed the Communist declaration that they had become a parliamentary party. They pretended to follow the ideas of President Masaryk, whose name they bandied about, and recognized Beneš as the country's leader. In fact, their program on paper was even more moderate than the leftist program that we in R3 were proposing.

If we were skeptical of Communist political leaders, we had only admiration for the heroic Red Army that was liberating us. Contact with the Soviets was our only hope of getting more arms and sending out whatever intelligence we had gathered. I was happy, therefore, when Robotka asked us to take Grňa to meet the Red Army that had reached Ivančice. The Soviets would take him on to Košice, where the leaders of the Czechoslovak government had gathered, waiting to return from exile.

This was bound to be an important meeting for the resistance, so before Grňa reached us, I decided that we'd better clear the road between us and the front. Aleš and I thus set out with thirty-five men, including Sandy, Loňka, and Sec, to take over the eastern highway between Velká Bíteš and Zastávka. One of our men knew a foot trail that would take us from Zastávka to Ivančice, where a division of Cossacks was positioned between Brno and the Austrian border, almost in the rear of the German troops that were still in Brno.

For miles out of Velká Bíteš we saw no one on the road. Then in Zbraslav, in a feisty spring wind that tore at our jackets, we came upon an isolated mill that six or seven Germans were using as a station while they guarded the road nearby. We were about fifteen, the others having branched off to patrol the intersections. The German soldiers spotted us at the same moment we saw them walking outside. Outnumbered, they made the fatal mistake of withdrawing into the mill, which we then surrounded.

All of us began firing into the building furiously. At the edge of my vision, on both the left and right, there was a blur of something flying out of the windows. All I could clearly see were rifles that two Germans held diagonally in front of them as they ran. Those two thus escaped, being beyond the reach of our fire. Perhaps that impulsive escape earned them recognition by the German government after the war—maybe even a medal and a small pension to enjoy with the rest of their lives. We had received only one machine gun in the drop, and Sandy was now using it for the first time. The rest of us had Sten guns with a very short range, so our shooting was mainly just supportive noise. After another minute, three more soldiers tore out of the mill's back entrance and hurtled into the barrage a few yards from Loňka, who hit all three. The mill now was quiet. Half of our men entered it cautiously and encountered two dead soldiers, each under a window, and one unarmed and unscathed German standing close by the front door, his hands outstretched and waving high above him as he shouted over and over in what he thought was Russian, "Don't shoot, surrender me! Don't shoot, surrender me!"

I was standing in the yard with the bodies. Suddenly, one of the dead men began writhing dreadfully. He had been shot three times in the face. Only a fragment of his head remained, but from this fragment came a steady shriek, not agonized, not even vocal, but a deafening, mechanical whine like the scream of metals scraping. "I must shoot him," I thought. But before I could move, Loňka had done it. His lips, bunched to one side as if trying to get out of the way, flinched as he fired, but when the chore was over, his mouth was almost tender. I saw Loňka's face many times when, going about my postwar life, I was peppered by the shrapnel of unwanted, piecemeal memories. The sickening face of the German did not come back to me— never. I succeeded in banishing it. But less excruciating images of the resistance, some of them merely poignant, remain beneath my everyday preoccupations like rust stains that no paint can cover permanently, always threatening to spot through the layers of commonplace years.

The mill shootout left us shaky as we went through the woods alongside the road, our German prisoner in tow. At the sound of a car, we lay down in the grass and, seeing that it was an official Nazi vehicle, blew it up with a hand grenade. As we progressed down the ribbon of gravel, we set up posts to make sure the way remained clear behind us. The one house we came to happened to belong to a known collaborator. Overwrought, four of my men bounded up the stairs over his store while the rest of us stood guard in the thin sun of the late afternoon. "We are the partisans," they shouted, when he opened the door, his wife behind him in the shadows.

"What do you think?" he protested. "I didn't do anything."

"Ah, no?" replied Sandy. "We hear rumors. We hear that you report everything you see around here to the Germans. You supply them with information. They supply you with cigarettes. Isn't that right? Isn't that right?" I heard slaps, then the woman's voice, anguished.

"You come here today and abuse us. They'll come tomorrow and kill us for helping the guerrillas."

"Take all of it," the man said. "The cigarettes, even the food. But please, leave me a note saying you seized it against our will. I have to have something I can show to the gendarmes and the Jagdkommandos in Bíteš, or we'll be shot."

It was dark when we finished. Throughout the night, General Luža would keep everything off the road from Bíteš to Zastávka, so that Grňa could ride in safety the next morning at least as far as the front. The secondary arteries—between Velká Bíteš and Tišnov, for example—were earthen roads where every vehicle traveled in a furious aura of yellow dirt. Our patrols were watching all these crossroads, too, so as to keep the route clear.

I had no idea then that Grňa's trip was not worth the trouble we were taking to facilitate it. I later learned that the journey to Košice was a completely silly mission. President Beneš and the officials of the London government returned in the wake of the German evacuation to set up a postwar administration. Beneš had long before determined that the survival of Czechoslovakia depended on our accommodation to both the western powers and the Soviet Union. His signing of the Soviet-Czechoslovak alliance treaty in Moscow in 1943 showed that he had made up his mind to come to terms with Stalin and with the Czechoslovak Communists who spent the war in Moscow—men such as Klement Gottwald, the chairman of the Czechoslovak Communist Party, Rudolf Slánský, Jan Šverma, and Václav Kopecký. By the winter of 1944–45, as the Soviet army covered more and more of our country, the balance between the democratic parties represented by Beneš in London and the Communists led by Gottwald in Moscow shifted in favor of the Communists. By the end of the war, it was a foregone conclusion that the London group would be replaced by a new government in which Communists would participate conspicuously. The exiled leaders of several parties in fact went to Moscow in March 1945, where, under the leadership of Gottwald, plans for the postwar government were laid out.[3] From Moscow, Beneš and exiled politicians went directly to Košice—a large town in eastern Slovakia that the Red Army had liberated as it advanced westward—and set up there until they could repossess Prague.

During the whole of the war, we resisters had heard from both London and Moscow, from Beneš and Gottwald, "The main front is at home. It is the home resistance, the people now sacrificing and suffering, who will form the postwar government." Stalin himself must have had substantial knowledge about the leaders of the home resistance; during the war, I later found out, he inquired of Slánský, "Who is this General Luža?" Nevertheless, the government announced in Košice was an appalling assemblage of old politicos culled from the numerous and ineffectual prewar parties, and Communists. As everything was being done under the aegis and pressure of our

3. Beneš did not take part in the meetings, on the ground that as a constitutional president, he stood above what he took to be party politics. Josef Korbel, in *The Communist Subversion of Czechoslovakia, 1938–1948* (Princeton, 1959), rightly blames Beneš for thus leaving the London democratic exiles leaderless and in disarray.

Soviet liberators, Beneš was obliged to install Communists in favored positions in the government. The new prime minister was Zdeněk Fierlinger,
formerly ambassador to the Soviet Union, a social democrat from the old-
boy pool who collaborated so closely with the Communists that he earned
the popular sobriquet of "Quislinger." Gottwald was deputy prime minister.
Instead of resisters, Communist Party members and democrats back from
exile held all the major posts, many of them absent during the terrible years
of the occupation. Some people held office as independents but were Communists in everything but name. General Ludvík Svoboda, for example, who
spent the war abroad and returned to fill General Ingr's shoes as minister of
national defense, was not a formal member of the party but certainly took
his orders from the Communists. The new government had not one single
representative from the Czech home resistance, and few with the guts to
stand up to the Communists.

Meanwhile, the situation in the western part of Czechoslovakia was confused, with the Germans being harried by free-for-all local outbursts against
them as they withdrew. It was not always clear whether Germans or Czechs
were in control of a particular town. Grňa believed that before he could engage in any political discussions with the returning government officials, it
behooved him to consult the collective resistance leadership. That, of course,
was not feasible. With the Germans still remaining in many areas, it was
impossible for us to communicate with all the resistance heads, even if we
had known who they were. Grňa therefore made the ridiculous decision to
abstain from questioning the makeup of the new government. He would go
to Košice with the sole mission of getting us more military supplies. He
would possibly resuscitate the idea of a national insurrection, if the leaders
seemed receptive to it, but he would not bring up any issue of political
power.

It should have been clear to Grňa, as it was to us by then, that the Red
Army did not want us to liberate ourselves. The Soviets never supplied arms
to our resistance. According to the Soviet scouts we met who confirmed our
suspicions, the Soviets figured they needed no help from us. They wanted
intelligence from us and guerrilla fighting. They did not mind the western
Allies dropping us a few guns with which to impede German movements.
But they did not want an independent-minded, well-equipped army in the
area they intended to occupy, a force to be reckoned with by the new government. Grňa's whole trip was therefore wrongheaded. Arranging for the

drop of weapons was an errand anyone could have taken care of, if the Allies were of a mind to supply us. Grňa should not have been in Košice at all, but rather in Prague, at the center of the revolution that was brewing there. But if he did meet leaders in Košice, his express purpose should have been to protest our exclusion in the new distribution of power.

I assumed that Grňa was going to Košice as the leader of our home resistance to present our case to President Beneš and set forth our expectations. I thought it was important for his entourage to exude an air of competence and control, so I prepared his escort to the front with high seriousness and quite a bit of pride. A member of General Luža lived in Zastávka and owned a motorcycle that he had kept concealed throughout the war. On the morning of the trip, he served as our scout, going ahead of us on the motorcycle and taking reports from the patrols at the intersections along the way. He then drove back to tell us all was clear. I intended to take two cars—assuming our temperamental Praga Baby would start—carrying a party that would include Karel Kristek (we were going through the area of his command and using his men as patrols), Aleš (he spoke Russian), Sec, and me. We would meet Grňa at Gustav Kristek's sawmill in Ludvíkov and bring him to Zastávka, where a guide would lead us across the front as far as the district city of Ivančice, captured a few days before by the Cossacks but still surrounded by Germans. The auto trip would take only about thirty or forty minutes if we encountered no trouble—"trouble" meaning Germans. The Russians at Ivančice would take Grňa to Košice to meet our government.

"Why all this?" asked Grňa when he saw the motorcycle and two cars. He had arrived in Rudolf Sedlák's serviceable cart and had perhaps expected to walk the twenty miles to Ivančice.

"For you," I answered. "In half an hour we'll be in Zastávka."

We sped along the empty road, Grňa on one side of the backseat and I on the other. Father hovered between us. At each point where a side road entered the highway, two of our patrols were stationed. To Grňa's open-mouthed amazement, the men saluted, military fashion, as our cars passed. "You like playing soldier, don't you?" I heard Father say inside my head, in the easy, intimate tone we had developed since his death. When he was alive, even our silences had sometimes been fenced with a vague tension that left my throat aching.

"Come, now, Father. Aren't you impressed with your effete scholar? Look at Grňa. He's practically awe-struck." Grňa was in fact so impressed that he gave out promotions on the spot. Aleš and I, who started the trip as un-ranked commanders, returned a captain and first lieutenant of the partisans.

"It's time for you to live in the world like a man without a father," Father said, so softly that I almost missed it. The cars had stopped, and everyone was getting out.

"I'll let go when I'm ready," I told him, and turned my thoughts to our guide, who was pacing in the woods.

I was disconcerted by this vaunted front that we were crossing. Exactly where was it? I expected a crowd of soldiers whom we would have to slip past. We met no one. Apparently, the front in this area simply meant a line of retreating German soldiers and civilians who wanted to keep their com-munication line secure and a line of advancing Soviets somewhat behind them. We crossed a railroad track going from Brno to Třebíč. That was the front. By then, we were on foot and were walking alone. If one of us were stopped, the others could try to escape, every man for himself. But we were not stopped. We soon realized we had reached the no-man's-land between the two armies. Though the war literally surrounded us, everything near us was dead quiet. People were even working in the fields. At Zábřany, with great relief, we saw our first Red Army patrol, three Cossacks.

"Spotted any Germans?" they asked us anxiously.

"Nobody," we answered. The Cossacks smiled broadly.

At Zbýšov there were more Soviets, patrolling nervously. A German plane flying high overhead was shooting at no one in particular, letting the Rus-sians know he was there. To this day, I don't know why. At last came Ivan-čice, held by a Cossack division. We were taken to the commander, Major General Bělous, who provided a special car to take Grňa to Košice. I turned over the German plans for the fortification of Brno and started back the way I had come.[4]

Grňa had quite a trip after I left him with the Cossacks. His escort to Košice was a Russian war correspondent who pined to see the city of Mozart and Beethoven. So Grňa and the escort took a detour to Vienna and tooled around the great capital before they found their way to Bratislava and then to Košice in Slovakia. Cloistered as he had been in the countryside, hiding in a house without electricity and therefore unable even to read after dark, Grňa was probably as eager a tourist as the Russian.

---

4. For submitting these plans, the General Luža group was awarded a special citation from the Red Army.

Otherwise, his trip to Košice was a disaster. Grňa was received by Defense Minister Svoboda, President Beneš, Drtina, and Rudolf Slánský. Besides the Communists and a few worthy others, Grňa found ensconced around Beneš the usual desiccated politicians back from their safe exiles and behaving as if nothing had happened. We learned much later that the Košice men were nervously expecting Grňa to demand that resisters be given significant posts. They had even speculated about what he would say. But he made no demands for representation, nor had he intended to. Perhaps he planned to confront the leaders later in Prague. If so, he should have gone at once so as to met them at the airport when they came from Košice. As it was, he arrived five days after them.. Not having been at all involved in the Prague uprising or the transfer of power from the Germans, Grňa had no political authority with which to coerce the Fierlinger group into sharing power with us. No one took him seriously.

I returned from my trip with Grňa to find the Group of General Luža blissful with activity. Our headquarters, where I also slept, was a paneled "luxury" hut that Sandy built deep in the forest. There reports were coming in steadily that General Luža was destroying cars and killing German soldiers every day on the nearby roads. One of the raids PAM 5 carried out in my absence yielded forty pairs of boots and twenty blankets, along with food and uniforms. We were no longer afraid of the German tanks and had taken to attacking small clusters of them from our hideouts along the roadside. The tank drivers couldn't take the behemoths into the thick forest. They were never sure how many of us were in a particular place, so they did not dare leave the protection of their rolling fortresses. They were reduced to shooting furiously into the opaque woods. Our harassment was not very decisive, of course. We could only force the Germans to send out convoys of tanks, but we had no intention of attacking these more formidable units.

We were in the last days of the war, square in the path of retreat, with thousands of grim-faced German troops trying to get to some part of the Protectorate still occupied by the Nazis. From dawn to dark the roads were black with cars loaded to the roofs with Germans soldiers and civilians, massive convoys surrounded by tanks, heading to Bíteš and Meziříčí and beyond. Thousands more were on foot, dragging their belongings, a human corridor inching over the hills. An airplane motor would growl faintly in the distance, hardly louder than a hungry stomach, and the concourse would stop like stones in the road. The crowd would listen for four or five seconds, then vanish. Suddenly, the road would be bare as far as the eye could see. A small, single-engine Russian plane would then come into view—a scout trying to locate the German units. All would be still except for the airplane's motor as it flew in desultory circles. The plane would finally wander away and in an instant the road would again be teeming, with hardly a foot of space between the bodies. Horses bobbed up and down on the human tide, surrounded so closely by pedestrians that from a distance, they looked as if they, too, were being carried like bedrolls on the shoulders of the refugees.

In the beginning of our fighting, our objective had been simply to make movement difficult for the Germans and wherever possible to seize one more rifle, one more pistol, thereby leaving one less for them. But by April, our hope was to block the roads and hamper the retreat so that the Nazis might be trapped behind enemy lines. Hermit and I decided to concentrate PAM 5 on the Brno-Jihlava-Prague road, the main route out of Brno, and make it the center of all-out guerrilla warfare.

We forgot, in those wonderful, dizzying days, that war is hell and that this war had been the worst of hells for five years. By day, we were attacking every German group that we could reasonably hope to defeat. By night, we met semipublicly in the Turk's tavern at Nine Crosses to plan the next day's raids. The Russians in PAM 5 often gathered there for lunch, too, filling the place with German uniforms, since those were the only clothes they had, their Sten guns next to them on the benches like so many bassoons at a concert intermission. Since we now could arm people from the villages, we were joined by men in the vicinity who lived at home but could participate in specific actions. Hluboké became a sort of partisan community. The Germans were everywhere in their Wehrmacht uniforms. Our men were in Wehrmacht uniforms. Vlasov teams wandered the forest in their rags. The old village was suddenly bursting with activity, with thousands of people trying frantically to get somewhere else, and hundreds of other people on the go, up and down the roads and paths but going nowhere.

The surreal character of those days dominates my memories like a crude, painted backdrop—vivid, skewed, and sometimes whimsical. Cattle and sheep roamed everywhere in the woods, driven by the retreating Germans and abandoned when their guards, conscripted peasants, fled from the partisan fighting. We had no shortage of meat. Even after the war, one saw scattered, underfed cows all over the area. Side roads were dotted with burntout German cars; they had been set on fire either by us or by Red Army bombers to keep them from being of further use to the Germans. We as-

signed the villagers the task of burying the German soldiers we shot. Sometimes the grave diggers spat on their bloody charges; sometimes, their minds
preoccupied with other things, they merely shoveled the corpses impassively
into unmarked holes. The old Radomír, like the present one, would have
reflected that a naked Übermensch looks like any other son, father, or
brother—human and frangible. But the partisan Jáchim only thought of
them as so many contaminants that had to be deposited as far as possible
from the water supply. A thrilling sense of abnormality pervaded us, like the
nervousness that sweeps a crowd entering the tent of a grotesque spectacle,
and there were hours when the fighting was a heroin of queasy, unpardon-
able pleasure.

I loved it, every minute of it. From morning to night I was busy getting
supplies, receiving reports, sending instructions, dispatching groups. When
I read the events posted in my diary, in my youthful, former penmanship, a
lifetime comes back to me. On April 25, Gustav Kristek with his Brno men
damaged the treads of two German tanks with our new antitank ammunition. The Germans had to send a third tank to the rescue, and the partisans
hit that one, too. On April 26, near Tišnov, we killed six German military
and seized a motorcycle and a truck; at Svatoslav, we shot three more soldiers. On the twenty-eighth we learned that Brno had fallen. The Germans
wanted at all costs to keep the main road open and its communications intact; therefore, we tried to blow up every small bridge in the area so the
enemy would be forced to stop and repair them. Every day came a report of
three to five Germans shot, often on the connecting roads. The dead soldiers
were listed indifferently with their equipment, as if the partisan making the
report had walked over the area of the skirmish and written down what was
on the ground, man or metal, as he came to it. On the twenty-seventh, three
soldiers, one car, three bicycles, two officers on motorcycles, a revolver, and
a rifle, which, like most German weapons, was better than our unreliable
Sten guns, and therefore valuable booty. In another strike on the twenty-
seventh, we killed four German soldiers on motorcycles and bicycles. Elsewhere that day, according to my diary, we captured three soldiers, a car,
three bicycles, a motorcycle and two German officers. On April 28, near
Hermit's house: two trucks and one car seized, one first lieutenant and three
SS men killed, seven Russian prisoners freed. "Killed a few rangers known
as informers," my diary adds on the twenty-eighth, as if precision were not
necessary. Also on that day, another detachment captured twenty German
soldiers, fourteen rifles, and three pistols. On the same day, on the road be-

tween Náměšt' and Bíteš, we stopped a tank, using a log in the road as usual. While we were hiding in the woods, the frustrated gunner started shooting blindly at the obstacle in his way, assuming we were near it. We were gratified to see we were making the Germans tense. On the thirtieth, exultation! We seized a munitions truck full of machine guns, an antiaircraft machine gun, antitank weapons, and ammunition. On and on went the reports, one or two or five a day until the end of the war, usually with some German fighters killed.

We lost amazingly few men in these attacks, although now and then we suffered a casualty. Our strikes were carried out according to certain tacit rules. We did not intentionally harm German civilians, and everyone, even the Russians, stopped shooting the instant an enemy signaled his desire to surrender.

Otherwise, I cannot claim much hesitancy about dispatching the Germans, for they were almost all men under arms. Even when the enemy does you the favor of being as despicable as the Nazis, it is hard for average people with average upbringings to be complacent about taking human lives. It was not, however, hard for us. For the first time in years, we were finally fighting, not hiding, crouching in corners, running, humiliated, bullied. Ours was no longer the war of a small nation that could be readily sacrificed, but a colossal war supported by millions. We were part of a great camp that included Russians and Americans, all fighting a common evil.

However, ours was a separate war in the sense that we were quite distinct from any military. A soldier has a duty to kill when ordered, without requiring any other justification. If he loses a battle, the regular soldier is taken prisoner and treated with certain protections outlined by the Geneva Convention. But if we partisans lost a battle, we had no chance of returning for the next war; we were hanged. All of us were volunteers, under no obligation to follow orders with which we did not agree. The only authority was one's own conscience; the only commitment was a moral commitment. We took all of the responsibility for our actions, and all of the consequences.

At the very end, we were capturing twenty or thirty troops together. Once our Tišnov group took seventy-five German soldiers near Kuřímská Nová Ves whom we turned over to the approaching Red Army. They didn't put up much of a fight, knowing the war was at an end. The Germans were never demoralized or disorganized as we might have expected. But they did show an awareness that the cause was lost and not worth the sacrifice of their lives. For example, some of the men of General Luža routinely slept in a forest

hut. I gave repeated instructions that they were never to sleep without post-
ing sentries. I suppose one or two nights they disobeyed the order and nothing happened. Then it was four nights, then a week they let pass without a
sentry on duty. One dawn a Vlasov contingent on horses came to the hut,
looking for partisans. They opened the door and saw nothing, since the men
were sleeping in the attic. Instead of searching thoroughly, as they surely
would have done a few months earlier, they left, apparently not in a combat-
ive spirit.

Nobody was eager to kill women, even women who were ardent Nazi
supporters, though some were less hesitant about it than others. Once Loňka
and his group of Russians attacked three German cars in the usual way—
placing a log across the road so that the little convoy was forced to stop. The
cars turned out to be carrying between ten and fifteen Ordnungspolizei—we
had no compunction about shooting them—but also two women who admitted they worked for the Gestapo.

"Ah, so you, too, are engaged in torturing people?" Loňka asked, probably intending to let them go.

"No, no, no," the women protested. "We are secretaries. We don't do
anything like that. We type reports."

"Then we are in luck," he said mischievously. "The resistance needs typ-
ists. We'll take you to work with us."

At that, one of the women reached into her coat for a pistol, but Loňka
shot her before she could even cock it. The other woman meanwhile jumped
the gully on the side of the road and reached the edge of the woods before
she was stopped by one of Loňka's men taking leisurely aim and shooting
her in the back. Loňka reported the incident with his customary aplomb.
What is normal behavior at a battlefront would surely be identified elsewhere as gross aberrance. Throughout my weeks with him, Loňka exhibited
plenty of normal aberrance. He was a complicated fellow. Whenever he
made a strike, he gathered the boxes of the Germans sprawled across the
ditches, for every German soldier kept in his possession a little box containing his military papers. Loňka had a collection of them—his scalps, I called
them—stacked on a special shelf where he could show them off. On the
other hand, the chocolate his men found in German pockets he insisted on
saving for those partisans with children. Nothing delighted him more in
those sugar-starved times than to come upon a few bars of candy for the
little ones in his neighborhood.

Our efforts were working. We were slowing down the retreat, forcing the

Germans to use more and more men and tanks. At night, they couldn't move at all except in large numbers. But each day they returned to the task of keeping the main roads clear for their troop movements—quite a job, since the retreat stretched all the way to Kadolec and Křižanov. Large panzer units went through our area, tirelessly removing all the obstacles on the roads, their infantry raking the woods for partisans and partisan huts. Convoys of several German trucks or jeeps with mounted machine guns passed to and fro—without our interference, since we couldn't hope to overcome them, though every day we were getting more aggressive.

Now and then the Germans reminded us that they could still obliterate the partisans if they chose to be distracted from fighting at the front. They remained an organized army even while our guerrillas, also in German uniforms, moved as freely as if they, too, were retreating from the advancing Ukrainians. On April 30, one of our groups attacked a car with German officers going from Brno to Velká Bíteš on the highway. When the car passed our men stationed in the forest, the partisans shot at it, hitting at least one officer, who slumped forward in his seat. The car sped up and escaped. Around noon, the Czech partisans, still hidden in the forest, heard some fearful noise and saw a tank coming to the exact spot where they had earlier hit the German car. We were not especially afraid of one tank, which would be obliged to station itself on the edge of the woods and shoot indiscriminately into the trees. But that tank was followed by another and another—seven in all—coming to take revenge for the attack on the German officers. This was more than we bargained for. I was not among the group hiding in the forest, having moved to the other side of the road about five hundred yards away with our Brno contingent of sixteen or eighteen men, but I could see everything. The tanks were going very, very slowly, looking for us. From their hiding place, one of the Czechs opened fire with a machine gun—a stupid mistake that didn't hurt the tank but gave away the partisans' location. The Czechs followed up with hand grenades and more machine gun fire, but even though they were very close to the tanks, they were not having much effect. Taking their time, the tanks lumbered into a semicircle and pointed their guns at the invisible bandits, all of whom by now had flattened themselves on the leafy ground. The tanks then began shooting blindly and ferociously into the forest. Trees doubled over, their branches cracking liked snapped bones in the terrifying barrage. Birds and forest animals whose voices I had never heard shrieked above the din. The pounding went on and on—twenty minutes, forty-five minutes, an hour—with branches cracking each minute like thunderclaps, until I imagined that every tree within range had been wounded and half the men in our unit must be dead. If hell were noise, it would sound like this. After almost an hour, the explosions stopped. The Germans were apparently discussing whether to continue. They couldn't see anybody, but they were obviously afraid to risk leaving the highway to go in after the partisans. There was the possibility that the forest was mined or that the partisans might be able to get dangerously close with grenades and Molotov cocktails. After ten minutes of silence, one turret cover came up and a head wearing a black beret cautiously rose. The buttons on the German officer's black uniform glinted in the sun as, gaining confidence, he raised his binoculars. Then the partisans opened fire and he flopped over the side of the turret like a flour sack. All the tanks started shooting again, but this time only for two or three minutes. They had apparently run out of ammunition, and so turned and rolled toward Bíteš.

All work had stopped in Hluboké, where the people knelt in terror next to their plows and worktables and prayed for the partisans. I had been praying, too, and summoned the courage to survey our losses. To my amazement, none of our boys had been killed; only Gustav Kristek was wounded when a tree branch fell on his foot. We half-expected another assault of tanks or armored cars and were especially worried that the Germans might retaliate by attacking the Turk's tavern and the village. But none of this happened. We were still in the forest at dark, keeping a wary watch, when we spotted the silhouettes of some German infantry, a little band slipping between the trees. There was an exchange of fire, and then we discovered that the soldiers were not Germans at all, but members of PAM 5 in uniform, German uniforms, of course, who had heard the commotion and had come to help us.

For several months, R3 had been trying to organize a central body that could represent the entire home resistance at the end of the war. Štainer and Robotka had reestablished links with the illegal trade unions and were maintaining a contact with the Czechoslovak Communist Party in Prague. All the groups we could locate were to form a Czech National Council that could speak for the resistance with one voice. Since the German occupation made it exceedingly difficult for us to communicate in the underground, we were still talking in whispers and had no way of knowing all the resistance organizations. There were bound to be groups that would not at first be represented in the Council, but at least we thought we would have some of our

people in place, ready to take over the responsibilities of interim government when the Germans left. The members of the Council would, we
thought, form the core of the republic's first postwar cabinet. They might be
joined by a few of the politicians returning from abroad, but we expected
the primary officials to be people put forward by the home resistance. The
men who made up the Czech National Council when it was finally consti-
tuted were by no means exemplars of political vision. With some exceptions,
they were a frayed and feckless group of third-raters, our first- and second-
raters having been lost to the Gestapo. They had at least endured the war
and aided the struggle as best they could; they were deserving mediocrities,
interested in making up for all the misery people had suffered, as opposed
to many of the undeserving mediocrities returning from exile, interested
mainly in their careers. But because they were weak individuals, they were
even less capable than the exiles of standing up to the Soviets and insisting
on positions of power for the home resisters. Both the exiles and home representatives together were hardly more than a rowboat facing the tidal wave
of Communists that was about to engulf us.

Everywhere the situation was fluid. The Germans would leave a place.
The town would rejoice, tear down the German flags, obliterate the German
names on the buildings, and set up a committee for governing. Fearing that
their army's lines of communication might be threatened, the Germans
would sometimes halt their retreat, return, and reassert control. They would
reinstall the swastika flags, put the names back on the buildings, and arrest
the committee members, shooting or hanging most of them, before retreating again a few days later.

Then there was a startling, spontaneous development, a situation that
often occurs in the last spasms of war and yet is seldom expected: the country erupted in revolution. It was not an organized national rebellion such as
Father had planned, but a spate of uprisings that came quickly and unpre-
dictably in towns where the Germans were still on the way out. Like twisters
in the wake of a hurricane, the uprisings were random, disconnected, and
vicious. The first such revolt started on May 1 in one of the most important
railroad stations in central Moravia, the Přerov, just as the Russians were
about to move in. Without waiting for the Germans to leave, the population
declared the town liberated and hoisted the Czech flag. In town after town,
people began seizing the government, pronouncing the death of the Protectorate and appointing themselves the local representatives of the Czechoslovak Republic. In some cases, they tried to disarm the Germans and hinder

their retreat. In others, they let the Germans continue their business of getting out. In the middle of it all, every radio in Europe blared electrifying news: Hitler had committed suicide on April 30, 1945, effectively ending the Third Reich. The German troop commanders redoubled their efforts to reach the American forces and avoid surrendering to the Soviets, while the unorganized and unconnected uprisings continued sweeping the country, town by town. In most cases, the people had no weapons with which to attack the Germans. The insurrections thus consisted of raising the Czech flag and refusing to accept German authority. Sometimes the German commander in the region, not wanting to delay his withdrawal, chose to ignore what the local people were doing, so long as his own forces were not molested. But in other places, every impudence was answered with a furious reprisal.

Part of the impetus for the uprisings was that everyone knew the Germans were on the run and it was at last possible, though still dangerous, to retaliate against them. But there was more. As the Germans retreated westward, they had been emptying their concentration camps and transporting the inmates, especially Jews, ahead of the front. In the winter of 1944–45, we Czechs were still unaware of what we now call the Holocaust—unaware that Hitler had been systematically exterminating the Jews. From time to time, trainloads of Jews had passed through, or we saw ghastly columns of skeletons being marched from Poland to Germany. But, as all the prisoners we saw at any time during the war were in appalling condition, we did not realize that Jews were being treated differently than Soviets or Christian Poles.[5] The BBC was almost our only source of outside information, and it gave little idea of what was happening. Now, suddenly, one community after another in the Protectorate saw tens of thousands of naked starvelings packed into cattle cars or stumbling over the hills in forced marches. One saw the Germans mistreating them, these infested, dying animals that had once been Jewish teachers, housewives, and schoolchildren, saw the Germans stomping them with jackboots, slamming rifle butts into their skulls, or shooting them matter-of-factly. It shocked people who were past shocking, Czechs whose own relatives had suffered unspeakable deaths at the hands of the Nazis.

The Czech uprisings were futile, crushed in every place where the Ger-

5. Of the 250,000 persons in the Czechoslovak Republic killed by the Germans during the occupation, 154,000 were Jews.

mans responded to the provocations. As near to us as Velké Meziříčí on May
6, two days before the end of the war, some members of Tau and local Communists held a meeting in the city hall, acting as the restored local authorities. Tau was one of R3's most active branches, made up of survivors of Staff
Captain Moravanský's old group. They were the last of our fighters still
above ground, working legally in the Meziříčí district office. These men
never tried to disarm the Germans. They simply held a meeting to discuss
some sort of provisional government for the town after the Nazi evacuation.
Suddenly a passing Wehrmacht unit stopped with two tanks, arrested the
newly formed district committee and some of their aides—a total of seventy-two Czechs—tortured them hideously, and threw them in the Oslava
River. Among them was a young engineer, the devoted son of my protector
in Meziříčí, the Proletarian. In Třešt, the SS found forty-seven men under a
Czechoslovak flag discussing the German capitulation and put an end to it
by executing them all. My own men almost shared the same fate. Robotka
wanted us to occupy Bíteš and its two thousand inhabitants on May 7, at a
time when the town was still one of the German army centers. I told Hermit
the idea was nonsense, as our flimsy weapons could never challenge the regular Wehrmacht units. After we learned the fate of Meziříčí, the plan was
dropped.

The fever of revolt continued to break out in a dozen other places, erupt-
ing in Prague on May 5, 1945. The Czech National Council had for several
weeks been preparing an insurrection in the capital with remnants of ON
and groups of other former military people. On April 23, R3 had given
Nechanský and Klemeš false identity cards and dispatched them to the center of the agitation with their transmitter. I saw Nechanský as he was leaving
for Prague, buoyant and full of resolve as the Czech National Council's future military leader. He would help coordinate the insurrection, keeping in
radio contact with the government in Košice. However, the mass uprising
took the Council and the leaders by surprise and forced them prematurely
into the open. Before they could mobilize, a phalanx of ordinary citizens
and Protectorate policemen had seized the Prague radio station and was
broadcasting frantic calls to the population and the Allies for help. The underground military group Aleš, led by General František Slunečko and General Karel Kutlvašr—people who had put ON back together after General
Novák's arrest—were at first the de facto military directors of the revolt and
prepared the appeals for weapons. The Czech National Council assumed political control, if one may speak of control in a populous city still fortified

and occupied by the Germans. Kutlvašr and Nechanský tried to give the insurrection some martial management. Through the transmitter, they sent coded messages out to Europe, explaining the strength and location of the German units and making arrangements to receive heavy weapons—weapons that would never arrive. The whole citizenry threw up sixteen hundred street barricades, which were then manned by thirty thousand Czech civilians with no effective weapons. The barriers blocked every main thoroughfare and paralyzed German activities, especially the movements of tanks. As the Germans got out of their vehicles to remove the obstacles, they were picked off by snipers. They soon learned to shield themselves by seizing Czech women and children to use as hostages while they grappled with the barricades. The Vlasov troops that had been German collaborators now changed sides and fought alongside the Czechs. It was not manpower, however, that the Czechs lacked, but weapons. Men and women with rakes and pistols faced thirty to forty thousand trained fighters armed with tanks and artillery. Their battle raged for three days, broadcast all over Europe hour by desperate hour as they pleaded with the Allies to send arms.

All their appeals were ignored by the Americans, though General Patton and the Third Army were at the time less than fifty miles from Prague. General Eisenhower steadfastly refused to allow the American troops to move because Prague, according to the designations he and the Allies had agreed upon, fell within the Soviet zone of occupation. The Americans listened impassively to the anguished messages as two thousand Czechs were slaughtered. One secondary arm of the Red Army was near Bíteš, about 120 miles away, but it lacked sufficient tanks and manpower to attack Prague. The main force of the Red Army was in Saxony. Fearing that the Americans might be induced to help the insurrection and end up occupying Prague despite the Allied agreements, the Soviets regrouped their forces and moved thousands of tanks—an entire tank army—over the Sudeten mountains to the capital. The Germans, anxious to evade the Red Army and surrender instead to the Americans, abandoned the struggle. They capitulated to the Czech National Council on May 8, and marched westward to reach the American lines in Pilsen, carrying only their small arms. When the Red Army at last entered Prague on May 9, they found it in the hands of the Czech National Council, a situation that was not at all to Stalin's taste. The next day the Košice government arrived and, as one of its first actions, dissolved the Czech National Council—the voice of the resistance and the insurrection. During the uprising, the National Council had accepted the help of the Vlasovs, who were Soviet traitors. The Soviet government used this as a pretext for refusing to recognize the Council or have any dealings with it. Pressured by the Soviets, the Czechoslovak authorities demanded that the Council resign, effectively ending the possibility that its resistance members would play any part in the new government.

Neither Štainer nor Grňa had participated in the Prague uprising. They and many other resistance leaders were still scattered over the country when the fighting began. Grňa reached Prague only after everything was settled and the Czech National Council had been shoved aside by the new men. However, even if he had been at the table when the ministries were handed around, Grňa was not a sufficiently forceful personality to compel the appointments we wanted. If he had at least presented our demands, we might have come out as well as the Slovaks and not been completely shut out. The leaders of the Slovakian national uprising did insist on recognition and were included in the government for Slovakia, represented by the two main parties of their home resistance, the Democrats and the Communists. When I heard about the government that had been formed without us, I was bitter and repeated again and again to myself and anybody who would listen, "This is not what we've been fighting for."

The radio in our headquarters was suddenly soundless. "Stand by for an important announcement," said a BBC broadcaster whose usually suave voice I recognized. There was another long pause. Four Beethoven notes had signaled the start of every BBC newscast throughout the war but this time, there was no musical introduction, just a quivering voice delivering a message so momentous that only phrases of it penetrated my excitement: "German capitulation . . . unconditional surrender . . . armistice signed . . . end at midnight May 8 . . . historic occasion." There were prayers, I think, and some anthems, and then throughout the day more and more details that I didn't hear because I ran to Hluboké to share the news with my men.

On the main road we could still see the German convoys retreating in orderly columns, away from Brno toward Jihlava. The German soldiers were well behaved, nervously looking around for partisans, even as they marched past posters declaring that anyone who helped the partisans would be executed.[6] A tank accompanied the columns. Every three or four minutes the

6. The posters further stated that if partisans were allowed to operate within a community, the mayor would be held responsible with his own life.

tank fired, for no reason that I could see except to scare away Russians. Seeing a few wary Czechs near the columns, I carefully approached one of the German artillerymen, an impeccably dressed, twice-shaven, sparkling young officer.

"How's it going?" I asked him in German.

"Not too bad," he answered. "We're headed for Prague. Tomorrow will be the end of the war. Things could be worse." The whole world seemed headed for Prague. The entire highway from Brno to Velká Bíteš was now streaming with cars, carriages, military vehicles, buses, horses, and wagons.

The war did not end sharply in our part of the country but rather died by imperceptible degrees, like a patient still clinging to life after the priest has come and gone and the funeral arrangements are set. On the morning of May 9, 1945, we quite clearly saw Soviet aircraft attacking Bíteš—hours after the end of the war—apparently because there was a concentration of German troops there. Parts of Bíteš were thus destroyed by the liberators. Some of my friends who had survived the entire war were killed in the bombing on this day after the armistice. Otherwise, there was not the dramatic fighting I had expected, considering we were at the front. The Germans moved out, the Soviets moved in, and the front moved somewhere ahead of us.

At ten both the Kristek brothers burst into the headquarters near Bíteš shouting, "Jáchim, the Russians are here! The Russians are here! We saw the first Soviets going through Ludvíkov." We hurried to Kristek's sawmill two miles away to welcome our liberators. People were smiling and chuckling as they waited along the road as if for a parade—the first crowd of happy Czechs I had seen since 1938. A few were shaking their heads and weeping softly in a sudden access of pent-up emotion. It was foggy that morning, and we could not see the Soviets until they were almost upon us. These first arrivals of the Red Army, part of the Second Ukrainian Front under Marshal Radion Malinovsky, were officers—educated, well behaved, and well groomed. They had come into a party atmosphere in every community, from the Slovakian border to Bíteš, and had listened patiently to I don't know how many heartfelt, clumsy welcoming speeches accompanied by spring bouquets. Teenage girls, rakishly made up, climbed on the tanks to kiss and hug the soldiers; old people reached toward them tentatively to touch a sleeve or jacket flap. The Soviet officers, too, were happy. "Be careful," they warned us jovially. "Behind us are coming some others. Lock up your girls. And whatever you do, don't give them even a taste of slivovitz."

Within an hour of the arrival of the Soviets, I had been relieved of my revolver. "You won't be needing this any more," they assured me.

The next wave of the Red Army crashed into town and stayed a few days in homes in the vicinity, followed by the next and the next. Unlike the first army, these were young, crude, childlike, peasant draftees, fundamentally good-hearted, uncontrollable when in quest of děvočky and liquor, which was nearly all the time. Nevertheless, we were glad to see them, all of them. Their worst transgressions were venial compared to the savagery of the Nazis from whom they had rescued us.

I walked through Meziříčí, with its pleased but disconcerted residents coping as best they could with crowds of singing, drunken soldiers in streets that were unaccustomed even to litter. A Russian was leading five horses along the main road. I did not have to wonder how he came by five draft horses. Another approached me trying to make innocent conversation. He tapped his wrist. "Watch," he said in Czech. I nodded. "Give?" he asked, using the basic vocabulary that all the soldiers had mastered. As I took off my watch, he grinned encouragingly, showing teeth that had probably never been exposed to a dentist. He strapped the watch proudly to his wrist, adjusting all the other timepieces, a glittering collection of Omegas and Zeniths that covered his arm up to the biceps.

Most of the soldiers were billeted with Czech families for a few days' layover before continuing their march. As if they had entered an empty dwelling, some of them swept past their hosts and at once began ransacking cabinets and rummaging through drawers, relieving the owners of every drop of liquor. Since there were few drops of real intoxicants to be had, they drank rubbing alcohol and aftershave, draining every strong-smelling bottle in the house. More than one soldier died from an overdose of eau de cologne. Once drunk, they began good-naturedly shooting up the town. At first, people tried to complain to the commanders that troops were pillaging, or that a soldier had stolen someone's wedding ring. "Stealing?" the commander would exclaim in all earnestness. "Show me who it was and I'll have him shot!" And perhaps he would have. To the Soviets, two grams of metal were worth more than a life.

Every Czech has a toilet story about the Russians, stories that skeptical westerners attribute to cold war gossip. But I was myself sitting with some Czech friends in their home in Bíteš when three soldiers entered without knocking, presented papers showing their house assignment, and announced that they had been riding around in the sun and were thirsty. Before anyone could fetch them a drink, they had begun exploring the rooms, coming to the bathroom in the hall, while my friends followed behind, lamely welcoming them in Czech and offering some tea. One of the Russians spotted the toilet, and while everyone stood by, quite appalled, he dropped to his knees and stuck his head into it, cupping his hands into the water and finally drinking from it directly. He ended by rinsing his head and neck with the toilet water before giving his comrades their turn. "Please, young men," the woman of the house said, "we use that for something else—the other thing." When I had translated her plaintive message, the soldiers turned away with a shrug and their customary response, an expression I heard five hundred times in those days, "*Ničevo*"— "Who the hell cares?"

Red Army soldiers were going from house to house calling on the towns-people. Once inside the door, they indicated politely across the language barrier that they would like to meet the young ladies of the house, who at first needed no encouragement to satisfy their curiosity about the foreign young men. Hasty seductions ensued; that is to say, the Soviets thought what they did was seduction, but the girls thought they had been raped. In the countryside, where nubile women were fewer, a band of Soviets might pound on a door before bursting in and hastily seducing every female in the house including the great-grandmother. Then, their habitual good humor restored, they would urge gifts upon the distraught family, handing over their horses or emptying knapsacks full of jewelry on the kitchen table, such donations being easy to replace. Contrite in the face of tears, they would have given the girls back their virginity if they could have. I was glad that Vlasta and her sister were locked in their rooms in Radoškov, an hour away from the Red Army's path.

On May 11, our group began setting up a new district committee for Velké Meziříčí, twelve members to replace the former committee that the Germans drowned in the Oslava. Hermit became chairman of this district committee. I was head of the police and gendarmes. Kobylka and Sec were also members. When General Svoboda, Czechoslovakia's new defense minister, arrived on May 22, he ordered us to round up all the Germans, traitors, and collaborators within forty-eight hours. Since we had no internment camp, they were to remain at large, identified by a special band on their left shoulders. Czechs were forbidden to talk to them, an order that I doubt was ever violated, since all the Nazis and their sympathizers had long since left town. Instead of searching for unavailable Germans, Hermit and I saw to it that the Meziříčí District Committee filed a statement attesting to Count Lich-tenstein-Podstatzky's invaluable help to the resistance, so as to protect our supporter from any anti-German reprisals. Then I said good-bye to my friends, both the living and the dead, picked up my mother, and prepared to return to life.

X

The Brno we came back to was a wan city of damaged souls and demolished buildings. Our apartment at 4 Wurm Road was empty, the Gestapo having confiscated our furniture, except for one single piece. I stared at it, the flower-covered couch where I had done my homework through all my school years, and it stared back at me with sixty-four eyes—black-ringed bullet holes. Our clothes were few and shabby, but we were no worse off than many others who, returning from Nazi prisons or the underground, had nowhere to go. Hundreds of villas and houses had been left by the German population of Brno when they fled from the Russians, but they were now either appropriated by the new Czechoslovak officials and their friends or were given over to the Red Army, which looted them completely. Dr. Káňa took us in at first, and then we were assigned a furnished house confiscated from the Germans. Russian soldiers got a key to it and ransacked it, for they considered anything movable their war booty. However, it is hard even now to hold any grudges against the soldiers. Some of the Soviets had been fighting since 1941. Even men who were civilized and citified when the war began would have been brutalized by spending so much of their young lives on battlefields.

In June 1945, a month after the armistice, I registered in Masaryk University's law school. Walking from home to classes, I felt as if I were in foreign territory. Part of my alienation was the natural difficulty of adjusting to normal life. For fully a year after the war I reached instinctively for my pistol, which I no longer had, whenever a stranger approached me or opened a door unexpectedly. In part I was feeling delayed grief as I tried to reconstruct the world without Father in it. I felt as if there were a wall around me that was invisible to others but that I could see quite clearly, separating me from everyone except the few surviving friends who had been with me in the resistance. Everyone had suffered during the war, I reminded myself. Behind each face I met, there were experiences that could be neither forgotten nor shared. This girl had been raped, that man had seen his brother tortured; another had lost a child in a bomb attack. We were a country of victims. I was not the only one trying to break out of a past that kept me from seeing the world afresh.

But what, after all, was fresh about it? All around the university were posters announcing the new political structure, that is to say, the new power of Communists, who were the leading element in every administrative and political unit and were not timid about imposing their views. The Red Army, not the local Communists, had liberated us. Communists had not been leaders in the resistance except, in some places, at the very end. But here they were, running everything, and the returning democrats were submitting to them on every point. The Communists were not interested in promoting or honoring the resisters, and the resisters meekly allowed themselves to be shoved to the back of the crowd.

Soon we would hear that the democratic resistance had not been important, that it was the Communists in the underground who had waged the significant resistance struggle—propaganda generated from Moscow and repeated so insistently that perhaps people who had not themselves been part of the resistance started to believe it. President Beneš still enjoyed support, even from the reluctant Communists. In the months after the war he might yet have carried out reforms and restricted the Communists. He had always wanted to remain above political parties, a statesman presiding over the democratic process. In any case, he was ill. But disappointing as he was, he was a towering figure compared with others in the government after 1945.

As in the rest of central Europe, the first postwar government in Czechoslovakia was a National Front comprising several parties. The former agrarian party was accused of collaboration and outlawed; otherwise, the National Front was a genuine coalition of parties freely elected in 1946. The new government put forth what was known as the Košice program, though it was formulated in Moscow, calling for a purge of collaborators. President Hácha and all members of the Protectorate government were to be charged

with high treason. The program provided for fairly radical economic reforms, along with a foreign policy that would make Czechoslovakia an ally
of the Soviet Union, a bridge between East and West.

The Communists, however, had a great deal of backstage power in this
apparently democratic government. From the very beginning they insisted
on holding the crucial ministry of the interior, which controlled the police.
Svoboda, the pro-Soviet independent, was minister of defense, in charge of
the military. The counterintelligence department was a particular Communist stronghold, augmented by a newly created department of political education. A new ministry of information was created, headed by a Communist.
Cultural activities and the media now came under his control, so that
Czechoslovakia for the first time had a virtual propaganda office in the government. A prominent Communist was minister of education. The Communists ran most of the cities after the war and appointed themselves to
posts of authority at every level in the new administrative system. They occupied positions of power in the trade unions and in the workers' councils
in all the large factories. Thus the working class, the traditional support of
the Social Democrats, was taking its direction from Communists, as was the
peasant movement. Even the secretary general of the organization of resisters was a Communist. A Communist held the ministry of agriculture, which
meant that confiscated German land was awarded to Communist supporters—hundreds of thousands of acres left by the expelled Sudeten Germans,
along with farms, houses, and businesses of Germans who had voluntarily
fled. As German property was being distributed, people naturally wanted to
be invited to the banquet and so were induced to join the Communist Party
even if they had had no particular political ideology.

In many cases, neither excessive blandishments nor strong-arm tactics
were necessary for the Communists to secure their dominance over Czechoslovakia. I was amazed that individuals such as General Homola's son Losik
eagerly spouted Marxist rhetoric, constantly referring to "the Party" in the
reverent tones of a nun discussing the Holy See. Under our electoral system,
if the Communist Party received 38 percent of the vote in a national election, as it did in the election of May 1946, then by rights 38 percent of the
ministerial appointments should fall to Communists. The Soviets and by extension the Communists were very popular after the war, and in any case,
the Soviets had given us back our country. It was difficult at first to refuse
them whatever they wanted. Initially, many provincial and local appointments were simply informal arrangements, made in the absence of govern-

ment structure. Just as in 1989, there was a vacuum of power that the winning side filled without much opposition. In 1989, democracy was the gust that swept away the crumbling old order, and the United States was the hero of the hour. In 1945, it was the Russians who were heroes, and Communism seemed the strongest alternative to the hated Nazis. The democratic forces in our country had been disorganized by the war. Social democrats, for example, were split between pro-Communists and our traditional representatives whose ideas were similar to those of the British Labor Party. Should the democratic parties concentrate on strengthening our constitutional rights, or should they side with the Communists to achieve social and economic changes? All of them vacillated during the period 1945–1948, while in the same years the Communist Party leadership was strong and stable with Gottwald as chairman and Slánský as secretary-general.

As a sop to the democrats, the Communists agreed to Beneš' reappointment of Jan Masaryk as minister of foreign affairs, the post he had held in the London government. The son of the first president of Czechoslovakia, Masaryk was genuinely nonpartisan, dedicated only to defending his country's interests. However, the Communists insisted on creating a new post, state secretary of foreign affairs, where the Slovak Communist Vlado Clementis was installed to act as Masaryk's watchdog.

As for the resisters who were supposed to lead the new order, we were all, every one of us, waved aside. Grňa was appointed chairman of a resistance veterans association, the Association of National Revolution, a harmless post that removed him from political life. Štainer was appointed commanding officer of national security in Bohemia—a high-sounding title that meant he worked as a policeman. He was promoted to colonel—in the police force, not the army. Robotka, who had been a captain in the army before the war, was now moved up a notch to lieutenant colonel, which would have been his rank anyway if the six years of the war had not interrupted his normal progression in the military. No one cared about him. Hermit became head of a special office of the minister of national defense, giving certificates to surviving resisters and thus entitling them to certain emoluments—a nothing job that nevertheless required that fire-eating conservative to join the Communist Party. Rudolf Sedlák, the forester, became the caretaker—"administrator"—of the new summer residence of President Beneš, Castle Náměšt' nad Oslavou, Oslava being the river where the seventy-two resisters in Velké Meziříčí had ended their lives. Jedlička emerged from prison to join the provisional National Assembly but, seeing that he had no real future in political life, eventually returned to directing his clothing cooperative in Brno. All the outstanding resisters were thus relegated to second-class functions.

There were a few warm moments for us. President Beneš received Mother at Náměšť Castle and later surprised us by paying all of the expenses for her kidney surgery. I was awarded military decorations for my resistance activities. In 1945 the army under General Novák's supervision installed a bronze sculpture of Father at the Moravia-Silesia military headquarters in Brno. A plaque was inscribed: "He fought with the people / He died for the people / He was victorious with the people." Over two thousand people attended the dedication, at which Grňa was the main speaker—a fine, though temporary, commemoration of Father. Three years later, the Communist government removed both the sculpture and the inscription.

Our own lives, Mother's and mine, began to absorb that wonderful medicine for ravaged souls: routine. Now that I no longer needed to ration my studies to stretch my supply of books, I read my school assignments hungrily. The rest of my time I dedicated to the Social Democratic Party, the potential alternative to the Communists. In our red climate, it was futile to advocate anti-Soviet activity, but I thought social democrats of all parties could at least bind the Communists to their promises to preserve the Czechoslovak system. Joined by old friends such as Císař Fireman, I became a leader of the party's youth wing. Before long, I was in the thrall of political activism—making campaign speeches, directing other volunteers, and writing publicity, all the while trying to maintain my law school grades. I had a special feeling for both Vlasta and Věra. Since I had no time at all for any girl, it was an expedient feeling, a sort of nostalgia, that demanded nothing save the awareness of it. My inner life was littered with glimpsed horrors and fugitive sensations that hardly qualified as emotions. I was unable to collect a self to offer either woman, and equally unable to let one or the other go out of my life.

Mother's grief had been kept at bay during the tension of living underground. Life was supposed to be normal now, but all the satisfactions of normality were drained from it. When she came back from hiding, only emptiness was waiting for her. Though often possessive of me, she responded to my conversation with the eyes of someone adding figures in her head. She was not cold, exactly, but I think that, like me, she was preoccupied—gingerly testing and pricking the numbness within. It was hard for me, having commanded sixty men directly and eight hundred indirectly, to pretend to let her supervise me. I had expected to build on the closeness we had in the underground. She and I had never shared our inmost thoughts or expressed tenderness outright even before we went into hiding, but I had somehow pictured us going home after the war and accumulating layers of affection in the details of our daily life. Instead, our still house seemed inhabited by a whimper.

Then I met a girl entirely unconnected with the resistance. She was studying at the Drama Conservatory in Brno and was already well known as a radio actress, though I thought her face was too extraordinary to waste on that sightless medium. Libuše Podhrázská was the blithe spirit I needed to help me get over the war, turning up in zany outfits that appalled my mother, breaking into the loneliness and sedateness of our apartment with her magical, D-major voice, the voice of an oboe improvising waltzes. Her father was involved in the coal business, but she herself was focused on the arts, a world away from politics or military matters. Just as I was busy with sorting out the past, she was full of exuberance and the future.

The future, however, looked increasingly ominous. For three years after the war, the Communists allowed some political parties to operate in Czechoslovakia, in accordance with the letter of Soviet pledges to the western Allies. There was pressure on everyone to appear pro-Soviet in all the activities of life—school, work, and certainly politics—but the pressure was a kind of political correctness and not an actual abrogation of the Czechoslovaks' right of free speech. If an official wanted to commit political suicide, he could publicly attack the Soviet Union in a general way (though not Stalin), just as today an American official casual of his career may make a racial slur without fear of going to jail. But the pro-Soviet attitude that began as an obligatory courtesy became more of a requirement each day.

Democrats were undermined in every way, particularly the democratic leaders of the resistance. Nothing showed this more than the trial of Viktor Ryšánek, the squint-eyed Czech informant who almost succeeded in delivering Father and General Novák to the Gestapo. Ryšánek was brought before a special court set up to try collaborators. He had escaped from Czechoslovakia after the war but returned voluntarily, perhaps hoping that the Communist prosecutors would offer him leniency in return for helping them destroy the reputations of resistance leaders. While Ryšánek was in custody, the Communist police allowed him a Christmas vacation, bringing him home in a police car to his Brno apartment so that he could take a bath and visit his girlfriend. They were treating him as if he were a witness for the prosecution instead of a defendant. Who, then, was the defendant in the case? Why, the resistance, or rather the non-Communist resisters, who were cast as anti-Soviets. At his trial in October 1946, Ryšánek testified that the resistance had been clearly divided between pro-Communists and rightists. He claimed that he, Ryšánek, had always been a Communist supporter, though he did not explain how a pro-Communist could also work for the violently anti-Communist Gestapo. In setting a trap for Luža and his supporters, he was trying to eliminate reactionaries—the rightists who hampered the genuine efforts of Communist resisters. Luža, he asserted, winking thoughtfully at the paneled wall behind the judges, had even consulted with him about "getting rid" of Karel Štainer. Ryšánek left a sinister space around the words, so there could be no doubt that Father was contemplating Štainer's execution. General Ingr, he continued with the same careful emphasis, had disseminated secret orders to "purge" all Communists from the resistance.

Ryšánek was strikingly intelligent. I sat in the courtroom while he adumbrated these lies and noted how cleverly he was able to slide off the point of a question and introduce distractions. The prosecutors, who were in reality his coaches, could provide him with a drop of substance, and like a glassblower he could expand it, breathing it into it whatever shape they wanted. Two other Gestapo men corroborated his testimony that the resistance had been divided between Communists and rightists and that only the Communists were active. Robotka asked to take the witness stand and, demonstrating his courage once again, testified that there had been no such split among resisters. Furthermore, he denounced the Gestapo-like methods of the prosecution.

How could anyone believe that my father, hunted and hounded by the Germans, was in any way—directly or indirectly—helping them? Or even that he wanted to assassinate Štainer? Wring his neck, yes. But kill him? Of course not. The whole idea that the resistance was divided was nonsense. Everyone in the movement was oriented toward the left. Father was not a Communist, but he was a Russophile, and he was never opposed to working with any sincere resister. The Communist press nevertheless took up the fabricated issue of the "The Division." The trial merged into a larger campaign to compromise and isolate democrats in one organization after another. Eventually, they would be sufficiently vulnerable for an all-out Communist attack.

If the Communists had promised Ryšánek a reward, they cheated him, or changed their minds. Having extracted what they wanted from him, the tribunal sentenced him to death. He was hanged immediately after the trial. His cohort Jizera died in prison before coming to trial. Paprskář, who revealed the whole conspiracy to Robotka at the last moment, was given life imprisonment. Those trials were among several in which non-Communist resisters were forced to prove they had not been obstructionists in fighting the Germans. To his credit, Grňa also courageously denounced these Communist methods.

By 1947, Czechoslovakia was the last country in the Soviet sphere with a functioning parliamentary democracy. It seemed to me that any moment the Communists might throw out our constitutional rights and pull us under the Iron Curtain like the rest of eastern Europe. But instead of preparing for a possible Communist takeover, our politicians were squandering their resources fighting among themselves in trivial, bitterly partisan disputes. I was planning to run on the Social Democratic ticket in the May 1948 elections for a seat in the National Assembly. In the three years since the end of the war, the democratic forces had regained much of their strength throughout the country. It looked as though the Communists would lose seats in parliament and a Social Democrat would be the next prime minister. The question was whether the Communists would allow the elections to take place.

In the summer of 1947, I proposed forming a new movement to counter the Communists, a mass, nonpartisan umbrella organization that would include all the democratic groups in one lobbying force. Such a movement would facilitate our organizing street demonstrations or boycotts in the event of a threatened coup. Eventually I got to see the minister of justice, Prokop Drtina. Beneš had given his informal approval, according to his staff, but expressed uncertainty as to how such an endeavor could be financed and organized. But Drtina, himself one of the leaders of a socialist party, was not enthusiastic. "Our party is already trying to do what you are proposing, so we have no need of another organization," he said. Like other politicians, he was not convinced that the Communists would attempt a coup, and if they did, he said, "the existing political parties can meet the challenge." In other words, he and others were afraid of losing their positions of leadership if their parties were subsumed into a larger movement, so they would go on doing nothing while the Communists took over.

After my meeting with Drtina, I spoke to Mother. "If there is a Communist coup, I will be arrested. I can either go underground or try to leave. But this time it won't be a matter of hiding until the end of the war. There might not be a war. The Communists might simply remain in power for the rest of our lives."

"There would be nothing here for you to look forward to," she replied mildly. "You'd be better off going."

I did not have to wait long for the crisis. By the autumn of 1947, Stalin had decided to consolidate his hold on eastern Europe, "to throw reactionary forces"—meaning democrats—"out of the National Front," according to Slánský, and to establish a Communist dictatorship.[1] In September, three non-Communist ministers, Jan Masaryk, Petr Zenkl, and Prokop Drtina, received parcels containing bombs, assassination attempts that the three survived. The Social Democrats were too disorganized to respond effectively to this provocation. They did replace their pro-Communist chairman, Fierlinger, with the centrist Bohumil Laušman. But despite being a little more politically independent, the unlucky Laušman was a fellow traveler with the Communists and hardly the man to represent us in the confrontation they were precipitating.

Police investigations implicated Communists in the bombing. State security's response to that information was to dismiss the non-Communist police officials and hire its own lackeys. The showdown thus came on February 20, 1948, when twelve democratic cabinet ministers resigned in protest against cumulative outrages, including the Communists' packing of the police force. The ministers, thinking naïvely like parliamentarians, had counted on Beneš to refuse their resignations and either to call new elections according to customary procedure or carry out their demands to clean up the police. But their resignations were not refused. The next day this same police force, enlarged by newly hired Communists, took over the Prague radio, post offices, and telegraph and railway stations. By abandoning their posts, the ministers handed the Communists their opportunity, for they left Gottwald legally in power. Next he armed detachments of factory workers and paraded them through the streets of Prague in what were made to look

---

1. Quoted in Josef Korbel, *The Communist Subversion of Czechoslovakia, 1938–1948* (Princeton, 1959), 186.

like mass pro-Communist demonstrations. These "workers' militia" converged on the Old Town Square, where Gottwald whipped them up with speeches vilifying the ministers who had resigned. For some time the Party had been secretly setting up "action committees"—gangs of followers they could trust. Now these Communist action committees directed by Slánský sprang up in every government bureau, factory, and town—in fact, in every organized body in the country—and proceeded to purge them of democrats, throwing some 28,000 people out of office.

I listened to the radio from morning until night, hoping Beneš would call for massive resistance, but hearing instead how the Communists were taking over one office after another, denouncing the democratic leaders. I exhorted people to recognize that we were in the midst of a crisis and should fight for our freedoms. But there were no leaders for this fight. The baffled population was like an audience assembled with no one to talk to it. Beneš was silent. He prepared an address, I was told, but never gave it.

By February 25, 1948, I realized we had lost. I went to our Social Democratic regional committee building in Brno and found policemen in front of it. When I tried to go into the party secretariat, my office, a dozen people I had never seen blocked my way. Most of them were young workers from the Small Arms Factory, not quite sure if they were acting correctly in occupying the secretariat. They were silent except for two truculent spokesmen who kept repeating empty phrases about a "reactionary takeover" and shouting at me that "our democratic forces stopped your counterrevolutionary putsch." I, too, was loud and excited. There were police in the hall, but they refused to intervene.

"Don't you understand?" I screamed at the factory laborers. "This is the end of the democratic republic! We're going to be like the Soviet Union!" The left wing of our party, the Fierlinger faction, didn't understand, either. In spite of what they could see happening, they thought this was just another government crisis, another new government, and that after a time, the Social Democrats would return to power. With the resignations of the twelve ministers—whose offices were already occupied by Communist gangs—Beneš had appointed a new cabinet handpicked by Gottwald and then retired to his country residence, withdrawing completely from state affairs. The only force that could have prevented the Communist coup was the military, but under General Svoboda the army made no move to enforce the constitution. Beneš in any case never considered opposing force by force. To my astonishment, the Communists had taken over without any serious fight from the democrats, even though the majority of both Czechs and Slovaks wanted democracy. My only consolation, looking back on it, is that if the Communists won easily in 1948, they lost easily in 1989. But long, hard years passed in between.

Beneš certainly gets some of the blame for the overwhelming success of the coup. In my mellow moods, I can sometimes understand why he acted as he did during the Munich crisis in 1938, refusing to fight the Germans without commitments from the Allies. But I can never understand his spineless relationship to Stalin, beginning with the agreements he allowed to be concluded in Moscow at the end of the war. In 1945, Beneš enjoyed enormous popularity at home and abroad at a time when Stalin was anxious not to alarm his western Allies and was not, therefore, in a position to oust him. From the beginning, Beneš should have rejected the preponderance of Communists in the postwar government and especially the Communist monopoly of the security systems. He should have seen to it that the military was in a position to enforce our democratic institutions. Instead, at the behest of Gottwald backed by Stalin, Beneš abandoned General Moravec and General Ingr in favor of Svoboda. By the time the coup took place, Beneš had had several strokes. The fate of our democracy was in the unsteady hands of a sick man.

I was scheduled to take the third and last examination for my doctor of law degree in May, but when the agitation began, my professors took me aside. "Mr. Luža, don't wait a month," they advised me. "Anything could happen now. Take the examination at once, even if you are not completely prepared." Thanks to their advice, I now possess a completely useless degree from Masaryk University in Czechoslovak law. Walking near the campus, already feeling defeated, I ran into Ferdinand Richter's son, who told me the astonishing news that his father, Jedlička's good friend, had turned pro-Communist and accepted a high position in the new regime.

My professors were right, for on February 29, 1948, came a national radio announcement concerning me and about fifteen others. We had been expelled from all public functions by the self-appointed Central Action Committee purportedly speaking for the National Front. I had also been removed from the Social Democratic Party by its new pro-Communist directors. Besides being a "reactionary," I was declared an enemy of the people. Hermit, Císař, and I were among those thrown out of the organization of veteran resisters, accused of using the association to act against the "people's democracy." The news was carried in the press for several days. I realized that as soon as the Communists consolidated their new power, they would arrest me or try to compel me to become a cooperator.

After February, the Communists were left sole masters of the country. Prokop Drtina, having been forced out of his ministry by the action committees, attempted suicide by jumping out of a window. He broke his legs and shattered the bones in his feet. He spent excruciating months in the hospital and was then imprisoned for many years. Jan Masaryk, whose very name was synonymous with Czechoslovak independence, astounded everyone by remaining in the Gottwald government as foreign minister, thus legitimizing, in my view, the Communist regime. However, on March 10 his body was found in a courtyard of Czernin Palace in Prague, the seat of the foreign ministry. He had jumped or been pushed from a third-floor window. Everyone loved Jan Masaryk, from the British King George VI, who enjoyed his jokes, to the average Czechoslovak, who revered him as the son of our national hero. Masaryk's American mother was mentally unstable and he himself was manic-depressive. I believe he committed suicide in remorse at having made common cause with thugs and ruthless ideologues who spat on Czechoslovak independence and democratic principles.

Thousands of democrats were now stained as if they had committed heinous, unspecified crimes—people who were known as anti-Communists or individuals whose only offense was that they had demonstrated a capacity for leadership that would make them likely magnets for anti-Communist activity. Purges began—of the press, universities, civil service, sports clubs—in which anti-Communists, non-Communists, intellectuals, or simply people whose slavish adherence to the Communist Party line was in question were expelled from their offices and consigned to disagreeable jobs in mines, farms, and the like.

We had already contacted the youth sections of the Danish, Dutch, and Austrian Social Democratic parties and had been assured by the Austrians that they would help us escape in the event of a Communist coup. I had to find someone to guide us across four or five miles of an unmarked and uncertain border between our country and Austria. One of the members of General Luža had moved from Bíteš to southern Moravia, near the border. He arranged for a friend to take us—Libuše, Císař Fireman, me and four others. During the next year, many social democrats would follow us, including, of all people, Laušman. Considered a traitor to our party in 1948 when he served as deputy prime minister in the hated Gottwald government, in 1949 Laušman joined the exodus of politicians fleeing the Communists.

The best way to cross the border to Austria, we were told, was to go on foot from the village of Jaroslavice, where the patrol was reputedly lax, to Gross Kadolec in Austria. We left Prague on Easter Monday, hoping that after a big feast day the frontier guards would be even more sluggish than usual. When we reached Jaroslavice, our man was waiting for us at a bridge on the Moravian side and accompanied us through some vineyards. Near what I presumed was the border, he stopped. "We were supposed to have someone lead us across," I said. The man shrugged.

"I don't know anything about that," he said. "Just wait until ten tonight. Move quickly and go in twos, straight ahead until you see some lights. That will be a barroom on the Austrian side. Remember that you can't see the guards, but they can see you silhouetted against the sky."

We each carried one light suitcase with all the possessions we would bring to our new life. I took only my briefcase, breaking the handgrip as I yanked it free from some vines. I held on to Libuše tightly, knowing that if we were spotted and I had to decide whether to halt or to run, I would be making the decision for both of us. The border was not yet mined, nor were there then the bloodhounds, towers, and electrified wires that would soon surround our country. After fifteen minutes the lights of the pub glimmered through a mass of trees, signaling that we had left Czechoslovakia. The first part was behind us.

We had not, however, escaped the Communists, having crossed into the zone of Austria occupied by the Soviets. We were brought to Vienna by our Austrian friends. Unlike the Czechs, the Austrian Social Democrats were bitterly anti-Communist and took seriously their mission of sending us to safety. Perhaps because we were among the very first Czechoslovaks in political life to flee the new regime, two members of the Austrian cabinet and the secretary general of the Austrian Social Democratic Party came to greet us. The minister of the interior gave us false identity cards—my new name was Maurer.

"You'll have to cross the Enns River," the party secretary told us. "Your identity cards will be checked as your train leaves the Soviet side and checked again by the military when you arrive on the U.S. side. Whatever you do, don't talk to anyone on the train or to each other. No one must hear your Czech accents. Pretend to sleep through the whole trip." Our little band spread out in two or three compartments with fourteen eyes tightly shut and, I believe, all seven minds praying the same prayer as the train pulled out of the western railroad station in Vienna. The Soviet military control came through checking identities. The conductor came through taking tickets. Nothing happened. When the train pulled into the U.S. zone at the other side of the river, we saw the American soldiers and we knew we had made it. Libuše was shaking when we stepped down from the train in Linz. All of us got into a taxi—our last taxi ride in many frugal years, as it turned out—and went to a hotel in the center of town where rooms had been rented for us. We had, it seemed, succeeded in escaping.

From Linz we headed to Salzburg. Císař wanted to celebrate by treating us to a Pullman car and a good dinner on the train, complete with wine and dessert. Austria had been bombed almost to rubble and was then a much poorer country than Czechoslovakia—a comparison that would be reversed in fifteen years. We didn't imagine that anything, even train services, could be expensive in such conditions. We drank and laughed during that wonderful meal for the first time since the February coup. But when Císař got the bill, all smiles stopped. His face turned so red as he stared at it that I feared nosebleed. "Wrap up the leftovers to take with us," I whispered.

Thus it was that one month after the coup Libuše and I woke up on a Sunday morning in another country, surrounded by another language. Even the bicycle horns made a different noise in Salzburg. It had seemed easy, so easy, to leave. It would be impossible to go back. We lay in bed, listening to the street sounds, too full to speak. Everyone with us and the many who would follow gave up a great deal to reach this meridian. Císař left his wife, who decided not to accompany him. Laušman, too, would have to leave behind a wife and children when he came a year after us. Laušman's flight was particularly harrowing. Not only would his son-in-law (Nechanský, who had arranged the weapons drop to our resisters) be executed by the Communists, but when Laušman's family tried to follow him to Austria, they were caught at the border. Mrs. Laušman was released after some months in prison, but the daughter Věra, Nechanský's wife, spent years in Communist jails.

I had arrived in Austria without even an overcoat, but in a sense, I was better off than the others. I was no longer Luža in a country where the name alone created all sorts of situations. I could walk out of my father's vast shadow once and for all. My mother had an excellent pension of six thousand crowns a month. Considering that she paid only six hundred for our apartment, she would be fine without me. I had brought money to live on until we could get visas and jobs—the lump sum of 45,000 crowns that I received for my service in the resistance. The prospect of living abroad was exciting, and in any case, the alternative for me was a Communist prison.

Neither Libuše nor I had told our loved ones we were leaving, partly to avoid the draining emotional reactions and partly to shield them from reprisals by the Communists—Mother, for example, might at the very least have lost her pension for failing to divulge my plans. Libuše was nineteen years old. Her future in theater had looked promising. No one was persecuting her; she had little to fear from the Communists. She was close to her family—three sisters, a father, and a mother who taught piano. Her youngest sister was her "baby."

"We will probably be able to return in three or four years," I had told her when I asked her to come with me. "The Communists may soon be forced out, but one can never be sure. We won't be able to get married right away. This is a big decision, this leaving, maybe more important than marriage. Think it over well." I had looked despondently at her parents' house. It was full of pictures of her and her sisters and grandparents. All around were dolls kept from childhood, relatives, baking bread, patterned quilts, love. I had probably talked her out of coming with me. The face she raised to me was scribbled with pain.

"Why should I torment myself by thinking it over?" she answered. "I know in the end I'll go with you." We had no idea then, thank God, how long the Communist occupation would last. We did not realize that we had seen our grandparents for the last time. Libuše would be parted from her sisters for most of their lives before being reunited. Both our mothers would be old before we saw them just two more times.

Three months after our escape, I slipped back into the country, twice, on a secret mission. "Operation Old Man" was a covert plan to get Edvard Beneš out of Czechoslovakia and bring him to France. Beneš was practically our only international celebrity. If he could get out, he could draw world attention to the situation in Czechoslovakia. The first time I went back, I was stopped just as I crossed into Slovakia. I had to run back over tank ditches with the border guards shooting at me. The second time, I got to Prague and managed to communicate with Beneš through his adviser. This was the plan: Beneš and his wife would leave their country home for their usual drive but would pretend to have car trouble on the road. They would be picked up by our car and brought to a field we had chosen that was suitable for a landing. It was understood that the French would send a plane to get the couple to the French zone of occupation in Germany. From there they would be taken to Paris. It was a well-planned rescue. It never occurred to me that Beneš would decline to be rescued. At first he agreed to come. But the next thing we knew, word came back that the "Old Man" was sick, too sick to leave the country. Beneš was only sixty-four, but in worse shape than I realized. He died six weeks later, on September 7.

That was the end of the mission. I now had to get out of Czechoslovakia again. No one shot at me this time, but in the woods at the Austrian frontier every stone marker I came to was in Czech, which of course made me think, wrongly, that I had gotten lost and was still in Czechoslovakia. Round and round I circled in a panic. After four harrowing hours I finally came to a road and, with my pulse blasting in my ears, tried to read the license plates zipping by. Finally, something that looked like an old Czechoslovak sedan came wheezing along and I made out the license. Austria! I had managed again, for the last time, to crawl out.

By now the money I had brought with me was going fast. It was becoming clear to me that without anyone at war against the Communist regime, the only feasible resistance was psychological—to undermine Communist control over Czechoslovakia by disseminating information. That I could do from anywhere in Europe. I went to work for the western-backed anti-Communist organization that eventually became the Council of Free Czechoslovakia. The best thing about it was that it enabled Libuše and me to move to Paris. Once there, we lived like the refugees we were. Our place near Pigalle consisted of one room with no bath anywhere in the house. To get to the toilet and lavatory, we had to pass through the bedroom of our elderly landlord and his wife. Libuše's acting coaches, recognizing her talent and our penury, gave her free lessons while she learned all she could about makeup. But even though many people treated us kindly, we never felt at home in Paris. The notorious snobbishness of the French is real, and every exile I knew from Czechoslovakia felt it. The academics considered any education that wasn't French an inferior education. Some of the lectures at the Sorbonne were so magnificent that they sent chills down my spine. But these were random thrills, by no means what I experienced in most classes. I was dismayed by the uneven standard of life and culture in the various parts of France. On one hand, there was Paris, with its theaters and venerable architecture, its brilliant existentialists leading postwar intellectual movements.

On the other hand, life in the provinces was more primitive than anything we had ever known in Czechoslovakia or war-torn Austria. In Limoges, I saw a horse and cart making its rounds to each cottage, pumping raw human sewage into a disposal tank.

Paris was a stopping place for émigrés on their way to someplace else, and we loved meeting all the Czechoslovak literati going into exile. But the news of home was always sad. In September 1948, we found out that Libuše's epileptic sister had died two months earlier during a seizure in the bathtub. Because of repairmen in the house, this one time the bathroom door had been locked; the family had been unable to reach her in time to prevent her from drowning. Libuše's quickness turned into nervousness, her liveliness into intensity. She laughed abruptly and wept anxiously, sometimes both together and, at the age of twenty, was diagnosed with an ulcer.

But the best things, too, happened to us in Paris: we finally got married. I was an eager bridegroom, tired of living in sin, for in 1949, only Orwell's proles cohabited without benefit of matrimony. The Parisians didn't mind; they considered us bohemians—literally and figuratively—too lower-ordersy for our morals to matter. But we knew if we had lived together openly in Czechoslovakia, our acquaintances would never have become our friends, and our friends would have kept us away from their children.

Our wedding was a discount ceremony with fifteen other couples. First a lady deputy mayor, a Communist, checked our permits. Since Libuše was underage and needed proof of her parents' consent, we had brought an affidavit from UNESCO approving of the marriage plans.

"You expect me to accept this?" the woman barked. "You should have stayed in Brno with your mother, Little Girl. How old are you? Sixteen? Seventeen? Did you lie about your age, too? So if your parents don't object to your getting married, why didn't you stay and have your own officials marry you?" she demanded, knowing full well why we didn't stay with our "own" officials. She was stamping the marriage license even while she upbraided us, so that the end of the harangue merged with the beginning of the general ceremony. She stopped once in her breakneck nuptial recitation to remark that Libuše would do well to reconsider marriage to someone with my dim prospects, while Libuše, as her last unmarried antic, placated me by slyly mimicking the diatribe. Our wedding took five momentous minutes. It was over before our two witnesses had figured out exactly where to stand. By the time I had been pronounced a man and she had been most solemnly pronounced a wife, all the couples in the hall were laughing openly. Then our little party went out for lunch and a movie.

As a present to ourselves—a singular extravagance—we had made reservations in a hotel near the Champs Elysées for the night. Our bridesmaid, Milada, walked along with us past the snow-gowned statues of the Place de la Concorde and into the carpeted hotel. But she stayed so long congratulating us that she missed the last metro and had to spend the night with us— our chaste wedding night—in our costly room. She tried to make up for it. We were living in a flat where the landlord provided a stove but we were obliged to furnish the coal. The next evening Milada saw to it that the coal stove was blazing when we returned home.

Our interim in Paris stretched unnoticed to half a decade. The postwar years turned into cold war years, and our dream of traveling and then returning home yielded to the realization that we might never be able to go back. In Czechoslovakia, Stalin had firmly established a terrorist state, at first persecuting mainly democrats and Catholics, but then attacking his own Communist minions so as to replace the local leaders with more servile apparatchiks. In November 1952, the so-called Slánský trial began, named after the secretary-general of the Party who was the main target, the most powerful Czechoslovak Communist after Klement Gottwald. There was plenty of blood on Rudolf Slánský's hands, even though his own young daughter had been kidnapped in the Soviet Union during the war and had never been found. Along with Slánský, Vlado Clementis and twelve others were publicly tried for treason, sabotage, and espionage. All but three of them were Jews. Eleven of the group were hanged.

Every victim was coerced into implicating others, until accusations against a widening circle of "Zionist conspirators," "CIA lackeys," and "western lapdogs" destroyed all sense of personal security in our country. Every human bond was broken by the state. Children were forced to denounce their parents, employees were recruited to spy on their supervisors, and the single most fearsome entity in life was the Communist government, especially for those who were part of it. Gottwald went to Moscow, apparently in good physical and political health, to attend Stalin's funeral in March 1953. When he returned to Prague, it was announced that he had caught pneumonia and then that he had died.

The terror abated but did not end with Stalin's death. Laušman, who had left Czechoslovakia the year after us, disappeared from Austria in December

1953. I have lately taken a particular interest in poor Laušman. In 1995, I discovered that during the years 1948–1953 the Communists took special notice of two Social Democratic leaders who had escaped the country: Bohumil Laušman and me. The Czechoslovak foreign intelligence service planned to end our anti-Communist frolics abroad, hoping to capture us separately and bring us back to Prague. Laušman was in fact visited by an Austrian Social Democrat, a double agent with a backup crew, who slipped a drug into his wine and kidnapped him from Salzburg. He was thrown into a Czechoslovak prison where he died some ten years later. As for me, Czechoslovak intelligence reported that it never succeeded in getting close enough to me to seize me. The office finally concluded that one provocative kidnapping in Austria was enough.[2]

Meanwhile, the situation in Paris was changing for us refugees. Washington, D.C. had become the center of Czechoslovak resistance to Communism, with the United States subsidizing exile organizations from all the Iron Curtain countries. The Free Europe Committee, the Assembly of Captive Nations, and other such groups were being established in the United States after 1948. Many of the exiles were moving to New York. I was thirty-one years old. It was time for me to get a serious profession, time for us to find a real home. In 1953, therefore, we left Europe behind.

New York was terrifying and exhilarating. We caught its energy, tried to be informal like Americans, and educated ourselves in the museums, theaters, streets, and subways, talking up a storm to everybody. Americans never noticed mistakes in English. Everywhere we went in the United States, we felt an excitement, a freshness that made us aware for the first time of the stodginess of other places. We amused ourselves composing imaginary postcards to our families. "Dearest Mamička," Libuše wanted to write, "You can't imagine how many cars there are in America. Everything here is so cheap. Radomír bought a shirt for $3. The tops of the skyscrapers are sometimes hidden in clouds. I still long for all of you. Please forgive me for leaving without telling you. Your loving daughter, Libuše." The way we communicated in reality was quite different—some deliberately banal letters that were

2. Described in Václav Kvasnička, *Droga zvaná špionáž* (A drug called espionage) (Praha, 1994), 27. See also Radomir Luza, "Research Note: My Files at the Czech Ministry of the Interior Archive, Prague, May 1995," in Günter Bischof and Anton Pelinka, eds., *Austrian Historical Identity* (New Brunswick, 1997), 288–92.

opened by the authorities before Libuše's family received them. Word came back through a Czech escapee: "Don't write us at all. Every letter makes big trouble for us. We love you."

Long before we became United States citizens, we became Americans, albeit Americans with funny accents who were not quite sure what to order in restaurants. Or at least I often felt alienated from other Europeans, with their clannishness, superior attitudes, and narrow infighting. Then again, among Americans, I'd notice familiarity and political innocence, the way they had of putting their hands all over you, and I'd feel like a decorous Old World relic. My first job was with American Express near Wall Street. There in the heart of capitalist oppression, I had friendly bosses and long lunch hours. After being exploited all day, I had sufficient energy to attend night school at Columbia. New York University eventually offered me a full scholarship and awarded me a Ph.D. in 1959. Libuše answered a newspaper ad that she could barely read and was immediately hired as a manicurist in an exclusive French beauty salon on Fifth Avenue. Her salary was a comfortable forty dollars a week. What's more, despite her limited English and even more limited experience with hair coloring—where all mistakes were serious—she was trained and promoted and promoted and promoted until her salary had risen within a few months to $125 plus a commission. The salon presented her as someone "straight from Paris" with all the latest hair designs. Some of the shop's clients were my lifelong movie idols—poor tippers, as it turned out, with difficult skin. We moved to Queens and became solid Americans, with a used car, a window garden, and a basement full of unwanted possessions.

May is hot in New Orleans and the house was hot, even with oaks and sugar maples sheltering our old street. Though I had already reached the age when sitting on floors was uncomfortable, I sat on the carpet in our living room with the ceiling fan gently ruffling my piles of paper: notes for five books I had long since published, old student exams, age-splotched letters from people who meant nothing and everything to me. I was not trying to make sense of life that particular humid afternoon. I resented the unsorted boxes still ahead of me and the junk I had collected over the years. But under an armful of articles and six issues of *Past and Present,* I glimpsed a familiar brown smoothness—my briefcase with the broken handle, my sturdy friend that had come with me through frontiers, traumas, phases, and moods. Under the splendid old locks would be Father's letters written to me while we were both underground. I had saved my own messages and letters, too, after the war, retrieving them from the shelters where I had buried them in glass bottles. My diary would be there, along with the papers I had procured regarding Father's death and Grňa's eulogy to him.

I looked at the case a long time before taking it onto my lap. Father's penmanship was small and light, the writing of a monk rather than a general. My hands touched the faint, coded script like fingers remembering Braille, each word a world of meaning. There were more letters from friends than I had remembered. Some were in Hermit's square, strong hand; others were the labored words of people self-conscious with paper. Here was a testimonial from dear Mrs. Little Spruce. I had stayed with the Nováks about fourteen months, off and on. Father had lived with them from October 1, 1943, until the end of June 1944. But this letter was about my mother, who was with them only three months: "We were stunned that a lady of her intelligence and social prominence turned into the most helpful person in the house from the moment she came to Javůrek. We had Jiřina's baby and a large garden to tend. She took on the role of a domestic and nursemaid and was entirely convincing. We admire her for that."

In 1944, Mother stayed with the Homoláčs, Vlasta's family. "She did everything in the house—cooking, making beds, laundry, washing floors, weeding the garden, even taking care of the rabbits and poultry," Mrs. Homoláč wrote. "When we learned her name, we couldn't believe that the wife of such an important man had worked like any country peasant. We passed her off as a widowed aunt. We could have had ten 'aunts' if they were like her. The first hour she was here, she put on a work dress and it was as if she put on the life of the farm with it."

Josef Pavlas wrote to Mother directly two months after the war, when he found out who she was. The Pavlas family had sheltered Grňa and Štainer and had allowed the transmitter Calcium to be placed with them before they themselves were forced underground. Mother lived with Pavlas for most of 1943, posing as the widow of a low-level clerk. "You did so much for us in every way," Pavlas wrote. "It is hard now to believe that you were not accustomed to the hard work of the countryside. . . . [P]eople who visited all thought you were our servant. I noticed that the occasional workers we hired even took it for granted that you were their servant, too, as you were so modest. You took care of us as if we were your own family. Our little Anushka still cries sometimes, 'Where is my auntie? Won't she be taking me for walks any more?' Thank you for all your help in those difficult times. We hope you will think of us. We love you."

There were letters from the Hálas, who were with Mother when she found out Father was dead, and statements from the others Mother lived with, all amazed at her identity and full of affection for a woman they remembered as simple. After the war, Mother visited these friends, grabbing an apron and helping with lunch just as naturally as when pleasing them had meant the difference between safety and prison. I had never imagined Mother could be so strong and unassuming, prepared to do whatever had to be done without complaint. I loved her because she was my mother; others loved her simply because she was lovable.

At the bottom of the case was a long missive on lined paper, handwritten, from Mary Duhm, the last person to shelter my father and one of the last to see him alive. Hermit had contacted her after the war, I suppose, when he was trying to get recognition for people who had supported the resistance. It had been more than twenty years since I had seen Mrs. Duhm's letter. The Duhms had been pensioners in Říčany, near Prague. Their son was a resister, a close friend of young Josef Koreš, who accompanied Father to Hříště and shot himself in the field outside the inn. It would be like operating on myself to read that letter again. I picked up the folded packet like a surgeon lifting out an organ that will have to go back in undamaged. The paper clip had left its outline in rust on the corner of the first page.

August 21, 1946
Little Josef Koreš came to us. He was nervous, as though we had not always welcomed him in this house. "Would you consider renting me your spare room?" he asked. ". . . It's for my boss. He needs a shelter badly. . . . We are almost desperate."

"No, indeed," we answered. "We won't rent it to anyone. But we'll give it to our resisters. Of course. I'll go get it ready."

In an hour Koreš returned with a tall gentleman in a Hubertus. Even though he was unshaven, you could see he was a first class gentleman, but pale with being so tired.

"Please, could I trouble you for some water to wash with?" he asked. I thought of my son who at that same moment might be trying to find a hideout somewhere. The best way I could help him was to help Koreš and this gentleman. "While you stay, you will be my sons," I said. "Nothing I do for you will trouble me."

"Little Mother, I am so grateful to be here," the man answered, and Koreš' eyes filled with water.

They both liked the airy room, but we had to be careful because just below it was a room where we distributed ration stamps. Many people came in and out to pick them up. We had a signal for warning them to be very quiet, and during the entire time they were upstairs, no one in our nosy village had the slightest suspicion that anyone lived in the house with us.

I did not disturb them except to knock three times when I brought their meals. Each time I came, the gentleman had a book in his hand. I think he knew everything in the whole world. Once as he took the tray, he pressed the calluses on my hand. "After the war, Mamička, we will see to it that parents like you can provide for their children without having to work this hard."

He would let me know whenever he was planning to go out, and tell me the exact hour of his return. That way I could watch the road and make sure no one was looking. But once he was in a big hurry and came out without waiting for my sign. Just as he was leaving the garden, our neighbor came in the gate on her bicycle.

"Have you seen my husband?" I asked her. "This man wants him. Perhaps you can come back in an hour, Sir, and he might be back." Then to the neighbor I said, "It must be some German."

"He looks like a German," she agreed.

"Ich bin Deutscher?" laughed the gentleman when he came home that night. "Little Mother, you are clever."

But I scolded him. "Just you wait next time and don't leave until I tell you it's safe." We had one or two other incidents. Once when company was here I looked out the window and saw him on his way home. I ran outside and told him, "Someone is here. Play like you're an inspector." Then I went in. In a few minutes came the knock on the door. "Open up! It's the Control!" The trick worked. The last thing anybody wanted to meet was an inspector. The two guests left out the back door.

One Sunday, my sister-in-law caught me taking lunch upstairs to the room. "Oh, are you taking in boarders again?" she asked.

"No. Only Mrs. Raskotnik from Prague is here for a few days with her husband. They are not well. Both of them are running fever."

"Well, Koreš," the gentleman said, when I delivered the lunch, "I don't mind being Mr. Raskotnik, even with a fever, but you have to be Mrs. Raskotnik." Koreš folded the napkin on his head and tied it under his chin like a kerchief, so they had a little fun while I went back downstairs.

Every evening we turned on the news from London. The gentleman knew many languages, so he listened in French, Russian, and English and translated for my husband while I stayed out in the garden, watching to make sure no one surprised them. At the end of the broadcasts, my husband would call me and the gentleman would explain it all again to me. "Mamička," he said one night, "the news is good and getting better. The end is coming soon." He showed us how the front was advancing both in the east and west, and everything he told us came out to be true.

Koreš went out almost every night. In the evening when I brought meals, he was usually still in bed. "You see there, Mamička, Koreš is exhausted," the gentleman smiled. "He goes to see his girlfriend and she wears him out." I thought to myself it was not girls Koreš was contacting at night. My nephew Karel Müller was helping the gentleman, too. He would leave messages for him behind the books in the first floor hall.

One day the gentleman said, "Little Mother, this coming Thursday makes three years that I have been underground."

"We will celebrate it," I said. "We'll have a nice dinner and plenty of cakes for a party."

Koreš left that night to go to a meeting with an officer and came back very upset. Suddenly Karel Müller, too, came in almost without speaking to me and ran upstairs with the gentleman.

A calendar turned its pages in my mind. That would have been September 26, 1944. They had just found out that Ouředník had been shot on the thirteenth and that Jiříkovský was in the hands of the Gestapo. Jiříkovský had on him the name "Rast'a"—Váhala—and Váhala knew where Father and Koreš were hiding.

Without waiting for me to tell him it was safe to go, the gentleman was running down the stairs with a rucksack.

"What's happened?" I asked. The gentleman was nervous. He pressed my hand and held it as if he might kiss it.

"I have to leave, Little Mother. Thank you."

Karel Müller and Koreš were making sure that nothing was left in the room and I ran up to help them. All of them were in a great hurry. "Koreš," I said. "Just stay here."

"No, no," he answered. "We have to go. For your sake, too. We'll give you. . . ." But before he finished, all three of them were out the door, and we never saw them again.

I had stood with giants in the resistance, none braver than my father, who left his walk in my body and his voice in my mind. And all those who helped us were heroes, though some of them wanted no part of us when we stumbled into their lives, endangering them. The little people who fed us and hid us were in a way the most extraordinary of all—the Giant, the Proletarian, Mrs. Duhm, who protected Father until no one could protect him. She had no notion that he was a general. She had a child, elderly parents, a life as precious to her as ours was to us. Did she look at the stranger when she was asked to take him in and decide then and there to face the gallows, to watch her son tortured, if necessary—to risk all their lives? Did she decide to become a heroine, this humble lady, or was it simply that she felt too much compassion to turn Father away? Was the resistance, then, only a story of individuals making human choices that had nothing to do with political will?

The resistance did little to diminish German power or to further our national aims in the long run. No resistance movement could have significantly influenced the outcome of the war, which was won by Allied armies. And even victory over the Germans turned out to mean that Communist dictatorship replaced Nazi dictatorship in our country. We had sacrificed the great men of our nation only to face decades of repression from a different enemy. But that the resistance could never be extirpated in Czechoslovakia proves that individuals—plain, not especially thoughtful men and women—can stand up to overwhelming dread, moved by nothing more coercive than an impulse to do the right thing. I know that in every land and in every period there runs a deep cruelty in human beings, surfacing every day as Nazism or Stalinism or some barbarous ethnic hatred. But I know, too, that there is an ineradicable moral sense, as strong in the mailmen and mechanics of this world as in the prime ministers and generals. In the end, the resistance was not the story of a movement but of lonely individuals discovering courage in themselves and proving that random sanity can disrupt well-organized and systematic madness. The resistance left a rib of hard evidence to show that kindness—as persistent as viciousness and more pervasive than mere self-interest—breaks out where you least expect it.

The ceiling fan creaked on gently as I put the papers back in the briefcase. My daughter came in, looking like my mother, and picked her way across the living room. "Daddy," she chided, "are you still at it? You won't ever get cleaned out."

"Actually, I'm closer than you think," I answered. But she had already passed through, and I spoke only to myself.

EPILOGUE

It will come as no surprise that most of the friends and resisters mentioned in this book are dead now, along with the enemies. Nazism, which held half the world in terror, is nowhere a dominant force. Communism, which shaped millions of lives and whole continents, has collapsed in Europe. Even the country Czechoslovakia, that my father gave his life for, no longer exists. In another generation, perhaps, it will seem no more than a footnote. Even today, all that I've described happened in another century.

Grňa was reunited with his wife, who had been in a concentration camp since 1942. He was forced out of public life after the coup, and in 1950 was imprisoned for two years. He had completed his memoirs of the resistance, *Seven Years at the Home Front,* in 1949, a very candid account that the Communists refused to publish until the Prague Spring. Grňa never saw his book in print, however, as he died in 1967, a year before its publication.

Josef Robotka, like so many heroes, fell afoul of the Communists. After the war he was sent to train at a military academy in the Soviet Union, where he made some criticism of the Russians that reached the wrong ears. He was thrown out of the army; his military career was over. In 1949 he left home one day, telling his wife he was going to meet someone and would return in half an hour. Instead of the person he expected, he found the Communist police waiting for him in a car. His wife had great difficulty finding out where he was and, after discovering that he had been arrested, could never learn the charges. When she managed to visit him in prison in 1950, closely guarded, he was prevented from telling her that he had been tried and sentenced in a secret military court. "Please forget about me completely" was all he was able to say. Some time afterward she received a package with his clothes. He had been convicted of treason and hanged in 1952. In 1990 he was posthumously rehabilitated and promoted to the rank of general major.

Karel Štainer joined the Communist Party in 1945 and continued attacking Father. He alleged that he, Štainer, had purposely hidden information from Luža because Father was passing it along to Novák and leaders of other bourgeois groups. In 1947 Štainer published a book which provided some useful information about the resistance, but it was suffused with half-truths that offended Grňa, Robotka, Hermit, and others whose accomplishments he slighted. In Štainer's resistance, I hardly existed. Štainer remained police chief of Bohemia for a few years, but he proved too populist even for the Communists. In the 1950s, he wound up in prison, where he occupied himself by teaching his fellow inmates his own version of Marxism-Leninism. Once released, he opposed the regime and got in touch with me through Váhala. After the Velvet Revolution, I submitted a long, strong letter recommending his promotion to general in the Czechoslovak army, the rank posthumously awarded to Robotka and other rehabilitated fighters. Despite our differences, I felt Štainer deserved recognition for his many contributions to the resistance. But the ministry of national defense denied him any honors, following instead the recommendation of military men who had been Štainer's fellow inmates in prison, the captive audience for his Communist rhetoric and bumptious ways. He died cranky and old in 1990. In his will, he barred any representatives of the military from attending his funeral.

Like me, Hermit was fired from his positions and expelled from the resistance organizations during the February coup in 1948; however, he was not further persecuted by the Communists. He spent the rest of his life collecting folk songs, an old hobby of his, and dodging his wife's attacks. He died in the late 1950s.

Rastislav Váhala joined the Communist Party in 1945 but was eventually expelled. He had been the attorney for the imprisoned General Heliodor Píka, head of the Czechoslovak military mission in Moscow during the war and one of the first people hanged after the coup. Váhala did everything he could to save Píka, and by 1948 or 1949, he had lost his illusions. He became part of the anti-Communist resistance within Czechoslovakia and was one of my most important secret contacts during my years abroad. Because he was allowed certain travel visas, I met him several times in Yugoslavia and Austria before his death in 1988.

General Novák became military commander of Moravia at the end of the war. He joined the Communist Party, but as he was close to Otto Šling and to Jan Šverma's widow, he was considered a member of the Slánský faction that came under attack. In 1950 Novák was arrested and tortured by the Communists, as he had been by the Nazis, and sentenced to a long prison term. He was released after six years, rehabilitated in 1965, and died poor in 1988.

General Ingr was appointed ambassador to the Netherlands in 1947. After the February coup, he continued working against the Communists as head of the democratic Czechoslovak foreign intelligence service in Washington, D.C. Still a chain-smoker, he left little trails of tobacco in his wake all through the corridors of the capital. He died of a heart attack in Paris in 1956.

Císař Fireman, having come out of the Gestapo prison, left the country with me in 1948. He eventually settled in Milan and continued his profitable work as an exporter. He died in the late 1950s, relatively young.

Kravka, Mrs. Little Spruce, Božena Foral (the maid who saved our lives several times), and the mailman Hlaváček, the Fast One, resumed their quiet lives after the war, avoiding the new menace of Communism. Malý, the Little One, who first brought me from the bus station in Javůrek to my life underground, went into a series of depressions after the war. He finally committed suicide by slashing his throat with a razor.

Like me, Jan Sec was forced to escape in 1948. His wife, Fanynka, apparently could not get out with their two children, or perhaps there was some alienation between them, as was rumored. Sec died at the end of the 1950s in Canada. Fanynka remained in Brno until her death in 1997.

Teta Tíni grew fat as a pigeon after the war and rarely left her apartment, but she had many guests whom she always treated to a delicious lunch served on dainty china. She still played the piano pretty well, despite chubby fingers burdened by rings that she could no longer remove. She continued to enjoy life in what she described as her "rather advanced" years, as if getting old were an accomplishment like getting an advanced degree.

Karel Kristek escaped in 1949 and went to Venezuela. Gustav was jailed by the Communists. After his release he suffered from serious ailments and had to have his leg amputated sometime in the 1980s. His wife did not remain with him in the hospital during this ordeal. He died quite alone. In

1949 Whiz Staller escaped to the West with his family and settled in the United States.

After my escape, Věra was interrogated several times as to my whereabouts—frightening interrogations during which the questioners threatened reprisals against her family if she withheld information. She was constantly watched by the authorities until she married a man not suspected by the Communist Party. She and her husband, a professor of electrical engineering, live in Brno.

Vlasta suffered a tragic fate. That good, reckless girl, who deserved to spend the rest of her life as an honored citizen, was instead tried by the Communists on trumped-up charges of treasonable activity. Not yet twenty-five, she was sentenced in 1949 to twenty years in prison. She spent eleven years—eleven lifetimes—in revolting conditions in dungeons all over Czechoslovakia, enduring every deprivation and humiliation. Her younger sister Otilia was also imprisoned and died young, in the early 1950s. Oto Homoláč, who was not permitted any contact with his daughters, escaped to Austria in 1949 and then emigrated to the United States, where he died. The Homoláčs' large holdings had been confiscated. The mother, penniless, was obliged to live with relatives. When Vlasta was finally released in 1960, she was still considered an enemy of the state, employable only as a waitress or maid. She eventually married and had a daughter. Her rehabilitation in 1989 allowed a few assets to be restored to her but did nothing to repair the shattered lives of that close, wonderful family.

Libuše's family was only harassed. For years each of them was hauled in again and again for the ordeal of interrogation: Who had helped Radomír escape? Had Libuše communicated with the family? Who were Luža's contacts inside Czechoslovakia? Even Libuše's little sister was questioned, though she was only seven years old when we fled. Another sister was denied entrance to medical school, despite an outstanding academic record, because there was a "traitor"—Libuše—in the family. We received a few letters from Libuše's mother and my mother in their own handwriting, but we surmised that the government sponsored the correspondence in the hope that we would write back and reveal some information.

Both Libuše's parents and my mother were, however, encouraged by the Czechoslovak authorities to meet us in 1964 in Vienna, where we had returned for a few years. Libuše's family was allowed to come again in 1966 for one week. We were all baffled by the government's sudden leniency, but jumped on the opportunities to visit. For the first time in sixteen years we saw our loved ones, older and much changed, as we were ourselves. Their visit passed like a minute, though we got up early and talked late into the night to make the days last as long as possible. Restrictions on travel were reimposed after those two visits. Following the Soviet invasion of 1968, we never saw our parents again. Libuše's mother and father died in the 1970s; my mother passed away in Prague in 1985.

I was lucky, so lucky, to witness the Velvet Revolution, to see that democracy—inefficient, fickle, uncontrollable, and wonderful—had again erupted in my country. Father's reputation, even his lapidary honors were restored. His bronze statue, removed by the Communists from the military headquarters in Brno, had been destroyed, but the plaque honoring him was reinscribed, and the site was dedicated to him once again in 1990. This time, more than four thousand people attended the ceremony—twice the number attending the original dedication. Father came, too, at least in spirit.

The end of Communist authority meant that we could return home. In 1990, we saw our country for the first time in forty-one years. The experience of going back to Prague, Brno, Bíteš, Velké Meziříčí, and the rest both agitated and eased me—eased my émigré's chronic sense of bifurcation. Since our escape, I had lived many places without ever feeling settled. Suddenly given the choice at long last of returning to the Czech Republic permanently, I chose to stay in America, having become more assimilated than I realized while my mind had been occupied with other things. Moreover, Libuše's health problems made it impossible to leave the United States, with its Medicare system. My decision surprised me. When my plane brought me back to New Orleans, I felt again the enormous energy and progressiveness that I had felt in first seeing America. This time I was no longer an exile. Whether landing in the Czech Republic or the United States, I was landing at home.

With the fall of the Communist regime, I gained access to my secret police files in the ministry of the interior. It was soon clear why the two visits from our families had been allowed in the sixties. Though Vienna was a free city not under Communist or Czechoslovak control, Czechoslovak foreign intelligence agents had nevertheless managed to install listening devices in our apartment at Sonnenweg 113. They hoped that I would confide my activities to relatives and friends who might visit. The Communist secret service had duplicated my house keys and had long been coming in and out when we were not at home, even entering when our son and daughter were alone with their godmother—herself a secret Communist agent. They even went so far as to rent an apartment near mine to service their operation. The interior ministry archives listed no less than twenty-five informers—my Czechoslovak "friends" abroad—and over five hundred reports on my daily life and subversive projects. Those projects consisted mainly of writing and publishing anti-Communist journals, quite openly and publicly, so all their espionage yielded little that they did not already know. I was stunned and delighted to learn of all the dogged activity against me. I had no idea I was considered such an important adversary.

Libuše and I became United States citizens in 1959. She sang me through the years in strange countries, her oboe improvising fluently and naturally in any tongue, while I, who spent months drearily memorizing declensions and irregular verbs, still drink and dream in Czech. Wherever we went in those years abroad—Vienna, Paris, New York, New Orleans—Libuše provided me with an Old World life of thrifty elegance and as much equability as I could hope for from a little pepper. Despite my mother's reservations about my wild girl, the marriage lasted. When Libuše died in August 2001, we had been together more than fifty years.

Since we did not get to live long in our native land, we ought at least to be dead there. Our ashes will rest in our beloved homeland, and the urns will be marked in Czech, though our kids and grandkids will mourn in English. To assuage my niggling sense of disloyalty to both my countries, I plan to apply to heaven as a dually patriotic Czech-American.

AFTERWORD

This book is mainly based on 108 hours of tape recordings provided to me by Radomir Luza in which he generally described his wartime experiences. Those original recordings will be deposited in the Hoover Institution archives at Stanford University. A great deal of information not included anywhere in the tapes was provided by Radomir during our discussions as I was writing the book.

—CHRISTINA VELLA

BIOGRAPHICAL SKETCHES

Practically all Czech names are accented on the first syllable. Accented vowels are lengthened—slightly exaggerated. All vowels are pronounced. When *i* appears with no accent, its sound is between the *i* in *bit* and the *ee* in *beet*. *Ř* is a subtle *rzh* sound, difficult to represent accurately. *R* with no mark is often rolled.

"ALEŠ." See DMITRIJEV, ALEXANDER ALEXEJEVIČ.

APPEL [ah pel], JAROMÍR [yar o meer]. Attorney in Brno. General Vojtěch Luža's contact to Prime Minister Eliáš and to underground groups in Prague from 1939 to 1941. Arranged for financial assistance to the families of imprisoned resisters.

BACHMUTSKY [bakh moot skee], NIKOLAJ [nik o lai] PAVLOVIČ [pav lo vitch]. Cossack. First lieutenant of Red Air Force, shot down near Leningrad in 1941 and taken prisoner by the Germans. Escaped POW camp in 1943. Sheltered near Kadolec by Mayor Kobylka. Commanded a contingent of partisans in the Bohemian-Moravian hills. Killed in shootout with the Germans on December 7, 1944.

BENEŠ [beh nesh], EDVARD. 1884–1948. President of Czechoslovakia 1935–38, 1940–48. Adopted the political philosophy of Thomas Masaryk. Professor of sociology in Prague. Joined Masaryk in exile during the First World War to work for Czechoslovak independence from the Austro-Hungarian Empire. Represented Czechoslovakia at the Paris Peace Conference in 1919. Served his country as foreign minister (1918–35), premier (1921–22), and leader of the Czech National Socialist Party, a liberal and nationalist party. Became president of Czechoslovakia at Masaryk's retirement, but resigned and went into exile after the dismemberment of his country by the Munich Pact. Resumed the title of president in London in 1940. Returned to Prague and was confirmed in office in 1945 and reelected in 1946. In June 1948, following the Communist coup of February, resigned on grounds of illness, refusing to sign the new constitution, and died shortly thereafter.

CHMELA [khuh mel a], LEOPOLD. Member of Ambassador Heidrich group. Met Radomír Luža in Okarec.

CIKRLE [sik er leh], FRANTIŠEK [fran ti shek] ("SANDY"). Worker from Brno, recruited by Gustav Kristek for General Luža group in spring 1945.

CÍSAŘ [tsee sarzh], JOSEF [yo sef] ("CÍSAŘ FIREMAN"). General manager of a publishing company in Prague. Organized a mass network of volunteer firemen's associations throughout the Protectorate. Became the third member of the Council of Three (Rada tří, or R3). Arrested by the Germans in 1944. Escaped the country in March 1948 and went to Milan. Died in late 1950s. His wife, MARIE CÍSAŘ, served as Radomír Luža's liaison to President Beneš in 1948.

CLEMENTIS, VLADO. Slovak Communist state secretary in ministry of foreign affairs, 1945–48. Executed in Slánský trial, 1952.

DMITRIJEV [duh mee tree yev], ALEXANDER ALEXEJEVIČ ("ALEŠ" [ah lesh]). First lieutenant in Red Army, captured by the Germans. Escaped POW camp in 1943. Sheltered by Hermit. Commander of a detachment of escaped Soviet war prisoners, PAM 5 of the General Luža group. Lived in Leningrad after 1945.

DRACHOVSKÝ [dra khov skee], JOSEF [yo sef]. Professor at Charles University and a resister.

DRTINA [der teen a], PROKOP. Member of PÚ; joined Beneš in exile in 1940. Minister of justice in postwar Czechoslovak government. Arrested by the Communists in 1948.

DUHM [doom], MARIE. Provided Vojtěch Luža's last shelter, near Říčany, in 1944.

ELIÁŠ [el ee ash], ALOIS [al o ees]. Former French legionnaire and division general at the time of the German occupation. Friend of Vojtěch Luža. Served as prime minister of the Protectorate from 1939 to 1941, while secretly assisting the resistance. Maintained close contacts with both the underground and President Beneš in London. Arrested by the Germans and sentenced to death in September 1941. Executed June 10, 1942. His wife, JAROSLAVA ("SLÁVKA"), served as a liaison between Vojtěch Luža and underground leaders in Prague.

FORAL, BOŽENA [boh zhen a] ("BOŽENKA"). Maid of the Luža family. Lied to the Gestapo when questioned about the family's whereabouts. She and her husband, FRANTIŠEK, disposed of weapons for the Lužas.

FRANK, KARL HERMANN. Deputy leader of the Sudeten German party, 1937–38; SS police chief and state secretary, later minister of state for Bohemia and Moravia, 1943–45. Responsible for brutal repression of the population during the occupation.

FRAŠTACKÝ [frash tatz skee], RUDOLF. Director of a sugar export company in Bratislava. On business trips to Switzerland carried messages and microfilm from the Czech resistance that would eventually reach the Czechoslovak exile government in London. After 1945, a leading member of the Slovak Democratic Party. Escaped to Switzerland in 1948. Eventually settled in Toronto and became a banker. Died in 1988.

"THE GIANT." See ONDRA, JOSEF.

GOLIAN [go li an], JÁN [yahn]. Lieutenant colonel in Slovak army, later promoted to general. Military commander of the failed Slovak national uprising against the Germans, August 1944. Executed by the Germans.

GÖRING [ger ing], ALBERT. Brother of Reich Marshal Hermann Göring. Worked in Prague and had contacts with Karel Staller.

GOTTWALD, KLEMENT. 1896–1953. Helped found the Czechoslovak Communist Party, serving on the central committee beginning in 1925. Fled to Moscow before the German occupation. Returned in 1945 as chairman of the Czechoslovak Communist Party and served as first deputy premier in the coalition government. Became premier of Czechoslovakia in 1946. Succeeded Beneš as president after the Communist coup in February 1948 and served until his own death in 1953. Made the country a satellite of the USSR.

GRŇA [grn ya], JOSEF [yo sef]. Professor of Finance at Technical University in Brno. Leading member of the resistance network PVVZ. Went into hiding on September 3, 1941. Was the second member (with Vojtěch Luža and Josef Císař) of the Council of Three. Imprisoned by the Communists 1950–52. Died in 1967.

"THE GYPSY." See SERINEK, JOSEF.

HÁCHA [ha kha], EMIL. Succeeded Beneš as president of Czechoslovakia before the war and was forced by Hitler in March 1939 to accept a German Protectorate over Bohemia and Moravia for which he served as president, the powerless Czech authority in the German-controlled government. Died in 1945.

HÁLA [hah la], JOSEF [yo sef]. Miller near Javůrek who provided cover to Milada Luža, Radomír's mother.

HANÁK [han ahk], RUDOLF. Brigade general, associate of Vojtěch Luža in Brno. Arrested in 1941.

HAŠEK [ha shek], EDUARD. Country estate owner in Okarec. Friend of Vojtěch Luža from the 1920s, he provided shelter and financial assistance to resisters.

HEIDRICH [high drikh], ARNOŠT [ar nosht]. Ambassador, frequent Czechoslovakian representative to the Geneva disarmament conferences in the 1920s, confidant of President Beneš, and one of the resistance leaders who survived the destruction of the principal resistance networks in 1941–42. Arrested by the Germans in 1944. Served as secretary general in the ministry of foreign affairs, 1945–48. Escaped to the West and died in Washington, D.C., in 1968.

"HERMIT." See INDRA, BOHUSLAV.

HEYDRICH [high drikh], REINHARD. 1904–42. Forced to resign from the German navy in 1931 for misconduct. Joined the SS and won Heinrich Himmler's confidence. Became deeply involved in planning the extermination of the Jews. Appointed acting Reich protector of Bohemia and Moravia in 1941, succeeding von Neurath. As SS-Obergruppenführer and head of Reich security forces, earned the nickname "Hangman of Europe" for his brutal methods and numerous executions. Assassinated by Czechoslovak paratroopers on May 27, 1942.

HLAVÁČEK [hla vah chek], JOSEF [yo sef] ("THE FAST ONE"). Postal carrier in Javůrek who carried messages for the resistance, helped organize the underground, and assisted the Luža family.

HOMOLÁČ [ho mo lodge], OTO. Captain of the Czechoslovak Legion in World War I and largest farmer in Radoškov. Provided shelter to resisters. Escaped Czechoslovakia in 1948. Died in the United States in the 1950s. OTO and wife ANNA were parents of VLASTA HOMOLÁČ.

HOMOLÁČ, VLASTA ("DUŠAN"). Courier and liaison in the resistance. Arrested by the Communists in 1948, was cut off from communication with her family, and spent eleven years in prison. Later married, had a daughter, and lives in Brno.

HONZA, JAROSLAV [yar o slav]. Mayor of Hříště whose offhand report to a gendarme of two strangers in the village resulted in the deaths of Vojtěch Luža and Josef Koreš.

HÖRNER [her ner], JIŘÍ [yee rzhee]. Gendarme in Přibyslav, shot during Radomír's reprisal but not killed.

HUTTER, JOSEF [yo sef]. Professor at Charles University prior to the occupation and his participation in resistance.

ILJIKČAN [il yik chan], JAKOV [ya kov] TĚVOSOVIČ [tev o so vich]. Armenian officer of the Red Army General Staff. Escaped from German POW camp in 1943. Assigned by R3 to initiate contact between the Czech resistance and the Red Army. Killed in eastern Slovakia in May 1944.

INDRA [in d ra], BOHUSLAV [bo hoo slav] ("HERMIT"). Staff Captain of Czechoslovak army. Owned a brick factory in Pánov. Sheltered Vojtěch and Radomír Luža. Appointed commander of the group "General Luža" in April 1945. Promoted to lieutenant colonel after the war and worked in the ministry of national defense in Prague, in charge of resisters' affairs. Expelled by the Communists from the army and all veterans' organizations in 1948. Died in 1961. His daughter, MILENA, became a teacher after the war and lives in the Czech Republic.

INGR [een gr], SERGEJ [ser gay]. Division general before the war. Minister of national defense in the London exile government, 1940–44. commander in chief of Czechoslovak armed forces, 1944–45. Purged by Communists in 1945; rehabilitated in 1947. Appointed envoy to the Netherlands. Worked in Washington, D.C., for liberation of Czechoslovakia from the Communists. Died in Paris in 1956.

JEDLIČKA [yed litch ka], FRANTIŠEK [fran ti shek]. Director of a clothing cooperative in Brno. Facilitated material support to Czech resisters in Berlin and Breslau prisons. After 1942 served as liaison between Vojtěch Luža and Prague underground. Imprisoned by Germans 1944–45. Member of National Assembly, 1945. Withdrew from politics to live in the countryside in 1948.

JÍNA [yeen a], JAN [yahn]. In diplomatic service prior to his arrest in 1939. After 1945, head of political section of presidential office. Provided the contact between President Beneš, Josef Císař, and Radomír Luža in 1948 in the failed mission to bring Beneš to the West. His wife, ÁŠA [ah sha], also served as a liaison to Beneš.

JIŘÍKOVSKÝ [yi rzhee kov skee], FRANTIŠEK [fran ti shek]. Army staff captain in Prague and active in underground. Together with Josef Císař, invited Vojtěch Luža to move to Prague in mid-1944. Arrested by the Germans in September 1944. In 1945 joined the public police force in Prague.

JIZERA [yi zer a], STANISLAV. Lieutenant colonel of Czechoslovak army prior to the war; later a Czech Gestapo informer.

KÁŇA [kahn ya], BOŽENA [bo zhen a]. Dentist, wife of brigade general BONIFAC KÁŇA, whom the Nazis tortured to death in 1941. Associate of Vojtěch Luža and had contacts with both the Brno and Prague underground. Allowed Milada Luža to stay with her and avoid arrest by the Gestapo, but after 1948 cooperated with Communist security agents and informed on Mrs. Luža.

KLEMEŠ [klem esh], JAROSLAV [yar o slav]. Radio operator dropped into the Protectorate by the U.S. Army Air Force in February 1945 as a member of the Platinum team. Arrested by the Communists after 1948. Rehabilitated and promoted to colonel in 1989. Still living in the Czech Republic.

KOBYLKA [ko bill ka], JAROSLAV [yar o slav]. Mayor of Kadolec. With his mother, BOŽENA, and his sister, provided hiding places and support to General Luža, Radomír, and Bachmutsky. Died in the 1950s.

KONEČNÝ [ko netch nee], SLÁVEK. Childhood friend of Radomír Luža.

KOPECKÝ [ko peck ee], VÁCLAV [vah tslav]. Czechoslovak Communist, became prominent in the postwar Communist-dominated government.

KOREŠ [ko resh], JOSEF [yo sef]. Lieutenant in Czechoslovak army reserve. Aide-de-camp to General Luža in Říčany. Assassinated with Vojtěch Luža in October 1944.

KRASAVINOVA, RUFINA NIKOLAJEVNA ("Rufa" [roof a]). Nurse in team of Red Army paratroopers dropped into the Protectorate in October 1944. Bachmutsky's love, carrying his unborn child when she was killed in action on February 8, 1945.

KRÁTKÝ [kraht skee], JAROSLAV [yar o slav] ("Zdena" [zden a]). Major in Czechoslovak army. Dispatched from London to Bratislava in 1944. Main liaison between the Slovak resistance and the London government. Asked by General Ingr to make contact with General Vojtěch Luža. Executed by the Germans in 1945.

KRAVKA [krav ka], ČENĚK [chen nyek]. Fought with Vojtěch Luža against the Bolsheviks as a member of the Czechoslovak Legion in Russia, 1917–20. Noncommissioned officer and aide to Luža. Helped Luža find shelters, 1941–43. Recruited resisters to build a strong local base around Velká Bíteš.

KRISTEK, GUSTAV. Architect in Brno. Head of the Brno detachment of "General Luža." Arrested by the Communists after 1948.

KRISTEK [krees tek], KAREL. Owned a sawmill near Velká Bíteš, which became the center of guerrilla activities. Escaped to Venezuela after 1948. Returned to Czechoslovakia in the 1980s.

KROFTA, KAMIL. Foreign minister of Czechoslovakia 1936–38. Member of resistance center PRNC, 1942–44. Died 1945.

KUNDERKA [koon deir ka], STANISLAV. One of the gendarmes who shot Vojtěch Luža and was killed in Radomír's attack on the Přibyslav station.

KUTLVAŠR [koot ul vah shr], KAREL. Division general before the occupation. Military leader of Prague uprising in May 1945. Arrested by the Communists after the 1948 coup and sentenced to life in prison. Released in 1960. Died 1961.

KVAPIL, JAROSLAV [yar o slav]. Prominent Czech writer. One of the leaders of the anti-Austrian resistance in World War I. Cofounder of Preparatory Revolutionary National Committee (PRNC). Arrested by the Germans 1944. Released at the end of the war. Died 1950.

LANG, THEODOR. Colonel of Protectorate government troops. Formed an underground resistance group that made contact with General Vojtěch Luža. Arrested by the Germans in 1944 and died soon afterward.

LÁNY [lah nee], EMIL [e mil]. Judge. One of the leaders of PRNC. Arrested by Germans and died in May 1945.

LAUŠMAN [laush man], BOHUMIL [bo hoo mil]. Member of Political Center in 1939. In exile in London during the war. Social democratic pro-Communist leader. Returned to Czechoslovakia in 1945 as minister of industry. Chairman of Social Democratic Party in 1947. Endorsed Communist coup in 1948, but escaped Czechoslovakia in 1949. Kidnapped by Communist security forces in Salzburg, December 1953. Died in prison near Prague, 1963.

LENC [lehnk], first name unknown. Speaker for Communist youth group Vanguard in Brno.

LICHTENSTEIN-PODSTATZKY [likh ten shtine pod stat skee], COUNT ALOIS [al o ees]. Estate owner in Velké Meziříčí. With his wife COUNTESS JOSEFINE (née HARRACH), donated between two and three million crowns to the Czech resistance. After 1948, lived in exile in Chile. Died in 1982. Family returned to Czechoslovakia after 1989.

"THE LITTLE ONE" ("MALÝ"). See TLAČBABA, BOHUMIL.

LOŇKA [lon nyk a], first name unknown. Prominent Soviet member of PAM 5.

LOUCKÝ [low tzkee], VĚKOSLAV [vyek o slav]. Associate of Radomír. Sheltered the transmitting station "Anna" that established contact with the London government. Put on trial with Nechanský in 1950.

LUŽA [loo zhah], BOHUSLAV [bo hoo slav] ("Slávek"). Brother of General Vojtěch Luža. Mayor of Uherský Brod and member of the National Assembly, 1938. Died in Buchenwald, 1945.

LUŽA [loo zhah], LIBUŠE [lee boo sheh], née PODHRÁZSKÁ [pod hrahz skah]. Born 1928. Married Radomír in 1949 in Paris. Mother of RADOMIR, JR., born 1963, and SABRINA, born 1965. Died 2001.

LUŽA [loo zhah], MILADA [mil a da], née VEČEŘOVÁ [vetch er a]. Born in Uherský Brod, 1898. Mother of RADOMÍR, born in 1922. In hiding 1942–45. Died in Prague, 1985.

Luža [loo zhah], Radomír [rad o meer]. General Vojtěch Luža's son. Born in Prague, 1922.

Luža [loo zhah], Vojtěch [voy tyekh]. Born in Uherský Brod, 1891. Division general in Czechoslovak army. Military commander of Moravia-Silesia, 1937–39. Military leader of resistance group Council of Three ("Rada tří" or "R3"). Killed October 2, 1944. Promoted to army general in memoriam, 1989.

Macek [mats ek], Josef [yo sef]. Economist, prominent social democrat. After 1948 escaped to the West and settled in Canada.

Maloušek [mal o shek], František [fran ti shek]. School principal in Kadolec and resister. Committed suicide in Brno Gestapo prison, 1944.

Malý ("The Little One"). See Tlačbaba, Bohumil.

Masaryk [maz uh rik], Jan [yahn]. Foreign minister, 1945–48. Son of Thomas G. Masaryk. Died in March 1948 in unclear circumstances, apparently committing suicide.

Masaryk, Thomas G. First president of Czechoslovak Republic, 1918–35. Died 1937.

McCarthy, Thomas. Commander of B-24 Liberator plane shot down near Tišnov in April 1945, whose crew was sheltered by the General Luža group. Nephew of President Franklin D. Roosevelt.

Mečíř [meh cheerzh], Bohuslav [bo hoo slav]. Head of the Přibyslav gendarme station, one of the assassins of Vojtěch Luža who was himself killed by Radomír's group.

Mezník [mez nyeek], Jaroslav [yar o slav]. Prominent resister. Committed suicide in Gestapo prison in Brno.

Moravanský, Jan [yahn]. Legionnaire in Russia. Major in Czechoslovak army. Head of Obrana Národa group around Velké Meziříčí and early associate of General Luža. Arrested in 1944.

"MRS. LITTLE SPRUCE." See NOVÁK, KAREL and LUDMILA.

MÜLLER [myew ler], KAREL. General Vojtěch Luža's aide in Říčany, among the last people to see him alive.

MUSIL [moo sil], CYRIL. Long-distance ski racer before the war, then innkeeper in Studnice, near Nové Město. Provided hiding places for General Vojtěch Luža, Štainer, Grňa, Svatoň, and Soška. Arrested by the Communists after 1948. Escaped from the notorious Leopoldov prison, a fortress in Slovakia, and fled to the U.S. occupation zone in Germany. Eventually settled in Canada, where he died.

NAVRÁTIL [nav rah teel], JOSEF [yo sef]. Přibyslav gendarme who, hearing of the presence of Vojtěch Luža and Koreš in Hříště, called Mečíř and asked for help in investigating their identities. Requested transfer immediately after the assassination and thus escaped Radomír's reprisal.

NECHANSKÝ [nekh ahn skee], JAROMÍR [yar o meer]. Czechoslovak army captain. Son-in-law of Laušman. Commanded the Platinum parachute team dropped into the Protectorate in February 1945. Arranged for drops of weapons to the resistance by U.S. Army Air Force. Sheltered near Velká Bíteš with Radomír's assistance. Took part in Prague uprising in May 1945. Involved with Communist military counterintelligence. Executed by the Communists in 1950 because of his contacts with U.S. intelligence.

NOVÁK, KAREL and LUDMILA ("MRS. LITTLE SPRUCE"). Karel was the schoolmaster in Javůrek until his retirement. Ludmila was the confidante of the Lužas and helped them all in many ways. At various times, the Nováks hid Vojtěch, Milada, and Radomír Luža in the house they shared with their daughter JIŘINA [yi rzhi na], son-in-law, and grandson.

NOVÁK, ZDENĚK [zden nyek]. Czechoslovak army general, politically conservative. Member of ON and military representative of PRNC, 1942–44. Main contact of General Vojtěch Luža to these underground groups. Arrested in 1944 by the Germans. Joined the Communist Party in 1945 and became commander of Moravian military region, 1945–50. Imprisoned by the Communists 1950–52. Died in 1988.

Ondra, Josef [yo sef] ("The Giant"). Blacksmith near Nové Město. Hid Vojtěch Luža and Radomír and arranged for hiding places for their cohorts. Assisted in Radomír's attack on the gendarmerie in Hříště.

Ouředník [oo rzhed nyeek], Josef [yo sef]. District director of Protectorate Health Insurance in Benešov. Senior aide to Vojtěch Luža and Císař. Killed in action by the Gestapo on September 13, 1944, in Prague.

Pánek, Josef [yo sef] ("The Proletarian"). Producer of blinds and shutters in Velké Meziříčí. Hid Radomír in his attic.

Paprskář [pap risk arzh], Karel. Czech Gestapo informer in Brno who, instead of leading the Gestapo to General Luža, decided to collaborate with R3.

Pařil [parzh il], Josef [yo sef] ("Pepek"). Member of Kobylka's support group in Kadolec. Helped Vojtěch and Radomír Luža and Nikolaj Bachmutsky.

Pavlas, Josef [yo sef]. Gamekeeper near Velké Meziříčí. Sheltered Grňa, Štainer, Milada Luža, and paratroopers. Forced to go underground in fall 1944.

Pavlíček [pav lee chek], Václav [vah tslav]. Mailman, assisted Jan Pliczka in Bohdalov. After the war, married Božena, Mayor Kobylka's sister.

Pechan [pekh an], Miloslav ("Míla"). Radomír's school friend. Escaped Czechoslovakia in 1948. Lives in Toronto.

Peller, František [fran ti shek]. District attorney in Brno. Associate of General Luža, 1940–42.

Peschl [pes chul], Celestina [tsel es tee na] ("Teta Tíni"). Radomír's maternal great-aunt.

Píka, Heliodor. Division general. Head of Czechoslovak military mission in Moscow, 1941–45. Deputy head of general staff, 1945–48. Arrested by

Communists in May 1948 and sentenced to death on trumped-up charges of treason. Rastislav Váhala was his defense attorney. Executed June 1949.

PLICZKA [plitch ka], JAN [yahn]. Worked for state finance office in Prague. Provided contact between R3 and Prague underground. Met Radomír in Bohdalov.

POKORNÝ (first name unknown). Schoolmaster in Katov. Sheltered Vojtěch and Radomír Luža.

"THE PROLETARIAN." See PÁNEK, JOSEF.

PRUDKY [prood kee], FRANZ. Sudeten German member of Brno Gestapo beginning in 1939. Gave Jedlička, his former employer, useful information for the resistance.

RAKOVÁ [rah kov a], MARTA ("VEČEŘA"). Czech informer for the Gestapo. Executed by resisters in Radomír's group.

RICHTER [rihk ter], FERDINAND. Jedlička's friend. Representative of the Beneš Socialist Party in the National Assembly, 1935–38. One of the leaders of Political Center. Arrested in fall of 1939. Sentenced to death and pardoned. President of Supreme Land Court in Brno, 1946–48. After February 1948 coup, became deputy chairman of the Communist-controlled National Assembly. Died 1950.

RICHTER [rihk ter], FRANTIŠEK [fran ti shek]. Managing director of a publishing company. Leader of PRNC, 1942–44. Arrested by the Germans and committed suicide.

RICHTER [rihk ter], LUDMILA. Wife of FERDINAND RICHTER. Arranged contacts for the General Luža group and provided information to R3.

ROBOTKA [ruh but ka], JOSEF [yo sef] ("RUDOLF"). General staff captain in Czechoslovak army. Joined ON in 1939. While living legally in Velká Bíteš, became senior military aide, courier, and a main contact to underground networks for Vojtěch Luža. Military commander of R3 for Moravia after November 1944. Promoted to lieutenant colonel after the war but arrested and executed by the Communists in November 1952. Posthumously rehabilitated and promoted to major general after 1989.

Ročejdl [ro chey dl], Jan [yahn]. Printer in Brno. Produced identity cards and "official" rubber stamps for R3 members. Recruited by Vlasta Homoláč in contact with Radomír.

Ryšánek [ree syan ek], František [fran ti shek] ("The Turk"). Keeper of Hluboké inn, near Bíteš, the center of guerrilla activities of the General Luža group.

Ryšánek [ree syan ek], Viktor. Czech informer for the Gestapo.

"Sandy." See Cikrle, František.

Sec [setz], Jan [yahn]. Bus driver in Bosonohy. Hid General Luža in his home. Went underground with wife Františka [fran tish ka] in 1944, sometimes hiding with Radomír Luža. Escaped Czechoslovakia in 1948. Died in Canada.

Sedlák [sed lak], Rudolf. Forester in Košíkov, near Bíteš. His house became Robotka's headquarters in 1945. Administrator of President Beneš' summer residence in Náměšt' after the war.

Šedý [shuh dee], Adolf. Went underground to evade being drafted for labor service in the Reich and worked with the resistance near Nové Město. Participated in attack on Hříště gendarmerie.

Šenková [shen kov a], Růžena [roo zhen a]. Provided shelter to Radomír in 1943.

Serinek, Josef [yo sef] ("The Gypsy"). Organized Soviets near Nové Město who had escaped from German POW camps. Became innkeeper after the war.

Sigmund, Miroslava ("Mirka"). Wife of prominent businessman and resister. Befriended Milada Luža in Gestapo prison, 1941.

ŠILINGER [shill in gher], ALOIS [al o ees]. Associate of General Vojtěch Luža.

ŠIROKÝ [shee rock ee], VILIAM. Slovak Communist leader, became premier of Czechoslovakia in 1953.

SLÁNSKÝ, RUDOLF. Secretary general of Communist Party of Czechoslovakia and a docile Muscovite, was nevertheless accused of treason in 1951, tried along with twelve others in 1952 in a notorious Communist purge, and hanged.

ŠLING [shling], OTTO. Powerful secretary of regional Communist Party committee in Brno. Executed after Slánský trial in 1952.

SLUNEČKO [sloo nyetch ko], FRANTIŠEK [fran ti shek]. Brigade general in Czechoslovak army. Member of ON, went underground in 1940, and re-emerged at the end of the war.

SOJKA [so yi ka], KAREL. Gendarme visiting Přibyslav who began interrogating Radomír during the reprisal attack and was killed along with the guilty gendarmes.

SOŠKA [sosh ka], EDUARD. Shopkeeper in Nové Město. Close associate of Lieutenant Colonel Svatoň. Killed by Gestapo, along with Svatoň, on November 1, 1944.

ŠTAINER [shty ner], KAREL. General staff captain in Czechoslovak army. Went underground in 1939; met General Vojtěch Luža in 1942. Following the deaths of Luža and Svatoň, became R3's military commander in Bohemia. Joined Communist Party in 1945. Arrested after 1948 coup and eventually became anti-Communist.

STALLER [shtal er], KAREL ("WHIZ"). General director of Brno Small Arms Factory. Met Luža in 1943. Provided intelligence and, because he resided in Bratislava, served as Luža's main connection to Slovakia. Escaped in 1949 to the United States, where he eventually died.

SVATOŇ [sva to nyeh], JOSEF [yo sef]. Lieutenant colonel in Czechoslovak army before the war. Head of large resistance group in eastern Bohemia.

Joined R3 in 1944. Deputy of Vojtěch Luža. Became R3's military commander after Luža's death. With Soška, killed by the Gestapo on November 1, 1944. Posthumously promoted to brigade general.

ŠVERMA [shver ma], JAN [yahn]. Czechoslovak Communist leader; died during the Slovak uprising in 1944.

SVOBODA, LUDVÍK. Lieutenant colonel before the war, minister of national defense, 1945. Army general. President of Czechoslovakia, 1968–75. Died in 1979.

"TETA TÍNI." See PESCHL, CELESTINA.

TLAČBABA [tlatch ba ba], BOHUMIL [bo hoo mil] ("MALÝ," "THE LITTLE ONE"). Worked at the Protectorate Bus Enterprises in Brno. Became one of Vojtěch Luža's aides. Went underground in 1944 and withdrew from clandestine activities. Committed suicide after the war.

TŮMA [too ma], LUDVÍK. Cavalry lieutenant colonel in Czechoslovak army. Aide to General Vojtěch Luža, 1939–41, until his arrest by the Germans.

"THE TURK." See RYŠÁNEK, FRANTIŠEK.

VÁCLAV (Pliczka's assistant). See PAVLÍČEK, VÁCLAV.

VÁHALA, RASTISLAV ("RAST'A"). Attorney in Prague. Vojtěch Luža's contact to trade unions and Communist resistance networks. Defense attorney to General Píka, 1948–49. Left Communist Party but remained in Czechoslovakia after the coup. Provided intelligence to Radomír, secretly meeting with him in Yugoslavia and Austria. Died in 1988.

VEČEŘA [vetch erzh a], KAREL. Radomír's maternal grandfather in Uherský Brod. Attorney.

VĚRA [vyer a]. Radomír's girlfriend before he went underground in 1942. Now resides in Brno.

VODA, SYLVESTR. Grain commissioner in Brno. Major in the Czechoslovak army reserve. First military commander of Brno, 1918–19. Vojtěch Luža's best friend. Arrested by the Germans September 30, 1941. Died January 1945.

VOLF, JAROSLAV [yar o slav] ("LEON"). Communist Party liaison to Robotka.

VOROSHILOV, KLIMENT. Soviet marshal and longtime aide of Stalin. Met Vojtěch Luža in 1936 in Moscow. Remarkably survived several purges and remained in powerful positions in the Soviet Union.

VOSTREJŠ [vos traysh], ARNOŠT [ar nosht]. Joined the General Luža group at the end of the war.

VOTAVA, JAN [yahn]. Innkeeper in Hříště, witness to assassination of General Vojtěch Luža.

WEINGART, KAREL. Head of the gendarme station in Říčany. Recruited by Kravka to provide information to Vojtěch Luža about movements of the German police.

ZAJÍČEK [za yee chek], FRANTIŠEK [fran ti shek]. Lieutenant in Czechoslovak army. Former military ski racer. During the occupation, district administration official in Velké Meziříčí. Aide to Štainer. After 1948 arrested with Robotka and sentenced to life in prison.

ŽALMAN [zhal man], OTAKAR. Czechoslovak army major in Brno. Aide to General Luža. Arrested by the Germans in 1943 and committed suicide in prison. In 1941–42, maintained communication with Vojtěch Luža through wife MARIE ŽALMAN.

"ZDENA." See KRÁTKÝ, JAROSLAV.

ZELENÝ [zel en ee], JAROSLAV [yar o slav]. Gamekeeper in Koníkov, near Nové Město. Provided shelter to Czech resisters and escaped Soviet war prisoners.

PRONUNCIATION OF CZECH PLACE-NAMES

Benešov (ben esh ov)
Bohdalov (boh dah lov)
Bosonohy (bos on oy)
Bratislava (brah ti slav a)
Brno (bur no)
Chotěboř (khot yeh borzh)
Daňkovice (da nyik o vi tseh)
Dářsko (dahrzh sko)
Domašov (do mah shov)
Domažlice (do mazh lit zeh)
Hluboké (hloo bo kay)
Hranice (hra nit tzeh)
Hříště (hrzheesh tyeh)
Ivančice (i vahn chi tseh)
Jaroslavice (yar o sla vee tseh)
Javůrek (ya voor ek)
Jihlava (yee hlav a)
Kácov (ka tzov)
Kadolec (kad o lets)
Katov (kah tov)
Koloděje (ko lo deh ye)
Koníkov (kon nyee kov)

Košice (ko shi tseh)
Kounic (ko nits) Student Home
Krásné (krahs neh)
Křižanov (krzhee zhan ov)
Kuřímská Nová Ves (koo rzhreem
    ska no vah vehs)
Lažánky (lazh ahn kee)
Ležáky (lezh ah kee)
Lidice (li di tseh)
Ludvíkov (lood vee kov)
Maršov (mar shov)
Moravská Ostrava (mor av skah o
    strav a)
Náměšť nad Oslavou (na myesht
    nad o slav o)
Nihov (ni hov)
Nové Město na Moravě (no vye
    myes to na mor ah vyeh)
Okarec (o kahr ets)
Olešná (o lesh nah)
Olomouc (o lo moats)
Ostrovačice (o stro va chi tseh)

Pánov (pahn ov)
Pilsen (pil zen)
Přerov (przheh rov)
Přibyslav (przhi bi slav)
Proseč (pro setch)
Račice (ra chi tseh)
Račín (ra cheen)
Radoškov (rad osh kov)
Říčany (rzhee cha nee)
Rosice (ro si tseh)
Ružomberok (roo zhom beh rok)
Studenec (stoo den ets)
Svatoslav (svah toh slahv)
Těšín (tyeh sheen)
Tišnov (tish nov)

Třebíč (trzhe beetch)
Třešt (trzhesht)
Uherské Hradiště (oo er skay hra
    dish tyeh)
Uherský Brod (oo er skee brohd)
Velká Bíteš (vel kah beet esh)
Velké Meziříčí (vel keh mez i rzhree
    chee)
Vlaším (vla sheem)
Vysoké Mýto (vee sok ay mee toh)
Wurm (voorm) Street
Zábřany (zah brzha nee)
Zastávka (zas tahv ka)
Zbýšov (zbee shov)
Zhoře (zhoh rzheh)
Zlín (zleen)

FOR FURTHER READING

No strictly objective and impartial study of the resistance was published in Communist-ruled Czechoslovakia between 1948 and 1989. However, from about 1963 to 1968, and again after 1985, historical writing was more balanced and reliable than in other years. This list of works in English, German, and French does not include the many important resistance studies written in Czech.

Radomir Luza's papers and documents pertaining to the German occupation of Czechoslovakia and the cold war era have been deposited with the Hoover Institution on War, Revolution and Peace at Stanford University.

Adler, H. G. *Theresienstadt: Das Antlitz einer Zwangsgemeinschaft.* Bonn, 1960.

   A standard work.

Beneš, Edvard. *Memoirs of Dr. Eduard Beneš: From Munich to New War and New Victory.* Boston, 1954.

   The account of President Beneš' activities from 1938 to 1945.

Bílek, Bohumil. *Fifth Column at Work.* London, 1945.

   A collection of documents on the subversive activities of the Henlein party in 1938, based on Czech archives.

Bosl, Karl, ed. *Handbuch der Geschichte der böhmischen Länder.* Vol. 4, *Der tschecho-slowakische Staat im Zeitalter der modernen Massendemokratie und Diktatur.* 4 vols. Stuttgart, 1968–70.

Part of a vast scholarly series by German historians.

Bradley, John. *Lidice: Sacrificial Village.* New York, 1962.

Brandeš, Detlef. *Die Tschechen unter deutschem Protektorat.* Vol. 1, *Besatzungspolitik, Kollaboration und Widerstand im Protektorat Böhmen und Mähren bis Heydrichs Tod (1939–1942).* Vol. 2, *Besatzung, Kollaboration und Widerstand im Protektorat Böhmen und Mähren von Heydrichs Tod bis zum Prager Aufstand (1942–1945).* München, 1969, 1975.

A solid study, based on primary sources, of Czech activities under the Nazi occupation.

Brügel, Johann W. *Tschechen und Deutsche, 1939–1946.* München, 1974.

An important work by a Sudeten German historian.

———. *Czechoslovakia before Munich: the German Minority Problem and British Appeasement Policy.* Cambridge, 1973.

An illuminating study critical of the Henlein party.

Bušek, Vratislav, and Nicholas Spulber, eds. *Czechoslovakia.* New York and London, 1957.

A comprehensive presentation of Czechoslovakia under Communist domination. Sponsored by the Free Europe Committee.

Chmela, Leopold. *The Economic Aspects of the German Occupation of Czechoslovakia.* Prague, 1948.

An assessment of Czechoslovak war losses and damages complied by Czechoslovak authorities. The author was head of the Czechoslovak National Bank after 1945.

Doležal, Jiří, and Jan Křen, eds. *Czechoslovakia's Fight: Documents on the Resistance Movement of the Czechoslovak People, 1938–1945.* Prague, 1964.

A selection of interesting documents; biased in favor of Communism.

Ducháček, Ivo. *The Strategy of Communist Infiltration: The Case of Czechoslovakia.* New Haven, 1949.

Short presentation of Communist methods used in the Prague February 1948 takeover.

European Resistance Movements, 1939–1945. Vol. 1, *Proceedings, First International Conference . . . 14–17 September 1958.* Vol. 2, *Proceedings, Second International Conference . . . 26–29 March 1961.* New York, 1960, 1964.

Filípek, Jan. *The Shadow of the Gallows: A True Story.* Palm Springs, Calif., 1985.

A story by a Czech resister.

Gedye, G. E. R. *Betrayal in Central Europe: Austria and Czechoslovakia, the Fallen Bastions.* New York, 1939.

Excellent firsthand account of the Munich crisis by an English reporter in Prague.

(German Federal Republic). Bundesministerium für Vertriebene, Flüchtlinge, und Kriegsgeschädigte. *Dokumentation der Vertreibung der Deutschen aus Ost-Mitteleuropa.* Edited by Theodor Schieder. Vol. 4, *Die Vertreibung der deutschen Bevölkerung aus der Tschechoslowakei.* Bonn, 1957.

Presents the German viewpoint of the transfer of the Sudeten Germans in 1945–1947.

Grant Duff, Shiela. *A German Protectorate: The Czechs under Nazi Rule.* London, 1942. Reprint, London, 1970.

Still useful.

Griffin, Joan, and Jonathan Griffin. *Lost Liberty? The Ordeal of the Czechs and the Future of Freedom.* New York, 1939.

An eyewitness report from Prague in 1938.

Heidrich, Arnošt. "Remembrance of Resistance Years, 1938–1945." In *On All Fronts: Czechoslovaks in World War II,* edited by Lewis M. White, 3:115–24. Boulder, 2000.

The story of resistance leader and ambassador Arnošt Heidrich, who became secretary general of the Czechoslovak ministry of foreign affairs in 1945 and escaped to the United States in 1948.

Horecký, Paul L., ed. *East Central Europe: A Guide to Basic Publications.* Chicago and London, 1969.

Important historical bibliography on Czechoslovakia.

International Military Tribunal. *Trial of the Major War Criminals before the International Military Tribunal, Nuremberg, 1945–46.* 42 vols. Nuremberg, 1947–49.

For Czechoslovak documents, see Vols. 10, 25–35, 37–40. Materials are not always reliable.

Ivanov, Miroslav. *Target: Heydrich.* New York, 1974.

A popular account of the assassination of Reinhard Heydrich based on original documents.

Kennan, George F. *From Prague after Munich: Diplomatic Papers, 1938–1940.* Princeton, 1968.

A collection of reports by the State Department diplomat and longtime advisor.

Korbel, Josef. *The Communist Subversion of Czechoslovakia, 1938–1948: The Failure of Coexistence.* Princeton, 1959.

A case study of Communist methods.

Krajína, Vladimir. "La résistance tchécoslovaque" (The Czechoslovak resistance). *Cahiers d'histoire de la deuxième guerre mondiale* 3 (1950): 55–76.

Král, Václav, ed. *Lesson from History: Documents Concerning Nazi Policies for Germanization and Extermination in Czechoslovakia.* Prague, 1962.

A translation from well-selected original documents deposited in the Central State Archives of Czechoslovakia.

———. *Das Abkommen von München 1938: Tschechoslowakische diplomatische Dokumente, 1937–1939.* Prague, 1968.

A collection of previously unpublished documents; includes some private papers of Czechoslovak foreign minister Kamil Krofta.

———. *Die Deutschen in der Tschechoslowakei, 1933–1947: Dokumentensammlung (Acta Occupationis Bohemiae et Moraviae).* Prague, 1964.

A collection of documents on Czech-German domestic relations.

Lettrich, Jozef. *History of Modern Slovakia*. New York, 1955.

A concise study of post-1918 Slovakia.

Lockhart, Bruce R. H. *Comes the Reckoning*. London, 1947.

A lucid presentation of the British attitude toward President Beneš and the Czechoslovak Republic during World War II by the British representative to the Czechoslovak exile government in London.

Luža, Radomír. "The Communist Party of Czechoslovakia and the Czech Resistance, 1939–1945." *Slavic Review* 28, no. 4 (December, 1969): 561–76.

———. "The Czech Resistance Movement." In *A History of the Czechoslovak Republic 1918–48*, edited by Victor S. Mamatey and Radomír Luža, 343–61. Princeton, 1973.

———. "Home Resistance. A View from the Front Line Trenches." In *On All Fronts: Czecholovaks in World War II*, edited by Lewis M. White, 3:103–13. Boulder, 2000.

Translated by the editor.

———. "The Liberation of Prague: An American Blunder?" *Kosmas: Journal of Czechoslovak and Central European Studies* 3 no. 1 (1984), 41–57.

———. "Rada Tří and General Luža." In *On All Fronts: Czechoslovaks in World War II*, edited by Lewis M. White, 3:90–102. Boulder, 2000.

Translated by the editor.

———. *The Resistance in Austria, 1938–1945*. Minneapolis, 1984.

Provides a conceptual framework and statistical analysis of resistance membership.

———. *The Transfer of the Sudeten Germans: A Study of Czech-German Relations, 1933–1962*. New York and London, 1964.

Details the postwar expulsion of the Sudeten Germans and provides information about the Czechoslovak wartime resistance and the Nazi policy of Germanization.

MacDonald, Callum. *The Killing of SS-Obergruppenführer Reinhard Heydrich, 27 May 1942*. London, 1989.

An informative account.

Mamatey, Victor S., and Radomír Luža, eds. *A History of the Czechoslovak Republic, 1918–1948.* Princeton, 1973.

The standard work on the subject.

Margoliová Kovalyová, Heda. *Prague Farewell.* London, 1988.

A memoir by the wife of a victim of the Slánský trial.

Mastny, Vojtěch. *The Czechs under Nazi Rule: The Failure of National Resistance, 1939–1942.* New York and London, 1971.

Good, though biased against the resistance.

Moravec, František. *Master of Spies: The Memoirs of General František Moravec.* New York, 1975.

An absorbing account by the head of Czechoslovak military intelligence before and during World War II. Published posthumously; contains some errors. Large sections omitted from the English version.

Rechcigl, Miloslav, Jr., ed. *The Czechoslovak Contribution to World Culture.* The Hague, 1964.

Studies and essays on Czechoslovak culture, arts, and science.

———. *Czechoslovakia: Past and Present.* 2 vols. The Hague and Paris, 1968.

A useful collection of articles on political, social, economic, and international problems.

Ripka, Hubert. *Czechoslovakia Enslaved: The Story of the Communist Coup d'Etat.* London, 1950.

A vivid eyewitness account by one of the ablest Czech democratic leaders.

———. *Munich, before and After: A Fully Documented Czechoslovak Account of the Crises of September 1938 and March 1939.* Translated from the manuscript by Ida Sindelková and Edgar P. Young. London, 1939. Reprint, London, 1969.

Still useful.

Schmidt, Dana Adams. *Anatomy of a Satellite.* Boston, 1952.

A story of the Communist takeover and its aftermath by a veteran foreign correspondent.

Smelser, Ronald M. *The Sudeten Problem, 1933–1938: Volkstumspolitik and the Formulation of Nazi Foreign Policy*. Middletown, Conn., 1975.

Intelligent and scholarly.

Society for the History of Czechoslovak Jews. *The Jews of Czechoslovakia: Historical Studies and Surveys*. Vol. 3. Philadelphia, 1984.

Szulc, Tad. *Czechoslovakia since World War II*. New York, 1970.

A survey by the New York *Times* reporter.

Taborsky, Edward. *Communism in Czechoslovakia, 1948–1960*. Princeton, 1961.

A reliable survey.

————. *President Edvard Beneš: Between East and West, 1938–1948*. Stanford, 1981.

A thoughtful political biography by a former personal aide to president Beneš in London.

Ullmann, Walter. *The United States in Prague, 1945–1948*. Boulder, 1978.

A valuable account.

White, Lewis, M., ed. *On All Fronts: Czechoslovaks in World War II*. 3 vols. Boulder, 1991, 1995, 2000.

A collection of eyewitness accounts.

Wynne, Waller, Jr. *The Population of Czechoslovakia*. Washington, D.C., 1953.

Zeman, Zbyněk A. B. *The Masaryks*. London, 1976.

A popular biography of President T. G. Masaryk and his son Jan.

Zinner, Paul E. *Communist Strategy and Tactics in Czechoslovakia, 1918–1948*. London, 1963.

A survey of Communist policies.

ABOUT THE AUTHORS

RADOMÍR LUŽA was born in Prague in 1922. He received a doctoral degree from Masaryk University Law School in 1948 and a Ph.D. in European history from New York University in 1959. He is professor emeritus at Tulane University in New Orleans, Louisiana, where for twenty-five years he taught modern European and German history. He is also professor of history at Masaryk University, having been appointed by President Václav Havel. In addition to six books, he has written over forty scholarly articles. He has received many awards, fellowships, and medals for his academic and political work, most recently from the President of Austria, who presented him with the Austrian Honorary Cross for Science and Art, First Class.

Professor Luža lives near Philadelphia. He has a son, a daughter, and two grandchildren. Libuše Luža died in August 2001.

CHRISTINA VELLA received her Ph.D. from Tulane University in modern European and U.S. history. She writes, lectures, and teaches in New Orleans, where she lives with her husband, Robert Riehl, and their two daughters.